Blessings and Prayers through the Year

A Resource for School, Parish, and Home

Elizabeth McMahon Jeep

Mary Beth Kunde-Anderson
Music Consultant

LTP
LITURGY
TRAINING
PUBLICATIONS

WLP WORLD
LIBRARY
PUBLICATIONS

Acknowledgments

We are grateful to the publishers who have given permission to include their work. Every effort has been made to determine the ownership of all texts and to make proper arrangement for their use. We will gladly correct in future additions any oversight or error that is brought to our attention.

Readings from the Old and New Testaments are taken from the *Contemporary English Version of the Bible,* copyright, © 1999 American Bible Society, 1865 Broadway, New York, NY 10023, and are used by permission of the American Bible Society. All rights reserved.

Blessing of the Cross, Litany of Saint Joseph, May Procession with Crowning of an Image of Mary are excerpts from the English translation of *The Book of Blessings* © 1988, International Committee on English in the Liturgy (ICEL) and excerpts from *A Book of Prayers,* © 1982, ICEL. The Opening Prayer for Saint Patrick's Day Mass is an excerpt from the English translation of *The Roman Missal* © 1973, ICEL. Used with permission. All rights reserved.

Prayer for All Souls' Day, Prayer for the Feast of the Immaculate Conception, Prayer on Martin Luther King Day, Blessing of Candles, Meal Prayer for St. Joseph's Day, Preparation of Ashes, Blessing for Placing Palm Branches in the Prayer Center, Blessing for Birthdays, Harvest Blessing for the Assumption, Magnificat are excerpts from *Catholic Household Blessings and Prayers* © 1988 United States Catholic Conference, Washington DC. Used with permission. All rights reserved.

Blessing for Saint Valentine's Day is adapted from *A Book of Family Prayer* (New York: The Seabury Press), 1983. Used with permission. Saint Patrick Loricae are taken from *Saint Patrick: A Visual Celebration,* Blanford Books, 1999. Music text for the Prayer for the Immaculate Conception @ World Library Publications. Used with permission.

Purchasing this resource does not grant permission to reprint all of the material it contains. It is illegal to reproduce copyrighted text and music without the permission of the copyright owner or licensing agent. In justice to the authors, composers, and employees of publishing companies, permission must be secured in order to photocopy any of the songs included in this resource.

The copyright holder or licensing agent is named at the bottom of each song. Mailing addresses are provided on page 234. When you write for permission, tell them which song, how many copies you want to make, and what you will be using them for. Each of the copyright holders and licensing agents has allowed their song to be included here trusting that parish and school staff members will act justly and lawfully.

The same guidelines apply to the prayer texts in this book. Permission should be received from the copyright owners mentioned above for their work listed. The remaining prayers may be copied by the purchaser of this book for one time use in a classroom.

BLESSINGS AND PRAYERS THROUGH THE YEAR: A RESOURCE FOR SCHOOL, PARISH, AND HOME © 2004 Archdiocese of Chicago: Liturgy Training Publications, 1800 North Hermitage Avenue, Chicago IL 60622-1101; 1-800-933-1800, FAX 1-800-933-7094, E-MAIL orders@ltp.org. All rights reserved. See our website at www.ltp.org.

Acquisitions Editor: Margaret M. Brennan
Design: Anna Manhart
Cover Art: Jui Ishida
Interior Art: Laura Montenegro
Typesetting: Jim Mellody-Pizzato
Print Buyer: Jean Troxel

BLESSINGS AND PRAYERS THROUGH THE YEAR vocal CD and accompaniment CD © 2004 World Library Publications, 3825 N. Willow Road, Schiller Park IL 60176-2353; 800-566-6150, www.wlpmusic.com, wlpcs@jspaluch.com. All rights reserved.

Project Manager: Mary Beth Kunde-Anderson
Producer, piano, guitar, percussion: Keith S. Kalemba
Singers: Norma Garcia and Michael Novak
Flute: Anna Belle O'Shea
Design: Denise Durand
Engineer: AirWave Recording Studio, Chicago

Printed in China.

ISBN 1-56854-369-7
CLASS

Table of Contents

Bless Us and These Your Gifts

When we bless—a person, an event, an object—we reveal its true nature. To bless a meal is to acknowledge what it is: a gift. None of us could create an ear of corn or build a peach. They spring from the earth, summer after summer, for our nourishment and delight, gifts to us from God.

When we bless a child we acknowledge that he or she is a gift, all gift. None of us could assemble a son or craft a daughter. They burst forth from our bodies, each one with his or her own abilities and proclivities.

What we did not earn or create can never be clutched and controlled as possession. It can only be acknowledged: This child is not my property; this child is my gift. When I bless this child, I remember.

Because the act of blessing helps us remember first who God is and what God does in and for the world, and then who we are before God and to one another, blessings have a privileged place among all the works of the baptized.

A blessing then is always a way of celebrating God's goodness, of naming and giving thanks for the mercy of God. It is a sign—something we can hear and see, perhaps feel—which in turn signifies the holiness of God, a holiness we share in and through Christ. That holiness extends even to objects when and as they are used for the work of God in the world.

One of the places where the good work of God is done is in school. Everything about school—desks and books and pencils and paper and teachers and fellow students—is there as a gift. We are to use these gifts to grow in the truth. It is right that we bless them, and ourselves, that we might always remember why we come, why we learn, why we teach, and why, what, and whom we celebrate.

Blessings are also a way for us to remember our neighbors, those known to us and those unknown to us. All of us—Christians, Jews, Muslims and unbelievers—are the children of God, created by God.

These prayers invite children into the rich tradition of Catholic practice as they also invite children to see and bless the wide world beyond our tradition. There are prayers for the earth we all share, and prayers for people whose traditions and practices we do not share.

Making Holy All Our Days

If blessings are a way to remember who God is and who we are before God, they also are a way to remember the cycle of hours and days, the weeks and the seasons that speak to us of the story of Jesus—the story that, through Baptism, has become our own. When all the world rushes from feast to feast (with the attendant reminder that we need to buy food and decorations and gifts for the feast) the Church remembers that there are fallow times, quiet times of watching. When the world proclaims that it is the shopping season of Christmas, Advent blessings root us in a time of waiting and hope. We remember that there are times that don't require any materials other than our hearts and minds and bodies, ours and those of others in our community.

Our bodies know the daily wisdom of cycles and seasons: We must sleep during each twenty-four hour period if we are to remain healthy. But if we spend each day, all day and night, in bed, our muscles will atrophy; even our skin will begin to break down and die. We live in a culture that says it is always time to feast, and so we grow fat. We live in a culture that says it is always time to work, and so we forget how to play. We live in a culture that says it is always time for information, and so we lose the gift of silence. Careful attention to the liturgical calendar forms us not only in the history and practice of the Church throughout the world and throughout all ages, but in personal wholeness and health as well. There are times for fasting as well as for feasting, times for dancing as well as for working. There are times for speaking and times for being silent, times for assembling as a community and times for being alone. There are times for mourning and times for rejoicing.

Kept faithfully, the calendar reminds us of God's good care. We are people who need and delight in the gift of day and night. Students can learn that this sensible and beneficent cycle is found in the rhythm not only of day but also of week and year, season after season, again and again, for as long as we live.

Feasts and Seasons

Knowing the Catholic ways of prayer means learning a vocabulary as well as a practice.

Using this book, students will come to understand the differences between the special days—solemnities, feasts and memorials—we all keep. A solemnity is a principal day and as such it holds the highest rank in the calendar. Every Sunday is a solemnity, as are Christmas and Easter. When a solemnity falls on the same day as a feast or a memorial, the solemnity always takes precedence. The observance of a solemnity begins with Evening Prayer I or First Vespers. Some solemnities have their own vigil Masses. Most students will be familiar with the Christmas Eve vigil Mass. Certainly they will understand the notion of a solemnity from their own lives. They know how that civic solemnity, the American Thanksgiving Day, is different from other Thursdays.

Feasts are days recalling significant events in the life of Christ, of the saints or of the whole Christian community. Students know family feast days from their own lives: birthdays, anniversaries, graduations, weddings, etc. All solemnities are feasts—Sunday, Christmas, Easter—but not all feasts are solemnities.

Some feasts are "movable," that is, they have no fixed date. Easter, for example, is always celebrated on the first Sunday after the first full moon after the vernal equinox. Simply put, Easter will fall on a Sunday somewhere between March 22 and April 25. Because Easter is movable, the feasts tied to its date, such as Ascension (forty days after Easter) and Pentecost (fifty days after Easter), are movable as well.

Other feasts are "immovable." Christmas is always celebrated on December 25. The day of the week changes but the date does not.

Most saints' days are memorials. Memorials are designated "optional" or "obligatory" depending on the saint's significance for the church. Students should come to know the patron of the diocese or city or parish or school. Perhaps the students could make a list of the patrons of each child in the class and then use this book to help keep those days.

Memorials rank behind solemnities and feasts. They are never kept during the week before Christmas, or during Holy Week or Easter Week.

Working with the liturgical calendar may seem difficult at first, but it can be a wonderful way to learn math—all that counting and figuring—as well as meteorology and history, and ethnic customs of every sort. Many lessons can be woven in and through the keeping of the calendar.

It might be interesting, for example, to consider all of the various Marian feasts. Why are there so many, and from so many cultures—from Our Lady of Guadalupe to Our Lady of Lourdes, healer and helper of the sick and suffering? Is there a value in keeping regional and national feasts? Is there a value in honoring so many aspects of Mary? Could we pare it down to a single "Mary's Day"?

Most students know how dependent they are on their mothers, and in how many different ways. She is the source of wisdom and the soother of upset stomachs, the cook and domestic confessor, the one who remembers that one child likes extra cheese on his pizza while the other can't stand the sight or smell of olives. Mothers—in all cultures, times, and places—have many roles, all of them important. How wise of the Church to acknowledge that we all need our mothers *and* Our

Mother, Mary, the *theotokos*, the God-bearer. In the Church, no one—even the ones whose mothers have abandoned us, or whose mothers are dead, or whose mothers are kept from us by illness or duty—not one of us is an orphan. Not one of us is motherless.

The Form of a Blessing

In our tradition blessings have a structure. Typically, the blessing has two parts: first, the proclamation of the word of God, and second, the praise of God's goodness and a prayer for God's help. These prayers give children an opportunity to learn the roles they will someday assume in the Sunday liturgy. One child can proclaim the word as others learn to hear and respond. All children might join in singing a psalm as the proclamation of God's word.

Another child can proclaim the goodness of God. Or all might join in a hymn of praise that acclaims God's goodness, such as "For Your Gracious Blessing" or "In the Lord I'll Be Ever Thankful." This does not mean that every student needs a book. The rite of blessing allows students to learn the liturgical cues they will follow all their lives. The invocation of the Trinity, "In the name of the Father . . . ," is always accompanied by the sign of the cross and always concludes with the assembly saying together, "Amen."

The proclamation of scripture always concludes with one of two formulas: "The word of the Lord" or after the proclamation of the Gospel, "The Gospel of the Lord." The assembly responds together, "Thanks be to God" or "Praise to you, Lord Jesus Christ."

In our tradition blessings are often accompanied by outward signs or gestures: the outstretching, raising or joining of hands, the laying on of hands, the bowing of heads, the sign of the cross, sprinkling with holy water, and the use of incense. These gestures are not merely interesting options, a way of spicing up the prayer with visuals. They speak to the mystery and truth of the Incarnation and to the mystery and truth of us as the people of the Incarnation. Jesus became flesh and so made all human flesh holy. We are a people whose every sacrament involves touch: the bath that is Baptism, the caress that is the Anointing of the Sick, the joining of hands that is Marriage. We are a people who know our bodies to be good, who gather each Sunday to feast on the Body and Blood of Christ that our own bodies might grow strong in the service of Christ and to Christ in our midst.

Because our whole body has been redeemed and made holy, we praise God with our whole body. We walk in procession. We sing. We kneel. We stand. We bow. We listen and speak. We bring our gifts *to* the altar and receive the Bread of Life and the Cup of Salvation *from* the minister. We eat and drink. We anoint one another and lay our hands in blessing. We offer an embrace of peace.

Because our whole body has been redeemed and made holy, we serve God with our whole body. We visit the sick. We feed the hungry. We clothe the naked. We come to those in prison. We pray for those in need.

Students may be familiar with the term "practicing Catholic." It is a good term and an important one, for practice involves more than thinking about a thing. No one calls *thinking* about scales a practice of them. No one calls *thinking* about jumping hurdles the practice of it. Thinking is surely a part of practice but not the whole. To practice one must do: place hands on the keys and play, lace on one's shoes and run. It requires the body, the use of the body. The same is true of our life of faith. We bless and are blessed, in mind and in body, with gesture and touch, with song and with silence, with works of mercy and healing.

Noah ben Shea has written that "Prayer is a path where there is none, and ritual is prayer's vehicle." May this book lead you to find paths in the wilderness, and may the blessings you learn by heart light your way.

—Melissa Musick Nussbaum

The Memorial of Kateri Tekakwitha 2003

About the Music

Expressing and strengthening faith through song is an essential, enlivening part of prayer. *Music in Catholic Worship* reminds us that "The quality of joy and enthusiasm . . . cannot be gained in any other way." Songs are included throughout *Blessings and Prayers* in several ways.

• Sometimes a commonly known song, such as "All Creatures of Our God and King" or "Now Thank We All Our God," is suggested within a particular prayer service. These are easy to find in most parish music missals or hymnals.

• In a few instances, when a song is particular to just one prayer service, the words are included within the body of a prayer service. These can be copied onto individual sheets, written on a board, or projected onto a wall or screen to facilitate participation. The *Las Posadas* song in Spanish and English on pages 51 through 53 is an example of text that can be copied.

• In addition, twenty seven songs with notes and words are included at the back of this book. These songs are useful for a number of different prayer services and can form a solid repertoire for prayer throughout the year. The titles are recommended in the notes before a particular prayer service.

How to Use the CDs

To facilitate learning the songs included in this book and singing them during prayer times, they are recorded on the two CDs in the back of this book. The first CD includes piano and voice to guide you and your students as you learn a song. The second CD includes only the piano part, to accompany you once you are confident with the singing. These songs do not require a soloist or cantor; everyone can sing them together. Many of the songs are successful without accompaniment; a cappella singing is a time-honored tradition in Catholic prayer.

Planning the Music

Many of these songs are well suited to any service within a particular season or topical section of this book. Here is a list for your reference and planning. The number following each title refers to the song numbers in the Song section beginning on page 233.

HARVEST TIME
Sing Out, Earth and Skies (22); Jubilate Servite (14); Sing to God with the Tambourine (23)

ADVENT
Awake, Awake and Greet the New Morn (2); In the Lord I'll Be Ever Thankful (12), O Come, O Come, Emmanuel

CHRISTMASTIME
Joy to the World (15); refrains of Christmas carols known by heart; a Glory to God setting from Mass

LENT
From Ashes to the Living Font (7); Lenten Gospel Acclamation (16); Jesus, Remember Me/Cristo, Recuérdame (13); Lift High the Cross (17)

EASTERTIME
Oh, How Good Is Jesus Christ!/¡O Que Bueno Es Jesús¡ (18); Celtic Alleluia (4); Shalom, My Friends (20)

PRAYERS FOR HAPPY DAYS
Sing to God with the Tambourine (23); Jubilate, Servite (14); In the Lord I'll Be Ever Thankful (12); Oh, How Good Is Jesus Christ!/¡O Que Bueno Es Jesús! (18)

PRAYERS FOR DIFFICULT TIMES
All Will Be Well (1); Come, All You Blessed Ones (5); Shalom, My Friends (20); Jesus, Remember Me/Cristo, Recuérdame (13)

Some songs can be used for a particular liturgical action or event regardless of the season. Using a song regularly helps students to learn songs by heart and to sing easily.

GATHERING
Come, Let Us Sing with Joy (6); Send Forth Your Spirit, O Lord (19)

WELCOMING THE WORD
If Today You Hear the Voice of God (11); Celtic Alleluia (4); Lenten Gospel Acclamation (16)

PROCESSIONS
We Are Marching in the Light of God/Siyahamba (26)

INTERCESSIONS
Hear Us, O God/Óyenos, Señor (10)

CLOSING
Go Now in Peace (9)

MORNING
This Day God Gives Me (24)

MEALS
Bless Us, O Lord (3)

—Mary Beth Kunde-Anderson

Part One

Seasons of
the School and
Parish Year

Autumn
September and October

In the northern hemisphere the autumn season is marked by shorter days, cooler weather, splashes of color on the tree, and the presence in grocery stores of pumpkins, squash, and Indian corn. The air is crisp, the colors are bright, and a new school year is beginning, full of promise and possibility. The opening of school has changed our activities to include time for study, team sports, and new friendships.

There are many feast days to enjoy during September and October. The feast of the Holy Cross on September 14 reminds us that the suffering and death of Jesus were not signs of defeat, but of God's saving love. It is a feast day for blessing the crosses in our classrooms or homes, a day often chosen for the first school Mass of the year.

We remember the Blessed Mother on the feast of her birthday, September 8, and a month later, October 7, we honor her under the title of Our Lady of the Rosary. In addition to the prayer for that day (on page 16), information on the rosary is given in Section Three, page 231.

In autumn, when the weather begins to chill and the days get shorter, nature is warning everyone to bring in the harvest. Winter, with its cold winds and empty fields, is not far off. In the Bible, angels appear in times of worry or distress. They are the sign of the support and guidance God gives those who listen and believe. Therefore, two feasts of angels are assigned to autumn, where they watch over those who fear the coming of winter or other difficulties.

The three archangels remembered on September 29, are Gabriel, who brought good news to Zechariah and to Mary; Raphael, who was healer and guide to the family of Tobias; and Michael, who won the battle with Satan. These powerful figures, in addition to the guardian angels whose feast is October 2, are excellent reminders of the loving and protective presence of God.

Autumn is part of what the church calls Ordinary Time. The name does not mean that this season is commonplace, something dull or boring. It is simply another way of calling it "ordinal" or "counted" time, because we are counting the weeks—the 27th Sunday in Ordinary Time, the 28th Sunday in Ordinary Time—until the year ends with the Solemnity of Christ the King.

Let us, with celebration and prayer, make each of these glorious autumn days count.

Meal Prayer for Autumn

Music options: Bless Us, O Lord (3) or In the Lord I'll Be Ever Thankful (12)

♩ begin or end with a song

LEADER   Let us offer God praise and thanksgiving.

✛ all make the sign of the cross

ALL   In the name of the Father, and of the Son, and of the Holy Spirit. Amen.

LEADER   Loving God,
          you set a table before us
          and fill it with good things.
          Teach us to share what we have
          so that no one who comes to eat
          finds an empty table.
          We ask this through Christ our Lord.

ALL   Amen.

LEADER   For the food we are about to eat
          and for the life that it nourishes,
          let us offer thanks to God.

✛ all make the sign of the cross

ALL   In the name of the Father, and of the Son, and of the Holy Spirit. Amen.

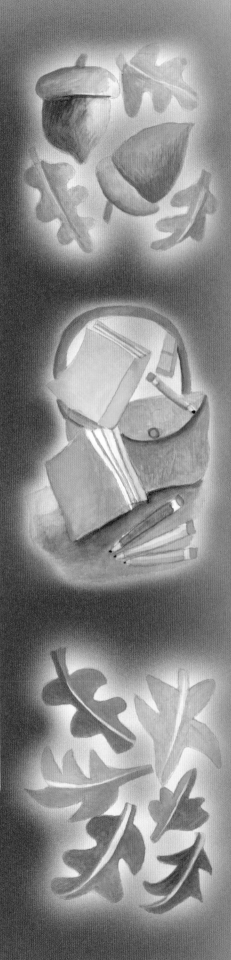

Prayer to Begin the School Year

The new year deserves a ceremonial beginning. Even if the whole school will celebrate an opening Mass, it is helpful for students in each classroom or department to gather for prayer on the first or second day of school. An informal blessing and a treat can help to immediately establish an atmosphere of prayer and friendship.

Preparation: Bring enough bread to be shared and a basket or other equipment to help share it. Choose a tasty, hearty loaf.

Select two leaders and one helper.

Music options: Come, Let Us Sing with Joy (6), Sing Out, Earth and Skies (22), Send Forth Your Spirit, O Lord (19), For Your Gracious Blessing (8)

♩ begin and end with a song

LEADER ONE Let us dedicate this year as we dedicate each day by signing ourselves with the cross of Jesus.

⁙ all make the sign of the cross

LEADER ONE It is good to begin our season of study in the autumn, when farmers are bringing in their harvest of good things to eat.

With God's unchanging kindness,
the work of the farmer
has brought wheat from the earth,
and the work of the baker
has provided bread.
So, with God's help,
our work in this class will bring us
nourishment and growth.

LEADER TWO Let us all say: Psalm 96:3–4, 11–13
Sing a new song to the Lord!

ALL **Sing a new song to the Lord!**

LEADER TWO Tell every nation on earth,
"The Lord is wonderful
and does marvelous things!
The Lord is great and deserves
our greatest praise!"
Tell the heavens and the earth
to be glad and celebrate!

Command the ocean to roar
with all of its creatures
and the fields to rejoice
with all of their crops.
Then every tree in the forest
will sing joyful songs to the Lord.

ALL   **Sing a new song to the Lord!**

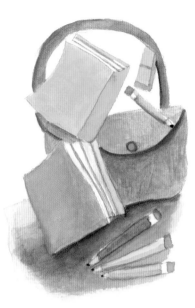

helper prepares the bread for sharing

LEADER ONE   God our Creator, provider of food
both for our bodies and for our minds,
bless this bread
as the sign of all the good things
we will share during this new school year:
increasing knowledge,
deepening friendships,
challenging activities, and
opportunities for leadership.
Bless us as we bite into the work of this year
ready to be nourished with your wisdom,
united in your love,
and strengthened by your presence
We ask this through Christ our Lord.

ALL   **Amen.**

 all make the sign of the cross

all enjoy the tasty treat

Blessing of the School

In September the school building can be a forbidding place for students and for teachers, even those who have been part of the school community for several years. A welcoming tour of the building can ease anxieties and help new students to start off on the right foot. It also can reinforce the understanding that school is a place where we work, grow and help one another, where we form friendships and share our hopes and dreams.

This ritual takes the form of a pilgrimage, a journey to survey and take responsibility for the space in which a great deal of living will be done during the coming school year. It is written as an annual event during the early weeks of the school year but may easily be adapted for other uses. It can be used by a class, a department, or the whole school.

Preparation:

1. Choose the STATIONS to visit and map your journey. Some possibilities are:
   - gathering spots: playground, cafeteria, assembly hall, school lobby
   - religious features: chapel or church, patron saint's image
   - nerve centers: lost and found area, offices of the principal, counselor, school nurse
   - safety features: fire alarm, security doors, off-limits areas
   - hands-on learning areas: gym, art and music rooms, library

2. Choose a GREETER for each station. The greeter will welcome the pilgrims and say a few words about that place, then send the pilgrims on their journey.

3. Choose MUSIC for the procession.

4. Make ADAPTATIONS. A large group might be divided into smaller processions following alternate routes. Younger children might make a series of short pilgrimages rather than touring the entire building at once. Children might carry something, such as flowers or drawings to be left at each station, fragrant herbs, pennants, ribbons, or rhythm instruments. The procession leader carries a candle or processional cross. The leader is followed by someone with holy water and by another person delegated to bless each station with the water as the procession moves through the building. Choices should be influenced by the degree of formality that is desired.

Music options: We Are Marching (26), Jubilate Servite (14), For Your Gracious Blessing (8)

LEADER   Let us offer God praise and thanksgiving.

⠿   all make the sign of the cross

LEADER   Today we visit the spaces in which,
through God's grace,
we are gathered in the name of Jesus,
filled with the Holy Spirit,
and formed into a community
of learners and friends.
On this journey
let us remember that God is with us
as we move through this building
and through the year ahead.

♩ begin the song as the group forms a line behind the leader and moves to the first station

at the first station all gather around the greeter

GREETER   Peace be with you.

ALL   **And also with you.**

the greeter tells about the place

the leader sprinkles water to bless the place

the greeter ends the blessing of this station with a "dismissal"

GREETER   As you now continue your journey
           may God be with you.

ALL   **And also with you.**

move to the next station, and the next, repeating the pattern of prayer, song and sprinkling until you return to your starting place

LEADER   Loving God, we praise and thank you
           for bringing us together.
           Bless all who pray and work and learn in this place.
           And grant a happy year to all the world.
           We ask this through Christ our Lord.

ALL   **Amen.**

Prayer for the Feast of the Birth of Mary

September 8

Preparation: The class might walk in procession to a statue of Mary in the church or in the garden of the school, or an image of Mary can be carried around the classroom. During the procession, the class can honor Mary with songs. Flowers can be placed at or near the statue.

Once the group is gathered, the following prayer is said. Select a reader.

Music options: Sing of Mary (21), We Sing of the Saints (27), with verse for feasts of Mary, or any familiar hymn to Mary

On this day we celebrate the birthday of Mary, the woman chosen by God to become the mother of the Savior. Because she is the mother of Jesus, she is also the mother of all who believe in him and follow his way. So we call her our Blessed Mother.

Long ago this was a day for a procession to the church of Saint Mary Major in Rome.

♩ begin and end with a song

LEADER   Let us begin our prayer.

⁛ all make the sign of the cross

READER   Listen to the words of the holy Gospel according to Luke   1:28–32, 38

The angel greeted Mary and said, "You are truly blessed! The Lord is with you."

Mary was confused by the angel's words and wondered what they meant. Then the angel told Mary, "Don't be afraid! God is pleased with you, and you will have a son. His name will be Jesus. He will be great and will be called the Son of God Most High."

Mary said, "I am the Lord's servant! Let it happen as you have said."

The Gospel of the Lord.

ALL   Praise to you, Lord Jesus Christ.

LEADER   Mary, our mother,
you sheltered Jesus in your own body,
raised him with a mother's care,
and followed him in faith.
With you, we celebrate God's saving love.
Let us all say:

ALL Hail, Mary, full of grace,
the Lord is with you!
Blessed are you among women,
and blessed is the fruit of your womb, Jesus.
Holy Mary, Mother of God,
pray for us sinners,
now and at the hour of our death. Amen.

Blessing of the Cross

SEPTEMBER 14, FEAST OF THE TRIUMPH OF THE CROSS

Preparation: To celebrate this feast, place flowers or incense near the classroom cross. If it is high on the wall, another can be brought for the occasion. Crosses brought from home can be placed on desks and blessed by their owners as the leader blesses the classroom cross.

Rehearse the response, "For by your holy cross. . . ." Practice how you will bow to the cross. Select a reader.

Music option: Lift High the Cross (17)

⋮ all make the sign of the cross

LEADER   We adore you, O Christ, and we bless you!

ALL   **For by your holy cross
you have redeemed the world.**

READER   Listen to the words of the apostle Paul
to the Phillipians   2:8–11

Christ was humble. He obeyed God and even died on
a cross.

Then God gave Christ the highest place and
honored his name above all others. So at the name
of Jesus everyone will bow down, those in heaven,
on earth, and under the earth. And to the glory of God
the Father everyone will openly agree, "Jesus Christ
is Lord!"

The word of the Lord.

ALL   **Thanks be to God.**

> The cross is the symbol for the way Jesus defeated sin, hatred, and death. The sign of the cross shows our willingness to follow Jesus and our joy at being part of his family. We first were signed with holy oil at Baptism, and our bodies will receive the sign for the last time on our day of burial. It is a pledge of our unity with Christ and his Church, and his saving love for us.

LEADER The sign of the cross shall be in the heavens
when the Lord comes.
Lift up your heads!
Your redemption is near when the Lord comes.

if incense is used, wave the smoke gently toward the cross

LEADER Loving God,
we have raised this cross
as a sign of our faith.
May we always hold fast
to the mystery of Christ's suffering
and enter the joy of his risen life.
He is Lord for ever and ever.

ALL **Amen.**

LEADER We adore you, O Christ, and we bless you!

ALL **For by your holy cross
you have redeemed the world.**

all make a deep bow toward the cross

 all make the sign of the cross

 end with a song

Prayer at the Autumn Equinox

SEPTEMBER 20, 21, OR 22

Preparation: The class should compose a number of petitions. Focus on groups of people or situations in the world that need God's help in finding peace, harmony, and equality. Select readers for the petitions.

Music option: Shalom, My Friends (20)

LEADER   Blessed be God, Creator of days and seasons.
          Let us all say:
          Blessed be God forever!

ALL   **Blessed be God forever!**

LEADER   Let us now try to make our bodies and minds
          still and peaceful.
          Let us ask God in our hearts for the peace and
          balance that we need.

          keep the stillness for a full minute or more

LEADER   Let us remember these intentions.

          those who are prepared offer petitions
          other petitions may be added

LEADER   Loving God, you give us hours, days and years.
          You give us a world to grow in.
          Let our work and our play,
          our sorrows and our joys,
          add to the rightness and balance of your creation.
          We ask this through Christ our Lord.

ALL   **Amen.**

♩ *end with a song*

When the exact middle of the earth, the equator, is turned exactly toward the sun, there are equal hours of daylight and darkness. The day on which this happens, once in the autumn and once in the spring, is called the equinox, or "day of balance."

From the autumn equinox the hours of darkness grow longer than the hours of daylight. Soon it will be dark before suppertime, and we will know that winter is coming.

Buddhists call the equinox *higan-e,* and they see it as a symbol of peace, equality, and harmony. We can use this day to reflect on the need for balance in our world.

For the day and exact time of the equinox, consult a science website.

Blessing of Flower Bulbs

SEPTEMBER 29, FEAST OF ARCHANGELS MICHAEL, GABRIEL, AND RAPHAEL

OCTOBER 2, MEMORIAL OF GUARDIAN ANGELS

Preparation: Purchase bulbs that grow well in your part of the country. Bring a shovel and copies of the song below, "Michael, Image of God's Justice." Gather where you will plant the bulbs—a sunny spot that is not too wet. Select a reader.

Music options: Michael, Image of God's Justice (sung to the melody of Beethoven's Hymn to Joy), We Sing of the Saints (27), with verse for September 29: Archangels

LEADER	Let us offer God praise and thanksgiving.

 all make the sign of the cross

LEADER	We remember the angels Michael, Gabriel, and Raphael, as well as the guardian angels, in the autumn when the earth is preparing for its winter sleep. Angels are messengers of God's loving care. They say to us, "Be hopeful. Trust in the Lord." To celebrate our trust in God, we will plant some flower bulbs. One day they will surprise us with their beauty.
READER	Listen to the words of the holy Gospel according to Mark 4:26–28
	Jesus said, "God's kingdom is like what happens when a farmer scatters seed in a field. The farmer sleeps at night and is up and around during the day. Yet the seeds keep sprouting and growing, and he doesn't understand how. It is the ground that makes the seeds sprout and grow into plants that produce grain."
	The Gospel of the Lord.
ALL	**Praise to you, Lord Jesus Christ.**
LEADER	Let us praise God, who has brought us into this autumn season.
ALL	**In the sight of the angels, I will sing your praises, Lord.**

The Bible tells us that angels are messengers from God who bring guidance and support in times of uncertainty. Michael, who defeated the disobedient angels, is a patron to defend us against evil. Raphael, who protected Tobias on a dangerous journey and cured his father's blindness, can be called upon when we need healing or guidance. Gabriel announced to Mary the coming of the Messiah. It is Gabriel who will announce with a trumpet the coming of Christ at the end of time.

The Church has assigned two feast days for angels in the autumn, when the earth begins to close down and people become concerned about survival during the cold, dark months to come. Angels remind us that God has not left us unprotected or alone. They remind us that spring will come, and the earth will come to life again in a blaze of color and warmth.

It is a custom to plant flowering bulbs on the feasts of the angels. Bulbs, like angels, are signs of hope. They are an autumn investment in the spring that is to come.

LEADER Let us praise God,
who will bring us through the winter cold.

ALL **In the sight of the angels,
I will sing your praises, Lord.**

LEADER Let us praise God,
who will bring us to the beauty of springtime.

ALL **In the sight of the angels,
I will sing your praises, Lord.**

LEADER Let us lift up the bulbs and pray.

Creator God,
we ask your blessing on these bulbs.
May they sleep safely in the winter earth
and awaken with joy in the warmth of spring.
May they remind us to trust in your promises.
We ask this through Christ our Lord.

ALL **Amen.**

plant the bulbs

♩ sing Michael, Image of God's Justice using the melody of Hymn to Joy

Michael, image of God's justice,
Angel warrior, God's right arm,
March beside us on our journey;
Ward off evil, fear and harm.

Gabriel, voice of God's salvation,
Messenger with news of grace,
Teach us of God's works and wonders
And the beauty of God's face.

Raphael, star to brighten darkness,
Giving friendship, giving sight,
Walk the path that we must travel,
Our companion through the night.

Joined in song by angel guardians,
Let our alleluias ring.
God is with us now and always.
Glory to our Lord and King!

Blessing of Pets

OCTOBER 4, MEMORIAL OF SAINT FRANCIS OF ASSISI

Preparation: An image of Saint Francis can be put in a place of honor. If the blessing takes place at school and the pets are left at home, photos or drawings of them can be posted on a bulletin board, or placed at the prayer center or shrine. If pets are brought from home, the blessing may take place outdoors. The pets' safety must always be kept in mind. Select two readers.

Music options: Sing Out, Earth and Skies (22), We Sing of the Saints (27), All Creatures of Our God and King

 begin and end with a song

LEADER   Let us offer God praise and thanksgiving.

all make the sign of the cross

LEADER   Let us bless the Lord,
            now and for ever.

ALL   **Amen.**

LEADER   Animals fill the skies, the earth and the seas. They are God's beloved creatures. Saint Francis remembered this. He called the animals his brothers and sisters. Today we ask God to bless these animals, our brothers and sisters. We thank God for letting us share the earth with such wonderful and amazing creatures.

READER ONE Listen to the words of the book of Genesis   1:20–22, 24–25

            God said, "I command the ocean to be full of living creatures, and I command birds to fly above the earth." So God made the giant sea monsters and all the living creatures that swim in the ocean. He also made every kind of bird. God looked at what he had done, and it was good. Then he gave the living creatures his blessing—he told the ocean creatures to live everywhere in the ocean and the birds to live everywhere on earth.

READER TWO God said, "I command the earth to give life to all
kinds of tame animals, wild animals, and reptiles."
And that's what happened. God made every
one of them. Then he looked at what he had done,
and it was good.

The word of the Lord.

ALL **Thanks be to God.**

LEADER O God our creator,
everything that has the breath of life
gives you praise!
We ask you to
watch over our pets and all animals.
Keep them in good health.
Guard them against trouble.
May the wisdom of Saint Francis
and our love for these animals
deepen our respect for all your creation.
We ask this through Christ our Lord.

ALL **Amen.**

 all make the sign of the cross

your pet deserves a treat

The Rosary

From its earliest beginnings, the Church has held Mary, the mother of Jesus, in great esteem. She is called the Mother of God, Mother of the Church, and our own Blessed Mother. Catholics can show their devotion to Mary by inviting her to pray with and for them. One way of doing this is by using the rosary and thinking about the events in her life and the life of her son.

For many centuries people have kept a count of prayers by moving their fingers over a string of beads or knots. In early days it helped people remember prayers that they knew by heart. Today it is an aid to counting repeated prayers. It often brings a sense of quiet and peace that helps people to reflect on the mysteries of the rosary.

For more information about the mysteries of the rosary, turn to page 231. There you will find a list of the traditional fifteen mysteries, as well as the five Mysteries of Light suggested by Pope John Paul II in 2002.

Preparation: When praying the rosary in school, we usually say one decade. To begin, a mystery—or event in the plan of God—is announced. Then the Our Father is said, followed by ten Hail Marys, and finally the doxology ("Glory to the Father . . ."). The following order of prayer includes both a decade of the rosary and a reading from the Bible. For a shorter prayer, omit the reading and say only three Hail Marys. Select a reader.

Music options: Sing of Mary (21), We Sing of the Saints (27), with verse for feasts of Mary, or any other hymn to Mary

♪ begin and end with a song

LEADER   Let us offer God praise and thanksgiving.

∴ all make the sign of the cross

READER   Listen to the words of the holy Gospel according to Luke   1:40–45

Mary went into Zechariah's home, where she greeted Elizabeth. When Elizabeth heard Mary's greeting, her baby moved within her.

The Holy Spirit came upon Elizabeth. Then in a loud voice she said to Mary, "God has blessed you more than any other woman! He has also blessed the child you will have. Why should the mother of my Lord come to me? As soon as I heard your greeting, my baby became happy and moved within me. The Lord has blessed you because you believed that he will keep his promise."

The Gospel of the Lord.

ALL   **Praise to you, Lord Jesus Christ.**

LEADER   The second joyful mystery: the Visitation.
Let us imagine ourselves with Elizabeth as she greets Mary. Like Elizabeth, we too announce that God has blessed her and her son, the fruit of her womb.

LEADER
Our Father, who art in heaven,
hallowed be thy name;
thy kingdom come;
thy will be done on earth as it is in heaven.

ALL
Give us this day our daily bread;
and forgive us our trespasses
as we forgive those who trespass against us;
and lead us not into temptation,
but deliver us from evil. Amen.

LEADER
Hail Mary, full of grace,
the Lord is with you!
Blessed are you among women,
and blessed is the fruit of your womb, Jesus.

ALL
Holy Mary, Mother of God,
pray for us sinners,
now and at the hour of our death. Amen.

repeat the Hail Mary nine more times, or for a shorter prayer,
two more times

LEADER
Glory to the Father, and to the Son,
and to the Holy Spirit:

ALL
As it was in the beginning, is now,
and will be for ever. Amen.

Harvest Time
November

Harvest festivals are the earliest and most universal form of prayer. There is nothing as powerful as the sight of food gathered from the earth to turn our thoughts to God, our Creator. Like the bountiful earth, God is generous with us. Harvest time reminds us to say "thank you!"

Harvest time also reminds us to pay attention to the beauty of growing things, from the rough brown potato to the brilliantly colored zinnia. The stunning beauty of the earth reminds us of the importance of caring for it.

It reminds us also that even as some people bring in rich harvests, others go hungry. The earth does not provide good weather and good soil in every location. But when people and nations create just systems of distribution, when they notice the needs of others and willingly share what they have, there is enough food for everyone.

Each culture has its own way of celebrating the harvest, but there are several elements in common. You will want to include these elements in your prayer during this season:

- prayers of thanksgiving
- a spirit of happiness and abundance (sometimes shown through music and dancing)
- the eating of food and the offering of food to the hungry
- decorative use of fruit, vegetables, grains, and flowers available in your region.

On page 20 there are some suggestions for using the fruits and vegetables of the harvest to decorate the prayer center and for sharing a nutritious treat.

Rosh Hashanah and Thanksgiving are harvest festivals. The prayer for Rosh Hashanah on page 219 suggests the sharing of honey-dipped apple slices. The sharing of food might also be included in your Thanksgiving prayer, see page 206. Be sure to look at your calendar and review the prayers in this book so that you can carefully plan your days of celebration.

Meal Prayer for Harvest Time

Music options: Bless Us, O Lord (3), Now Thank We All Our God, or another familiar hymn of thanksgiving

 begin or end with a song

LEADER Let us offer God praise and thanksgiving.

 all make the sign of the cross

LEADER   Blessed be the name of the Lord.
ALL   **Now and for ever.**

LEADER   Loving God, all that we have
            comes from your goodness
            and the work of those who love us.
            Bless us and the food we share.
            Watch over those who care for us.
            Open our eyes to the needs of the poor
            during this time of harvest and thanksgiving.
            We ask this through Christ our Lord.
ALL   **Amen.**

 all make the sign of the cross

Blessing of the Harvest and Harvest Prayer Center

The law of Moses commanded the people of God always to leave a good portion for the poor when they harvested their grapes or wheat or barley. During November people often collect clothing, food, or money for the poor as a way of sharing the bounty of the land as well as providing them a means of celebrating the Thanksgiving feast.

If the school or class does this, place the things you collect near your prayer center. These gifts really help other people. At the same time, they also represent the way we should care all year long about the poor, the hungry, and the homeless people of the world. If you bring together gifts for others, you may want to bless them before sending them out for Thanksgiving. A Blessing of Gifts is on page 207.

Rejoice in God's bountiful earth by sharing in its rich flavors. If the school has a stove, make a delicious vegetable soup. Each student can bring a single ingredient, such as a vegetable, herb, or salt. Students can wash, peel, and slice. While the soup is cooking, they might say the blessing prayer and then take turns reading aloud *Stone Soup*, by Marcia Brown.

You may prefer to bring a variety of fruits, along with a plate, knife, napkins, and other equipment needed to share it. Prepare some for eating and place the rest in a bowl in the prayer center.

Preparation: Celebrate the bounty of the land by bringing some of its products into the classroom. You might use vegetables to decorate the prayer area. Use vegetables that won't go bad if they sit without refrigeration, such as eggplant, cabbage, onions, potatoes, yams, green peppers, radishes, carrots, corn, acorn squash, and of course, pumpkins. Add fall leaves or grains from your area to make a beautiful display.

If you wish, prepare some of the food for eating. When food is offered, always be aware of students who have food allergies.

Place a bowl of holy water nearby. The prayer is marked for three leaders, but as many as six could take a turn. Select three (or more) leaders.

Music options: Sing Out, Earth and Skies (22), Sing to God with the Tambourine (23), For Your Gracious Blessing (8)

♩ begin and end with a song

LEADER ONE   I praise you, Lord God, with all my heart.

Let us all say, "With all my heart I sing praise!"

ALL   **With all my heart I sing praise!**

LEADER ONE   Our God, you deserve praise!   Psalm 65:1, 9, 10–12
You take care of the earth and send rain
to help the soil grow all kinds of crops.

LEADER TWO   Your rivers never run dry,
and you prepare the earth to produce much grain.

LEADER THREE   You send showers of rain to soften the soil
and help the plants to sprout.

LEADER ONE   Wherever your footsteps touch the earth,
a rich harvest is gathered.

sprinkle with holy water the fruits and vegetables
or other gifts of the land

LEADER TWO   Bless us, O Lord, and these fruits and vegetables
(flowers, grains) of the harvest season.

LEADER THREE May all who taste them be filled with joy;
and may they be for us
a sign of that final harvest
when all creation is gathered
into your kingdom,
to live with you for ever and ever.

ALL   **Amen.**

all make the sign of the cross

enjoy the food

Prayer at Halloween

OCTOBER 31, THE EVE OF ALL SAINTS' DAY

Preparation: The following prayer is an appropriate beginning for an all-school Halloween or All Saints' Day party, or for a parade of costumes. For a celebration within a classroom, the prayer can be shortened by omitting Psalm 96. Select a reader.

Music options: We Sing of the Saints (27), Come, All You Blessed Ones (5), When the Saints Go Marchin' In

LEADER   Let us offer God praise and thanksgiving.

all make the sign of the cross

LEADER   Great is the Lord, worthy of praise!
ALL   **Tell all the nations "God is Great";**
spread the news of God's love.

LEADER   Sing a new song to the Lord!   Psalm 96:1–3
Everyone on this earth,
sing praises to the Lord,
sing and praise his name.
Day after day announce,
"The Lord has saved us!"
Tell every nation on earth,

Days were once counted from sunset to sunset, and so Christian feasts begin in the evening before the day that is marked on the calendar. The evening (or "eve") of All Saints was called "All hallows evening." "Hallows" means holy. "All hallows evening was shortened to "Hallowe'en." The evening of October 31 begins our two-day remembrance of our ancestors and heroes of the faith.

Many Halloween customs were inherited from pre-Christian times, when people felt both respect for their ancestors and fear of death during the coming winter. After the harvest was collected and the days became short and dark, people made bonfires to welcome the spirits of the dead. The lights in jack-o-lanterns are the remains of this custom. The eerie faces carved in them are meant to scare away unfriendly spirits. Food offerings were left for the spirits, just as we give sweets to visiting trick-or-treat ghosts.

People once dressed up like their dead relatives or heroes to invite the spirits of those people to return and bless them. Today we sometimes dress as saints or heroes, and sometimes as ghosts or skeletons. The evening is a traditional time for singing, dancing, and storytelling around the bonfires, and for enjoying delicious treats.

Christians know that those who have died share now in the resurrection of Christ. With and in Christ we all triumph over death. We use these days to remember our departed saints and to retell their stories. Our Halloween customs help us to laugh at the idea of ghosts and to celebrate with costumes, masks, and games our joy at being part of God's holy people.

"The Lord is wonderful
and does marvelous things!"
Great is the Lord, worthy of praise!

ALL **Tell all the nations "God is Great";
spread the news of God's love.**

READER Listen to the words of the book of Revelation   7:13–14, 17

One of the elders asked me, "Do you know who these people are that are dressed in white robes? Do you know where they come from?"

"Sir," I answered, "you must know."

Then he told me: "These are the ones who have gone through the great suffering. They have washed their robes in the blood of the Lamb and have made them white. The Lamb in the center of the throne will be their shepherd. He will lead them to streams of life-giving water, and God will wipe all tears from their eyes."

The word of the Lord.

ALL **Thanks be to God.**

LEADER Let us pray.

May God be ever before us,
leading the procession of saints.
May God be at our side
a companion on our journey.
May God be at the center,
the source of our joy and celebration.
We ask this through Christ our Lord.

ALL **Amen.**

LEADER Great is the Lord, worthy of praise!
ALL **Tell all the nations, "God is Great";
spread the news of God's love.**

 all make the sign of the cross

♩ sing a song and begin the procession

Litany of the Saints

Preparation: Ask students to think about saints who are important to them, or who are patron saints. Important names that are not included in the litany below can be added.

Music options: The following litany may be chanted or spoken. End with We Sing of the Saints (27), Celtic Alleluia (4), or a familiar alleluia.

⁘ all make the sign of the cross

LEADER	ALL
Lord, have mercy.	**Lord, have mercy.**
Christ, have mercy.	**Christ, have mercy.**
Lord, have mercy.	**Lord, have mercy.**
Holy Mary, Mother of God,	**pray for us.**
Saint Michael,	**pray for us.**
Holy angels of God,	**pray for us.**
Saint Abraham and Saint Sarah,	**pray for us.**
Saint Isaac and Saint Rebekah,	**pray for us.**
Saint John the Baptist,	**pray for us.**
Saint Joseph,	**pray for us.**
Saint Peter and Saint Paul,	**pray for us.**
Saint Mary Magdalene,	**pray for us.**
Saint Stephen,	**pray for us.**
Saint Agnes,	**pray for us.**
Saint Martin,	**pray for us.**
Saint Margaret,	**pray for us.**
Saint Catherine,	**pray for us.**
Saint Benedict,	**pray for us.**
Saint Francis,	**pray for us.**
Saint Clare,	**pray for us.**
Saint Dominic,	**pray for us.**
Saint Theresa,	**pray for us.**
Saint Elizabeth Ann Seton,	**pray for us.**

other names of saints, especially student and school patrons, may be added

November, the time of harvest and the beginning of the earth's winter sleep, begins with a double feast in remembrance of those who have died. The saints, people already "harvested" into God's kingdom, are remembered on November 1, All Saints' Day. On November 2, we pray for all family members and friends who have died. We pray that they too are numbered among God's holy ones. Each saint has something to teach about living as faithful Christians, and we rely on them to pray for us. We know that they will ask God to strengthen and protect us. This is a good time to learn more about our patron saints.

This day is a solemnity, the highest rank in the Church's order of celebrations. It is also a holy day of obligation, which means that Catholics participate in the Eucharist on this day if they can. These honors show us how important it is to be active members in the sacred

exchange of love and sup-
port that exists between
those who have died and
those who are still living
on this earth.

On the day of our Baptism
the church used the Litany
of the Saints, calling upon
many saints by name, asking
them to pray for us. We
use it again to celebrate and
honor them.

LEADER   **ALL**

All holy men and women,   **pray for us.**

LEADER   Let us take a few moments in silence
to pray with all the saints.

allow a minute or two of silence

We praise you, O God, and we honor all your holy ones.
We ask the help of those men, women, and children
who struggled against evil and stood firm,
who loved one another,
who worked for justice and peace,
who healed the sick and fed the hungry.
We on earth and they in heaven
sing one song of praise.
We in grace and they in glory
form one communion in Christ, your Son.
Make us and all those we love
worthy to be called your saints.
We ask this through Christ our Lord.

ALL   **Amen.**

LEADER   Let us pray with the words that Jesus taught us.

ALL   **Our Father . . .**

♩ *end with a song or alleluia*

Prayer for All Souls' Day

NOVEMBER 2, COMMEMORATION OF ALL THE FAITHFUL
DEPARTED, ALL SOULS' DAY, *EL DÍA DE LOS MUERTOS*

Preparation: The following prayer is for friends and relatives who have died.
It can be used at any time, especially during the month of November. If you prepare
a classroom shrine, gather there to pray. A shrine can be as simple as a candle
placed next to a list of people the class wishes to remember. Or pictures, memorial
cards, or drawings of those people can be brought. Symbols of harvest and of death
and resurrection can be added. In Mexico, shrines for the Day of the Dead are
often elaborately decorated with many objects or *offrenda*. They include beans, corn,
pumpkins, gourds, bread, the crucifix, the paschal candle, candy skulls, skeletons
in bright party clothes, figures of the tree of life, or flowers, as well as remembrances
of those who have died during the past year.

A prayer for someone who has died very recently is on page 202.

Music option: Come, All You Blessed Ones (5)

♩ begin or end with a song

LEADER	Let us offer God praise and thanksgiving.

⁛ all make the sign of the cross

LEADER	Blessed be God
	who raised Jesus Christ from the dead.
	Let us all say: Blessed be God for ever.
ALL	**Blessed be God for ever.**
LEADER	In silence, let us take a few moments now to
	remember the dead.

allow a minute or so of silence

LEADER	Lord God, whose days are without end
	and whose mercies are beyond counting,
	keep us mindful that life is short
	and the hour of death unknown.
	Let your Spirit guide our days on earth
	in the ways of holiness and justice,
	that we may serve you
	in union with the whole church,

This is the day we set aside
to pray for all who have
died, especially our family
members and friends.
All those who are baptized
are members of the one
Body of Christ, whether they
are living or dead. Our love
and work on earth can
be a blessing to those who
have died, just as their love
is a blessing for the living.
We call the unity of love, con-
cern, and prayer the
"communion of saints."

In some places, families
and parish groups go to the
cemetery on November 2
with food, candles, and
photos of the dead. They pull
up the weeds, plant flowers,
pray, picnic, sing, and tell
stories late into the night.
In Latin America, *El Día de los
Muertos,* the Day of the Dead,
is not gloomy or sad. It is
a colorful, lively celebration of
our belief that in death, life is
changed but not ended.

Long ago in England, peo-
ple went from door to door
on this day and begged
for "soul cakes." They sang a
carol, "Soul, soul, soul cake!

Please, good people, a soul cake! One for Peter, two for Paul, three for God who made us all." This may be the beginning of trick-or-treating.

All the elements that are used to celebrate this feast day show the strong faith of Christians that those who have died in Christ are raised with him and share in his glory.

sure in faith, strong in hope,
perfected in love.
And when our earthly journey is ended,
lead us rejoicing into your kingdom,
where you live for ever and ever.

ALL   **Amen.**

LEADER   Eternal rest grant unto them, O Lord.
ALL   **And let perpetual light shine upon them.**

LEADER   May they rest in peace.
ALL   **Amen.**

LEADER   May their souls
and the souls of all the faithful departed,
through the mercy of God, rest in peace.
ALL   **Amen.**

all make the sign of the cross

Blessing of Musicians

NOVEMBER 22, MEMORIAL OF SAINT CECILIA

Preparation: The blessing can be used just for music teachers and leaders of song, for student musicians such as the band or choir, or for all together. Music students might bring their instruments to the gathering, or they could bring a ribbon-tied scroll of sheet music to represent instruments too large to carry. Use your best music during the ceremony.

If the blessing is part of the introductory rite of a school Mass, use the reading for the day and place the intercessions after the homily. A reflection may be given before the intercessions in any case. Musical versions of Psalm 150 appear in many hymnals.

For a shorter ceremony, use only the actual prayer of blessing, but by all means begin and end with a song.

Select a reader.

Music options: Jubilate Servite (14), Celtic Alleluia (4), Sing to God with the Tambourine (23), For Your Gracious Blessing (8)

 begin and end with a song

Saint Cecilia, an early martyr, was greatly loved by her friends in Rome. After her death they turned her home into a church. An early account of her life stated that Cecilia sang in her heart on her wedding day. When the story was copied, the words

LEADER Let us offer God praise and thanksgiving.

✦ all make the sign of the cross

LEADER On this feast of Saint Cecilia we gather to praise and thank God for the presence in our community of talented musicians, and to ask God's blessing on them.

Let us all say:
Sing praise to our God!   Psalm 150
His deeds are wonderful,
too marvelous to describe.

ALL **Sing praise to our God!**
His deeds are wonderful,
too marvelous to describe.

"in her heart" were left out, and later readers were pleased to know that she was so happy and talented that she sang at her own wedding. Saint Cecilia is now the patron of music and musicians. For centuries she has inspired people to write music in praise of God.

LEADER Praise God with trumpets
and all kinds of harps.
Praise him with tambourines
and dancing,
with stringed instruments
and woodwinds.
Praise God with cymbals,
with clashing cymbals.
Let every living creature
praise the Lord.

ALL **Sing praise to our God!**
His deeds are wonderful,
too marvelous to describe.

READER Listen to the words of the second book
of Chronicles   5:1, 3–5, 12–13

After the LORD's temple was finished, Solomon called together all the important leaders of Israel. Then the priests and the Levites picked up the sacred chest, the sacred tent, and the objects used for worship, and they carried them to the temple.

The Levite musicians were wearing robes of fine linen. They were standing on the east side of the altar,

27

LEADER   Continue to watch over your people, Lord.
          Feed, comfort, and protect them,
          now and for ever.
ALL   **Amen.**

the Blessing of Gifts for Giving to the poor can be used here (see page 207), or use the Blessing of Food for Sharing (page 206), or continue

LEADER   Let us lift up our hands to the Lord.

          At this time of Thanksgiving,
          may our gracious God,
          the giver of the harvest,
          bless and protect us.
ALL   **Amen.**

 all make the sign of the cross

♩ sing a song of thanksgiving and praise

Prayer to Christ our King

Preparation: Divide the group into Side A and Side B, and provide copies of the psalm for everyone.

Music option: Lift High the Cross (17)

 all make the sign of the cross

LEADER	The Lord is king!	Psalm 145
ALL	For evermore!	

SIDE A   I will praise you, my God and King,
and always honor your name.
Each generation will announce to the next
your wonderful deeds.

SIDE B   I will tell all nations how great you are.
They will celebrate and sing
about your mercy
and your power to save.

SIDE A   You are merciful, Lord!
You are kind and patient
and always loving.
You are good to everyone,
and you take care of all your creation.

SIDE B   Then everyone will know about
the mighty things you do
and your glorious kingdom.
Your kingdom will never end,
and you will rule forever.

LEADER   The Lord is king!
ALL   For evermore!

 end with a song

As the Church's year ends, our thoughts turn to the end of time, when Jesus will gather his people into glory. We use images and symbols to think about those events because no one knows exactly how it will come about. We say that it will be like a king welcoming people who have been on a long journey to his kingdom. But we do not have to wait until the end of time to become members of that kingdom. Christ our king has come to us! As the book of Revelation says, Jesus "is Lord over all lords and King over all kings. His followers are chosen and special and faithful" (16:14).

Matthew's gospel begins with wise men seeking the newborn "king of the Jews," and ends with Pilate asking, "Are you the king of the Jews?" In between those two scenes are stories of people who knew the answer to that question.

Jesus explained to everyone that his kingdom is not like worldly kingdoms, where rulers abuse power and burden their people. He does not rule with armies but with truth. He does not have a great palace but a great heart filled with love. In his kingdom the oppressed become free, the poor inherit the land, the merciful receive mercy, and the hungry eat like queens and kings.

ADVENT

Advent begins on the fourth Sunday before Christmas. It is a period of simple living and extra prayer as we prepare for the coming of Jesus our Savior. The first coming of Jesus, at Bethlehem, will not happen again. During Advent and Christmas we retell the story of that coming, but it reminds us to prepare for a new coming. In Jesus, God has come among us. He is with us still, and one day when his work is complete, he will gather us into his glory. Until then we wait, and we prepare.

During the weeks of December we hear the encouraging words of Isaiah and John the Baptist. One will come, they tell us, who will be called "Emmanuel," which means "God-with-us." "Prepare the way," they tell us, "make straight his path."

Jesus, the Prince of Peace, calls his followers to make their world loving and peaceful. So we take time during Advent to prepare gifts for others, and we are generous with signs of apology and forgiveness. Many schools and parishes prepare gifts for families in need and plan penance services.

Advent has many customs and traditions. There is the song of invitation, "O Come, O Come Emmanuel." Make an Advent wreath and gather around it for prayer each day. Remember the Advent saints. Set out an empty stable and bless it as a sign of preparation for the coming of Jesus. Use an Advent calendar and open up a window each day, or hang symbols on a Jesse tree. During the final days of Advent, keep the Christmas novena with added prayer (the O Antiphons, for example), or *Las Posadas.* Remember ethnic or local traditions.

There are so many possibilities for the celebration of these days that choices must be made. Look through the prayers and blessings in this section of the book to help you choose which of these customs will help you celebrate the holy season of Advent with simplicity and joy.

Christmas will be the second half of our two-part celebration of the coming of God among us. The very idea of Christmas fills us with expectation! But we don't want to rush into the customs of Christmastime before we savor each part of Advent. We will wait until after December 25 to enjoy Christmas decorations and stories, songs, and parties.

Meal Prayer for Advent

Music option: Bless Us, O Lord (3), or a familiar Advent hymn

LEADER   Let us offer God praise and thanksgiving.

O LORD

all make the sign of the cross

LEADER   Come, Lord Jesus!
ALL   **Come quickly!**

LEADER   Blessed are you, Lord, God of all creation:
in the darkness and in the light.
Blessed are you
in this food and in our sharing.
Blessed are you as we wait in joyful hope
for the coming of our Savior,
Jesus Christ.
For the kingdom, the power,
and the glory are yours,
now and for ever.
ALL   **Amen.**

O ROOT
OF JESSE

all make the sign of the cross

♩ *end with a song*

O KEY
OF DAVID

35

Welcome to the Gospel of a New Year

BEGINNING OF ADVENT, FOURTH SUNDAY
BEFORE CHRISTMAS

Preparation: Welcome the new Gospel at the end of the last gathering during Ordinary Time or before the beginning of the first gathering of Advent.

Statements describing the Gospels of Matthew, Mark, and Luke are printed at the end of this prayer. The two descriptive statements needed for the current year should be marked by the leader of prayer.

Where a three-volume lectionary is used for school Masses, both the "old" and "new" volumes are carried in procession. Otherwise, the one-volume lectionary or Book of the Gospels is carried, with additional students carrying icons of the two evangelists (pictures, or signs with the evangelists' names).

Select two readers.

Music options: If Today You Hear the Voice of God (11), Celtic Alleluia (4)

 begin with a song

LEADER   For the past year we have listened almost every Sunday to a reading from the holy Gospel according to N____. That Gospel has taught us many things about God's love.

READER ONE   read the appropriate descriptive statement (see end of prayer),

LEADER   Let us show our appreciation for the Gospel according to N____ with a deep bow (or a round of applause).
We will now close the holy Gospel according to N____. We will bring it back again in two years.

the lectionary or icon is placed on a side table

LEADER   Let us now welcome the holy Gospel according to N____.

the "new" lectionary or icon is raised for all to see

READER TWO   read the appropriate descriptive statement (see end of prayer)

The first Sunday of Advent begins a new Church year, and a "new" Gospel is opened for our reflection during the coming year. The Catholic liturgy provides a three-year cycle of readings for the major feasts and seasons of the year.

The Sunday Gospels are generally taken from Matthew during year A, from Mark during year B, and from Luke during year C. Portions of the Gospel of John are read each year (especially during year B, because Mark's Gospel is so short). In our daily prayer at school, we try to follow the Sunday readings as well as the spirit of the changing seasons.

LEADER Let us show our welcome for the holy Gospel according

to N____ with a deep bow (or round of applause).

Loving God,

we praise you for your living word

spoken to us through all eternity.

And we thank you

for the words of the holy Gospel

through which the voice of your son Jesus

calls us to follow him.

Strengthen us,

through the power of your Holy Spirit,

to answer that call

now and for ever.

ALL **Amen.**

LEADER Let us bow our heads and pray.

Loving God,

bless this sacred book,

and bless all who proclaim your holy word

with their lips

and with their lives.

We ask this through Christ our Lord.

ALL **Amen.**

continue with the prayer of the day, or sing an alleluia

Descriptive Statement: Matthew–Year A

The tradition of the Church teaches that Matthew was also named Levi. He was a tax collector whom Jesus called to become an apostle. The Gospel of Matthew tells us many things about the reign of God and the qualities necessary for a good disciple. Through the words of this Gospel, Jesus reminds us that he will be with the church until the end of time.

Descriptive Statement: Mark–Year B

The tradition of the Church teaches that Mark grew up in Jerusalem and became a missionary when he was still a very young man. He and Peter traveled to Rome where they preached the word of God. The Gospel of Mark was the first to be written, and it records many of Peter's stories about the life and wisdom of Jesus.

Descriptive Statement: Luke–Year C

The tradition of the Church teaches that Luke was a doctor and a missionary companion of Paul. Luke is a patron of artists, and his words paint a picture of Jesus as loving and kind, welcoming all and teaching of God's forgiveness. This Gospel gathers the stories and teachings of Jesus into an orderly account so that all who hear it can come to believe.

Blessing of the Advent Wreath

BEGINNING OF ADVENT

Preparation: The blessing prayer can be used at any time after the Advent wreath is prepared but before the first candle is lighted. A bowl of burning incense can be placed near or in the middle of the wreath.

The prayer is marked to show how five leaders can participate. If there are fewer leaders, they can take turns reading parts of the prayer.

Once the wreath is blessed, it should be used throughout the season. Open with the invitation, "Come, Lord Jesus," and the response, "Come quickly." Light the proper number of candles and proceed with daily prayer. Put out the candle(s) carefully when prayer is ended.

Music options: Awake, Awake and Greet the New Morn (2), In the Lord I'll Be Ever Thankful (12), For Your Gracious Blessing (8), O Come, O Come, Emmanuel

LEADER ONE   Let us offer God praise and thanksgiving.

:: all make the sign of the cross

LEADER ONE   Come, Lord Jesus!
ALL   **Come quickly!**

LEADER ONE   It is wintertime. Days are short and nights are long. We need the light of Christ. We need the warmth and joy of Christ. And so we gather around this wreath in hope.

gently wave the smoke of the incense toward all parts of the wreath, saying

Like smoke from this incense,
let our Advent prayers
rise to you, loving God.

LEADER TWO   God our creator,
by your word all things are made holy.
Bless this wreath
as a sign to us of Jesus our Light.

One of the strongest symbols of Advent is an evergreen wreath holding four candles. The circular wreath is a sign of God's loving care, which has no ending. The evergreen branches suggest the faithfulness of God, which is always alive and fresh.

During the first week of Advent, a single candle is lighted during daily prayers. Two candles are lighted during the second week, then three, and finally four. In this way the light gradually increases as we move toward the coming of Jesus, the Light of the world.

According to tradition, three candles are purple, while the candle for the third Sunday is a bright rose color. It is meant to lift our spirits, just as the liturgy for that day tells us to rejoice (*gaudete* in Latin)!

The wreath should be somewhat large and placed in a prominent place. It can be decorated with ribbons or symbols, but it should retain its simplicity and beauty. It might even be hung by wide ribbons from the ceiling, calling to mind a royal crown, or a victory wreath, or even the wheel of time.

The use of candles during the darkest and coldest days of the year is an ancient custom adopted in the sixth century by European Christians. The Jewish people have a similar tradition. Even as we light candles on our Advent wreath, they will be lighting the candles on their menorahs in celebration of Hanukkah, the festival of lights.

LEADER THREE   The circle of this wreath will remind us of the coming of Christ, whose love for us has no end. The light of these candles will remind us of the coming of Christ, who is the Light of the world.

LEADER FOUR   The green color of these branches will remind us of the coming of Christ, who brings us eternal life.

Let us bless the Lord.

allow a minute or two of silence

LEADER FIVE   By day and by night,
and through every season,
you watch over us, loving God.
By the light of this Advent wreath
we shall wait in patience for your Son,
our Lord Jesus Christ.
His coming comforts our fears
and brings hope to our waiting world.
All glory be yours,
now and for ever.

ALL   **Amen.**

 all make the sign of the cross

♩ end with an Advent song

Prayer for Opening the Advent Calendar

EACH DAY DURING ADVENT

LEADER   Bless the Lord on this Advent day,

               Bless the Lord and prepare his way!

ALL   **Blessed be God for ever!**

       open one door of the Advent calendar and discuss what you find there

LEADER   As we continue with the duties of this day

               let us pray:

               Come, Lord Jesus!

ALL   **Come quickly!**

In many countries an Advent calendar is used as to count the days until the solemnities of Christmas (December 25), Epiphany (Sunday after January 1), or the Baptism of the Lord (Sunday after Epiphany). The calendar is usually a paper poster or cloth wall-hanging with the necessary number of doors or pockets. Each day a door is opened to reveal a saying or person from the Bible or a symbol of the Advent season. Each surprise hidden in the door or pocket should help us to think about concrete ways to prepare for the coming of Jesus.

O ROOT OF JESSE

Blessing of the Jesse Tree

ANY TIME DURING ADVENT

Preparation: Prepare cards by writing on each one the name of a person from the scriptures, the place where the person's story can be found in the Bible, and some information about his or her role in preparing the people of God for the coming of the Messiah. If you think students might have a hard time thinking of symbols, a few suggestions might be added to the cards.

Each student draws a card. After reviewing the story of the person he or she has chosen, the student (or group of students) designs and cuts out a symbol to hang on the Jesse tree. When everyone is ready, the students take turns explaining their symbols and hanging them on the tree. The last symbol, placed at the top of the tree, represents Jesus, the long-awaited Savior.

Patterns for Jesse tree symbols are available at Christian bookstores, but it is usually better for children to create their own symbols for the tree.

A Selection of Figures for the Jesse Tree: The following list should be adjusted according to the students' age and familiarity with the Bible.

THE SPIRIT OF GOD moved over the waters of creation. Genesis 1:1–2 or 1:1—2:2 (dove, wind over water, days of creation)

ADAM and EVE in the garden, sinned. Genesis 3:1–6 (man and woman, tree, apple)

NOAH saved his family from the flood. Genesis 6:11–22; 9:8–17 (ark, flood, rainbow)

ABRAHAM went to a new land, was promised a large family, father of faith in the one God. Genesis 12:1–5; 15:1–6; Hebrews 11:8–10 (suitcase, map, tent, stars)

SARAH laughed at the promise of children. Genesis 18:1–14 (empty cradle, laughing woman)

ISAAC, son of Abraham, made peace. Genesis 26:23–33 (feast, peace treaty, well)

JACOB dreamed of a ladder going to heaven. Genesis 28:10–22 (ladder, rock)

JOSEPH wore a colorful coat and forgave and fed his brothers. Genesis 37:1–4, 45:1–11 (fancy coat, wheat, 13 brothers)

MOSES led the Israelites out of Egypt and received the Ten Commandments. Exodus 14:10–31; 19:16–19, 25; 20:1–17 (walking stick, water held back, chariots in water, fiery mountain, thunder and lightning, tablets of the law)

RUTH remained faithful to her husband's faith and family. Ruth 1:15–18 (wedding ring, road, two pairs of sandals)

SAMUEL heard God's call as a young boy and anointed the kings of Israel. 1 Samuel 3:1–10; 16:4–13 (bed, sleeping boy, jar of oil)

JESSE of Bethlehem was the father of David. 1 Samuel 16:4–13; Isaiah 11:1–2 (town of Bethlehem, man with eight sons, Jesse tree)

DAVID was a shepherd, killed Goliath, was king of Israel for 40 years, wrote many psalms. 1 Samuel 16:17–23; 17:41–50; 2 Samuel 5:1–5 (sheep, slingshot, harp, star of David, crown)

SOLOMON was a king known for his wisdom and for building the Temple. 1 Kings 3:3–13; 5:1–8 (lamp or book, temple)

ISAIAH spoke of the Messiah and his kingdom of peace. Isaiah 2:1–5; 7:13–14; 9:2–3; 11:4–8, 10–11 (pregnant woman, peaceful animals, broken weapons, farm tools)

JEREMIAH told of God's promises. Jeremiah 23:5–6; 31:31–34 (scales of justice, heart)

Creating a Jesse tree, a visual "family tree" that traces the spiritual ancestors of Jesus back to David and Jesse and other people from the Bible, is an Advent custom of recent origin, although hints of it can be traced to medieval manuscripts. It involves making hand-made symbols for all of those ancestors and hanging them like ornaments on a small evergreen tree, a bare branch in a vase, or a banner in the shape of a tree. It is a way to remember all of those people who faithfully waited for the Savior and prepared for his coming.

JOSEPH of Nazareth was Mary's husband. Matthew 1:18–25 (carpenter's tools, lily)

MARY was the mother of Jesus. Luke 1:26–38 (rose, lily, mother and child)

ELIZABETH and ZECHARIAH were parents of John the Baptist. Luke 1:5–17 (angel, altar)

JOHN THE BAPTIST baptized Jesus. Matthew 3:1–11, 13–17 (shell, font, water)

SHEPHERDS came to worship Jesus. Psalm 23; Luke 2:8–20 (angels, sheep, crook)

MAGI brought gifts to the stable. Matthew 2:1–12 (gifts, road, star, stable)

JESUS, the "son of David," came to save the world. John 1:1–18 (infant in manger, light, Good Shepherd—there are many symbols of Jesus)

Music options: For Your Gracious Blessing (8), O Come, O Come, Emmanuel, Advent songs, p. viii

O LORD

LEADER   Come, Lord Jesus!

ALL   **Come quickly!**

LEADER   God most merciful,
from the dawn of the creation
you formed a people
in strength and wisdom.
You blessed them with leaders and prophets,
men and women of holiness
who trusted in your promises
and longed for your coming.
We praise and thank you
for seeing the needs of your people
and preparing them for the coming
of Jesus, their Savior.

Loving God,
bless this Jesse tree
as a sign of our membership in your family of faith,
as a sign of our gratitude for all those
who prepared a way for us,
as a sign of our longing for you to be with us
now and always.
We ask this through Christ our Lord.

ALL   **Amen.**

O KEY OF DAVID

♩ sing an Advent song

LEADER   Come, Lord Jesus!

ALL   **Come quickly!**

Blessing of the Stable during Advent

Preparation: Some time during Advent place an empty stable near the Advent wreath and prepare it for the figures of Mary and Joseph, which should be added before leaving for the Christmas break. In some places students make additional figures of people typical of their towns (such as parents, grocers, nurses, farmers) or of themselves and place them around the stable to welcome Mary and Joseph. After the Christmas break, the figures of the Christ child and the shepherds are added, and at Epiphany, the magi. In some classes the groups of figures are positioned around the room and are gradually advanced toward the stable.

Use the following blessing of the stable during Advent and the blessing on page 72 after you return from the Christmas break and are ready to complete the scene.

Music options: For Your Gracious Blessing (8), O Come, O Come, Emmanuel, Advent songs, p. viii

In the year 330, the Emperor Constantine built a church in Bethlehem. Under the church was a series of caves, one of which, according to local tradition, was the place where Jesus was born. This cave became a sacred shrine for Christians, and over the years they filled the place with gifts of precious gold, silver, and jewels. Other churches copied the grotto, adding statues or pictures of the birth of the Lord. These too became richly decorated with offerings.

Saint Francis of Assisi had seen such shrines, and he thought that people needed a reminder that Jesus was born in a poor shelter, with a feed box as his cradle. He invited the people of Greccio to the simple stable he built beside his church, where they found real people and live animals acting out the story of the birth of the Messiah. Soon others were making simple crèche scenes for their homes and churches.

gather around the stable

LEADER   Let us ask God to bless us during this Advent season.

all make the sign of the cross

LEADER   As we have prepared our hearts, we also prepare this stable to receive the Lord Jesus when he comes.

Let us pray.

Loving God,
bless the home
we have prepared for you.
Its door is open
as a sign of our love
and hospitality.
We wait with bright hope
for your coming,
as we pray,
Come, Lord Jesus!

ALL   **Come quickly!**

end with a song

Blessing of Tangerines

DECEMBER 6, MEMORIAL OF SAINT NICHOLAS

Preparation: In some schools Saint Nicholas makes an unexpected visit on his feast day, asking the children if they can guess his name and tell his story. He scolds any who have been lazy about their school work, and then offers encouragement and pardon for all in the form of tangerines or candy canes. The tangerines are reminders of his bags of gold. Candy canes are signs of his bishop's crosier, which is itself a form of shepherd's crook.

Music options: We Sing of the Saints (27), with verse for December 6: Saint Nicholas, We Bring God's Holy Love (25), Advent songs, p. viii

 begin and end with a song

LEADER   On this day in Advent let us remember the holy Bishop Nicholas as we pray.

all make the sign of the cross

LEADER   Loving God,
you ask each of us
to show kindness and care
for one another.
We thank you for the witness
of good Saint Nicholas
who shows us the joy
of preparing gifts for others.

Let us pray.

We ask you, Lord, to bless these tangerines
which remind us of the gifts of Saint Nicholas.
As we share the freshness of this fruit,
so may we share in his love for the poor
and his care for children around the world.
We ask this through Jesus Christ our Lord.

ALL   **Amen.**

Saint Nicholas was a fourth-century bishop of Myra in what is now Turkey. He was known for his compassion and generosity. When Nicholas learned that a poor man's three daughters could not marry because they had no dowry (a money gift that all husbands required), he threw three bags of gold in through their window at night. Icons of the saint usually show those three bags of gold. Saint Nicholas may be, after the Blessed Mother, the most universally known and beloved of the Christian saints. He is the patron of Russia and Greece, as well as of children, travelers, sailors, unmarried women, and pawnbrokers (the three balls that usually hang over pawn shops, where money is lent to the poor, represent the three bags of gold). Under the title of Santa Claus or Father Christmas, he is credited with gifts left in stockings or shoes all over the world.

Christians in Scandinavian countries imagined Nicholas racing across the ice in a sleigh drawn by reindeer. Dutch settlers in New York called him Sinter Klaas, which soon became Santa Claus. In the nineteenth century, the artist Thomas Nast and the poet Clement Moore gave Santa Claus a red suit, white beard, and fat tummy, creating a figure that the good bishop Nicholas would hardly recognize!

Prayer for the Immaculate Conception

DECEMBER 8, SOLEMNITY OF THE IMMACULATE
CONCEPTION OF THE VIRGIN MARY

On the solemnity of the Immaculate Conception, we celebrate our belief that Mary was full of God's grace from the moment she was given life in the womb of her mother Anne. This privilege was given in preparation for her role as the mother of God. Mary did not earn this freedom in any way. It was simply a gift bestowed out of God's goodness.

Recognition of Mary's preservation from all sin began in the East, spread to the West in the middle ages, and was declared a dogma of the Church in 1854. Four years later, in 1858, Mary appeared to fourteen-year-old Bernadette Soubirous, in Lourdes, France. She said of herself, "I am the Immaculate Conception." The miracles of healing at the scene of the appearances quickly spread devotion to Mary under this title.

By the time European immigrants began arriving in the United States in large numbers, December 8 was a popular feast. Mary, under the title of the Immaculate Conception, is the patron of the United States. A very large basilica in Washington, D.C., the National Shrine of the Immaculate Conception, is dedicated to her.

This solemnity is a holy day and all Catholics participate in the Eucharist.

Music options: Sing of Mary (21), We Sing of the Saints (27) with verse for Feasts of Mary, Immaculate Mary, Advent songs, p. viii, or the following verse sung to the familiar melody of Praise God from Whom All Blessings Flow

> Behold a virgin bearing Him
> Who comes to save us from our sin.
> The prophets cry: Prepare his way!
> Make straight the path to Christmas Day.

LEADER   Let us begin our prayer on this feast of Mary.

✛ all make the sign of the cross

LEADER   We praise you, Lord,

in this daughter of Israel,

Mary, your faithful one and our mother!

We pray as she did:

may your name be holy;

may the hungry be filled

and the rich know hunger;

may the proud be scattered

and the oppressed raised up;

may your love be ever with your people.

We make our prayer always

through Mary's child;

he arose from her the sun of justice,

Jesus, who is Lord for ever and ever.

ALL   Amen.

LEADER   O Mary, conceived without sin:

ALL   Pray for us who have recourse to you.

 end with a song

Prayer for Our Lady of Guadalupe

DECEMBER 12, THE FEAST OF *NUESTRA SEÑORA DE GUADALUPE*

Preparation: Create a shrine around an image of Our Lady of Guadalupe. Decorate it with candles, bright flowers, pierced paper designs, or ribbons, and gather there for prayer.

Copies of the litany will be needed, unless the leader reads both title and refrain and invites the assembly to repeat it.

Music options: Sing of Mary (21), Las Mañanitas, Advent songs, p. viii, or another hymn to Mary

♩ begin and end with a song

LEADER   Let us offer God praise and thanksgiving
on this feast of Nuestra Señora de Guadalupe

 all make the sign of the cross

LEADER   Come, Lord Jesus!
ALL   **Come quickly!**

LEADER   Loving God,
you bless the peoples of the Americas
with the Virgin Mary of Guadalupe
as our patron and mother.
Through her prayers
may we learn to love one another
and to work for justice and peace.
ALL   **Amen.**

LEADER	ALL
Lady of Guadalupe,	**pray for us**
La morena of Tepeyac,	**comfort us**
Mother of the faithful,	**defend us**
Refuge of the oppressed,	**strengthen us**

In the year 1531, Mary appeared to an Aztec native named Juan Diego. He saw her dressed as an Aztec princess wearing brightly colored clothing. She had a sash around her waist that was worn by pregnant women. Mary promised to help all who called on her and asked that a church be built where she stood. When Juan Diego asked for a sign to convince the bishop of the vision, Mary guided him to a spot where roses were suddenly blooming where only cactus had grown. He filled his cloak with the roses and rushed to the home of the bishop. There he emptied his cloak in front of the astonished bishop and found not only the roses but the image of Mary imprinted on his cloak. That cloak, or *tilma*, is now placed over the altar of a great church that was built, as Mary had directed, on the hill of Tepeyac where an Aztec temple had once stood.

The vision and Mary's message brought faith and comfort to the Aztec people, who had been treated with great cruelty by Spanish explorers. Aztec women had been especially abused, and they were greatly honored by Mary's appearance in their features and clothing. Today the oppressed native peoples of the Americas see her as a promise of justice and a cause for hope.

Nuestra Señora de Guadalupe is the patron saint of Mexico, where her feast is often preceded by a novena. On December 12 people rise before dawn to sing *"Las mañanitas,"* often accompanied by mariachi music, before celebrating the eucharist.

Hope of the immigrant,	cheer us
Light of the traveler,	guide us
Friend of the stranger,	welcome us
Shelter of the poor and needy,	sustain us
Patron of the Americas,	unite us
Mother of many children,	watch over us
Star of the morning,	waken us
	to the coming of your Son, Jesus Christ, who arose from you the sun of justice and is Lord for ever and ever. Amen.

LEADER   God of mercy,
through the prayers of Our Lady of Guadalupe
help us to place our trust in you,
and with ever growing faith,
to care for the poor and needy
in your name.
We ask this through Christ our Lord.

ALL   **Amen.**

Blessing of Pastries

DECEMBER 13, MEMORIAL OF SAINT LUCY

Preparation: Place an image of Saint Lucy, if you can find or draw one, in your prayer area, or tie a red ribbon around a large white candle and let that represent the saint. Place bread or pastry there, ready to be blessed and shared. (A Swedish bakery might have something special to suggest.)

Music options: We Are Marching (26), We Sing of the Saints (27), Advent songs, p. viii

 begin and end with a song

LEADER   Let us offer God praise and thanksgiving
             on this Advent feast of Saint Lucy.

all make the sign of the cross

LEADER   Loving God,
             in the time of darkness
             you send us light;
             in the time of hunger, bread;
             in every time and country
             you send us saints
             to amaze us with the light of your grace
             and strengthen us with the warmth of your love.
             With Lucy and all your saints
             we wait in trust and joy
             for the glorious day of your coming.
             Lord Jesus,
             bread of heaven
             and light of the world,
             come quickly to your people.

             allow a moment of silence

LEADER   Let us pray.

             God of light,
             bless this food
             which we share.

Lucy's name means light, and this makes her a perfect Advent saint. Before the calendar was modernized many years ago, her feast fell on the day of the winter solstice, when darkness has its greatest hold on our world. Lucy (Lucia) was a third-century Italian woman who was martyred because she dedicated her life to Jesus and gave her dowry money to the poor.

Lucy is the patron of the eyes, the body's source of light, and her help is asked for any eye problems, especially the danger of blindness. At one time she was the patron of those who lighted the street lamps, and they went about their task on December 13 with great ceremony.

The people of Sweden, who live through the intense cold and long darkness of northern winters, have great devotion to Saint Lucy, and her feast is the start of Christmas cooking and festivity. In Swedish homes, schools, and businesses on this day, a young woman or girl dresses in a white robe with a red sash, and places a crown of candles on her head. She brings a tray of coffee or cocoa and pastry for a festive breakfast. She is helped by boys and girls in white who represent shepherds, magi, or other figures in the Christmas Gospel. They sing a song to the saint, and other carols. This custom reflects the tradition that Saint Lucy was seen bringing bread to the hungry during a famine in the middle ages.

Let it be for us
a sign of care for one another
and the heavenly banquet yet to come.
We ask this through Christ our Lord.

ALL   **Amen.**

give each person some of the bread or pastry; when all are served, conclude

LEADER   Come, Lord Jesus!
ALL   **Come quickly!**

enjoy the tasty treat in honor of Saint Lucy

Las Posadas (Lodgings)

DECEMBER 16 THROUGH DECEMBER 24

Preparation: Las posadas can be celebrated by a class, by the whole school or religious education community, or by the parish. It can be done on each of the novena days or just on the final day before leaving for the Christmas break. The traditional song, a dialogue between Joseph and the innkeepers, can be sung or spoken, or the children can ad-lib their dialogue.

For a classroom celebration, children can be divided into groups and placed in different areas of the space so that the travelers can move gradually toward the stable. In a school-wide celebration, the youngest class should begin the procession—dressed as Mary, Joseph, and angels (let all of them take the parts rather than choosing only three or four from the group), or carrying statues of these—and knock on the door of each classroom until reaching the chapel, church, school lobby, or cafeteria, where the eighth-grade "inkeepers" wait by the stable. This is the appropriate time for enjoying small gifts, traditional food and drink, and a piñata.

Everyone will need a copy of the dialogue. An English version is provided after the Spanish text. Parts marked A are said by the travelers; parts marked B, by the innkeepers.

Pedir Posada

A   **En el nombre del cielo os pido posada**
          pues no puede andar mi esposa amada.

B   **Aquí no es mesón, sigan adelante,**
          yo no puedo abrir, no sea algún tunante.

Las posadas (called *panuluyan* in the Philippines) are an example of the drama and ritual of Hispanic prayer. They are celebrated in various ways in countries like Mexico, Belize, Guatemala, Panama, and Nicaragua. The tradition combines the solemnity of the last days of Advent with the exuberance of a neighborhood festival. The name *"posadas"* means lodgings, or places to stay. The ceremony recalls Joseph and Mary's search for shelter when they arrived at Bethlehem. It also is a reminder of the homeless people who today are looking for lodgings.

During the novena, or nine days before Christmas, people dressed as Joseph

A	No seas inhumano, ténnos caridad
	que el Dios de los cielos te lo premiará.
B	Ya se pueden ir y no molestar,
	porque si me enfado os voy a apalear.
A	Venimos rendidos desde Nazaret.
	Yo soy carpintero de nombre José.
B	No me importa el nombre, déjenme dormir,
	pues que ya les digo que no hemos de abrir.
A	Posada te pide, amado casero,
	por solo una noche la Reina del Cielo.
B	Pues si es una reina quien lo solicita,
	¿cómo es que de noche anda tan solita?
A	Mi esposa es María, es Reina del Cielo,
	y madre va a ser del Divino Verbo.
B	¿Eres tú José? ¿Tu esposa es María?
	Entren peregrinos, no los conocía.
A	Dios pague, señores, vuestra caridad,
	y así os colme el cielo, de felicidad.
B	¡Dichosa la casa que alberga este día
	a la Virgen pura, la hermosa María!

Canto de conclusion. Todos adentro

TODOS 	Entren santos peregrinos, peregrinos,
reciban este rincón.
Que aunque es pobre la morada, la morada,
os la doy de corazón.
Cantemos con alegría, alegría,
todos al considerar.
Que Jesús, José y María, y María,
nos vinieron hoy a honrar (2x).

and Mary, or carrying figures of them from a nativity scene, are led by an angel from one neighboring home to another, where Joseph asks for lodging. The "innkeepers" turn the pilgrims away and join the procession as it moves to another home. At the final stop the pilgrims are again refused, but when they announce that it is Mary, Queen of Heaven, who asks for shelter, the doors are opened wide and all are welcomed. The figures are carefully placed in the stable, and all are given something tasty to eat.

Las posadas continue until Christmas eve *(Nochebuena)*, when the figure of the Infant Jesus is added to the stable scene. A lullaby is sung and all proceed to Midnight Mass. After that a final and more elaborate celebration is held. It includes music, food, and of course, the breaking of a piñata.

The piñata is thought to be a catechetical tool created by Spanish priests who came with the conquistadores. The traditional piñata is a clay or paper pot with seven horn-like protrusions representing the seven deadly sins. The people who attack the piñata are blinded by sin (blindfolded), yet use their faith (the stick) in their struggle against Satan (the piñata). And what a pleasure it is when someone is successful in breaking the power of Satan, and grace rains down!

Las Posadas Song

A
In the name of heaven,
please won't you open your door!
My dearest wife is so weary,
she cannot walk one step more.

B
I am not running an inn here
and I won't talk to a stranger.
You could be robbers or rowdies,
you could put us into danger.

A
See our need for some lodging!
Do not continue in blindness.
Then God in heaven above,
will bless you well for your kindness

B
Keep on your way! You're a bother.
I'll make you leave, heaven knows.
I have no time for your story.
I have no time for your woes!

A
I am the carpenter Joseph.
In Nazareth we began.
We need to rest for the night.
Please take us in if you can.

B
Whoever you are, kindly travelers,
we, too, have need of our rest.
I've said it over and over,
I cannot grant your request.

A
Look at the one who is with me,
and have regard for her plight.
She is the Queen of Heaven
asking to stay just one night.

B   How can this lady be royal,
coming to us with no crown,
walking alone on the dark streets,
stopping in our humble town?

A   This is my wife, holy Mary,
She is our queen as you heard.
Soon to give birth to a baby,
mother of God's holy Word.

B   Truly these strangers are Joseph
and Mary come from afar.
We welcome you holy pilgrims,
now that we see who you are.

A   May God reward you, good people.
You took us in from the cold.
Happiness, comfort, and peace:
blessings more precious than gold.

B   Happy our house for your presence!
Happy by you to be blessed:
Mary the virgin mother,
beautiful Mary our guest.

for the conclusion, when all are in the house

ALL   Please come in most holy pilgrims, holy pilgrims,
take your rest and never part.
Glad am I to make you welcome, make you welcome,
in my house and in my heart.

Let us sing in exultation, exultation!
on this day(night) so richly blessed.
Joseph, Jesus, Holy Mary, Holy Mary,
have become our honored guests.

53

O WISDOM

The O Antiphons: Daily Prayers for the Week before Christmas

DECEMBER 17 THROUGH DECEMBER 23

Preparation: At daily prayer on these days, listen again to the words of the prophets telling of God's promises to the waiting people of Israel. Pray the O Antiphon and conclude with the appropriate verse of "O Come, O Come, Emmanuel."

For a shorter prayer, or for younger children, light the Advent wreath, say the greeting, and move directly to the O Antiphon. Conclude with the Our Father and the closing dialogue each day.

A leader and a reader, as well as someone to lead singing, are needed for each day.

Music option: O Come, O Come, Emmanuel

December 17   O Wisdom

LEADER One of the prophets' ancient names for God was Wisdom. They wrote of Wisdom moving about the city like a beautiful woman inviting people to her home, where she would teach them to know what was good and just.

light the candles of the Advent wreath

LEADER Blessed are you, Lord, God of all creation:
in the darkness and in the light.
Blessed are you as we wait in joyful hope
for the coming of our Savior, Jesus Christ.

ALL **For the kingdom, the power, and the glory are yours, now and for ever.**

LEADER Come, Lord Jesus!
ALL **Come quickly!**

READER Listen to the words of the book of Wisdom   9:9–10

Wisdom has always been with you.
She knows your mighty deeds,
and she was there
when you created the world.

Wisdom knows what pleases you,
and she knows what is right
according to your commands.
So from your glorious and holy throne in the heavens,
please send Wisdom to work beside me
and teach me what is pleasing to you.

The word of the Lord.

ALL   **Thanks be to God.**

LEADER   O Wisdom, O holy Word of God,
You govern all creation
with your strong yet tender care.
Come and show your people
the way to salvation.

Let us pray with the words that Jesus taught us.

ALL   **Our Father . . .**

♩ sing the following verse of O Come, O Come, Emmanuel

O come, O Wisdom from on high,
Who orders all things mightily;
To us the path of knowledge show,
And teach us in her ways to go.
Rejoice! Rejoice!
Emmanuel shall come to you, O Israel.

LEADER   Lord our God, you bring light and joy
to the darkness of this world.
Let us carry your light in our hearts this day.
Come, Lord Jesus!

ALL   **Come quickly!**

put out the candles of the Advent wreath

O LORD

December 18   O Lord

LEADER   Out of respect, the Jews never say the name of God aloud. When reading from the scriptures, they call God "Lord." Christians also call Jesus "Lord." He is the fulfillment of the promise that God would one day come to live among the people to strengthen and redeem them.

light the candles of the Advent wreath

LEADER   Blessed are you, Lord, God of all creation:
in the darkness and in the light.
Blessed are you as we wait in joyful hope
for the coming of our Savior, Jesus Christ.

ALL   **For the kingdom, the power, and the glory are yours, now and for ever.**

LEADER   Come, Lord Jesus!
ALL   **Come quickly!**

READER   Listen to the words of the prophet Isaiah   40:3–5, 9

Someone is shouting:
"Clear a path in the desert!
Make a straight road for the LORD our God.
Fill in the valleys;
flatten every hill and mountain.
Level the rough and rugged ground.
Then the glory of the LORD
will appear for all to see.
The LORD has promised this!"
There is good news for the city of Zion.
Shout it as loud as you can
from the highest mountain.
Don't be afraid to shout to the towns of Judah,
"Your God is here!"

The word of the Lord.
ALL   **Thanks be to God.**

LEADER   O sacred Lord of ancient Israel,
         who showed yourself to Moses in the burning bush,
         who gave him your holy law on Sinai mountain:
         Come, stretch out your mighty hand
         to set us free.

         Let us pray with the words that Jesus taught us.
ALL   **Our Father . . .**

♩ sing the following verse of O Come, O Come, Emmanuel

> O come, O come, great Lord of might,
> Who to your tribes on Sinai's height
> In ancient times once gave the law,
> In cloud, and majesty, and awe.
> Rejoice! Rejoice!
> Emmanuel shall come to you, O Israel.

LEADER   Lord our God, you bring light and joy
         to the darkness of this world.
         Let us carry your light in our hearts this day.
         Come, Lord Jesus!
ALL   **Come quickly!**

put out the candles of the Advent wreath

December 19   O Flower of Jesse

LEADER   King David, the son of Jesse of Bethlehem, was the
         first great king of Israel. Long after he had died,
         the people longed for another great king who could
         lead them as he had done.
            Through the words of the prophet Isaiah, God
         promised that the Messiah would be a new branch
         on the royal family tree of Jesse and David.

light the candles of the Advent wreath

O ROOT
OF JESSE

LEADER   Blessed are you, Lord, God of all creation:
in the darkness and in the light.
Blessed are you as we wait in joyful hope
for the coming of our Savior, Jesus Christ.

ALL   **For the kingdom, the power, and the glory are yours,
now and for ever.**

LEADER   Come, Lord Jesus!

ALL   **Come quickly!**

READER   Listen to the words of the prophet Isaiah   11:1–4

The LORD says this:
"Like a branch that sprouts from a stump,
someone from David's family will someday be king.
The Spirit of the LORD will be with him
to give him understanding, wisdom, and insight.
He will be powerful, and he will know
and honor the LORD.
This king won't judge by appearances
or listen to rumors.
The poor and the needy will be treated with fairness
and with justice."

The word of the Lord.

ALL   **Thanks be to God.**

LEADER   O Flower of Jesse's stem,
you have been raised up as a sign for all peoples;
the powerful stand silent in your presence;
the nations bow down in worship before you.
Come, let nothing keep you from coming to our aid.

Let us pray with the words that Jesus taught us.

ALL   **Our Father . . .**

♩ sing the following verse of O Come, O Come, Emmanuel

58

O come, O Rod of Jesse's stem,
From every foe deliver them.
That trust your mighty pow'r to save
And give them vict'ry o'er the grave.
Rejoice! Rejoice!
Emmanuel shall come to you, O Israel.

LEADER   Lord our God, you bring light and joy
to the darkness of this world.
Let us carry your light in our hearts this day.
Come, Lord Jesus!

ALL   **Come quickly!**

put out the candles of the Advent wreath

December 20   O Key of David

LEADER   In today's O Antiphon, Jesus is called the Key
of David. People with keys are often people with
authority. Jesus is the key that opens the gate
of heaven for us.

light the candles of the Advent wreath

O KEY
OF DAVID

LEADER   Blessed are you, Lord, God of all creation:
in the darkness and in the light.
Blessed are you as we wait in joyful hope
for the coming of our Savior, Jesus Christ.

ALL   **For the kingdom, the power, and the glory are yours,
now and for ever.**

LEADER   Come, Lord Jesus!

ALL   **Come quickly!**

READER   Listen to the words of the book of Revelation   3:7–8, 11

The Lord says this: "I am the one who is holy and
true, and I have the keys that belonged to David.

When I open a door, no one can close it. And when I close a door, no one can open it. Listen to what I say.

"I know everything you have done. And I have placed before you an open door that no one can close. You were not very strong, but you obeyed my message and did not deny that you are my followers.

"I am coming soon. So hold firmly to what you have, and no one will take away the crown that you will be given as your reward."

The word of the Lord.

ALL **Thanks be to God.**

LEADER O Key of David, O royal power of Israel,
controlling at your will the gate of heaven:
Come, break down the prison walls of death
for those who dwell in darkness
and the shadow of death,
and lead your captive people into freedom.

Let us pray with the words that Jesus taught us.

ALL **Our Father . . .**

♩ sing the following verse of O Come, O Come, Emmanuel

O come, O Key of David, come,
And open wide our heav'nly home,
Make safe the way that leads on high,
And close the path to misery.
Rejoice! Rejoice!
Emmanuel shall come to you, O Israel.

LEADER Lord our God, you bring light and joy
to the darkness of this world.
Let us carry your light in our hearts this day.
Come, Lord Jesus!

ALL **Come quickly!**

put out the candles of the Advent wreath

December 21   O Dayspring

LEADER   In today's O Antiphon, we call Jesus the "dawn" or "dayspring." In wintertime nights are long and days are short. So we call on God to be light to us at this time of the winter solstice, the shortest days of the year. Just as the dawning sun soon rises high in the sky and shines brightly, we think again of the coming of Jesus who is our "sun of justice" and "light of the world."

light the candles of the Advent wreath

LEADER   Blessed are you, Lord, God of all creation:
in the darkness and in the light.
Blessed are you as we wait in joyful hope
for the coming of our Savior, Jesus Christ.

ALL   **For the kingdom, the power, and the glory are yours, now and for ever.**

LEADER   Come, Lord Jesus!
ALL   **Come quickly!**

READER   Listen to the words of the prophet Isaiah   60:19–21, 22

The LORD says this:
"You won't need the light of the sun or the moon.
I, the LORD your God, will be your eternal light
and bring you honor.
Your sun will never set or your moon go down.
I, the LORD, will be your everlasting light,
and your days of sorrow will come to an end.
I am the LORD, and when the time comes,
I will quickly do all this."

The word of the Lord.
ALL   **Thanks be to God.**

LEADER   O Dayspring,
splendor of eternal light,
sun of justice:
Come, shine on those who dwell in darkness
and the shadow of death.

Let us pray with the words that Jesus taught us.

ALL   **Our Father . . .**

 sing the following verse of O Come, O Come, Emmanuel

> O come, O Dayspring, from on high
> And cheer us by your drawing nigh;
> Disperse the gloomy clouds of night,
> And death's dark shadow put to flight.
> Rejoice! Rejoice!
> Emmanuel shall come to you, O Israel.

LEADER   Lord our God, you bring light and joy
to the darkness of this world.
Let us carry your light in our hearts this day.
Come, Lord Jesus!

ALL   **Come quickly!**

put out the candles of the Advent wreath

December 22   O King of Nations

LEADER   Today's O Antiphon gives two titles for Jesus. First
he is called the "king of all the nations," then he
is called Jesus our "keystone." The keystone is the
stone in the middle of an arch. It supports the other
stones so that the arch does not fall down. In the
gospel of Matthew, Jesus is also called a cornerstone.
The cornerstone of a building is perfectly straight
so that the walls built on it can be strong and true.

light the candles of the Advent wreath

LEADER   Blessed are you, Lord, God of all creation:
         in the darkness and in the light.
         Blessed are you as we wait in joyful hope
         for the coming of our Savior, Jesus Christ.
         Come, Lord Jesus!
ALL   **Come quickly!**

READER   Listen to the words of the prophet Isaiah   28:16–17

         The Lord says this:
         "I'm laying a firm foundation
         for the city of Zion.
         It's a valuable cornerstone
         proven to be trustworthy;
         no one who trusts it will ever be disappointed.
         Justice and fairness will be the measuring lines
         that help me build."

         The word of the Lord.
ALL   **Thanks be to God.**

LEADER   O King of all the nations,
         the only joy of every human heart;
         O keystone of the mighty arch of humankind:
         Come and save the creature
         you fashioned from the dust.

         Let us pray with the words that Jesus taught us.
ALL   **Our Father . . .**

♩ sing the following verse of O Come, O Come, Emmanuel

> O come, Desire of nations, bind
> In one the hearts of humankind;
> Come bid our sad divisions cease,
> And be for us the King of Peace.
> Rejoice! Rejoice!
> Emmanuel shall come to you, O Israel.

<table>
<tr><td>LEADER</td><td>Lord our God, you bring light and joy
to the darkness of this world.
Let us carry your light in our hearts this day.
Come, Lord Jesus!</td></tr>
<tr><td>ALL</td><td>Come quickly!</td></tr>
</table>

put out the candles of the Advent wreath

O
EMMANUEL

December 23   O Emmanuel

LEADER	Today's O Antiphon reminds us that God is with us always. The name Emmanuel means God-with-us. As we draw ever closer to the celebration of Jesus' birth, we are assured of God's presence in our lives and our world.

light the candles of the Advent wreath

LEADER	Blessed are you, Lord, God of all creation: in the darkness and in the light. Blessed are you as we wait in joyful hope for the coming of our Savior, Jesus Christ.
ALL	**For the kingdom, the power, and the glory are yours, now and for ever.**
LEADER	Come, Lord Jesus!
ALL	**Come quickly!**
READER	Listen to the words of the prophet Isaiah 7:13–14
	Then Isaiah said: "Listen, every one of you in the royal family of David. The LORD will give you proof. A virgin is pregnant; she will have a son and will name him Emmanuel." The word of the Lord.
ALL	**Thanks be to God.**

LEADER   O Emmanuel, king and lawgiver,
desire of the nations,
savior of all people:
Come and set us free,
Lord our God.

Let us pray with the words that Jesus taught us.

ALL   **Our Father . . .**

♩ sing the following verse of O Come, O Come, Emmanuel

O come, O come, Emmanuel,
And ransom captive Israel,
That mourns in lonely exile here
Until the Son of God appear.
Rejoice! Rejoice!
Emmanuel shall come to you, O Israel.

LEADER   Lord our God, you bring light and joy
to the darkness of this world.
Let us carry your light in our hearts this day.
Come, Lord Jesus!

ALL   **Come quickly!**

put out the candles of the Advent wreath

Blessing before Christmas Break

LAST DAY OF CLASSES BEFORE CHRISTMAS DISMISSAL

Preparation: Shortly before dismissal, the students gather so that the teacher will be able to bless each one.

Music options: Go Now in Peace (9), Advent songs, p. viii

♩ begin and end with a song

TEACHER   Let us begin our prayer.

⁘ all make the sign of the cross

The days of preparation are almost over. The temptation to begin Christmas festivities has been strong but we have maintained the Advent spirit of quiet and expectation. As the focus of celebration shifts from the classroom to the family home, it is good to provide a ritual of blessing and closure to the Advent days spent together.

TEACHER   May the Lord's face shine on us,
and may the Lord guide our feet
into the way of peace.
Blessed be the name of the Lord,
now and for ever.

ALL   **Amen.**

TEACHER   Let us put ourselves into the hands of the Lord
and pray that God will bless us and our families
during the coming holy days.
May all of us help to make our homes
places of joy, love, peace, and safety.
May we be generous and considerate,
not thinking only about ourselves
but helping others enjoy
the blessings of Christmas.

Please respond "Amen" as I bless each of you.

the teacher goes to each student in turn, traces the sign of the cross on
the student's head and says

TEACHER   N____, go with God.

STUDENT   Amen.

when these individual blessings are completed, prayer continues

TEACHER   My dear friends and students,
           may our loving God give you light and joy.
           And, until we gather here again,
           may God bless all of us.

all make the sign of the cross

Christmastime

December 25, The Birth of the Lord, through the Baptism of the Lord

Christmastime is a celebration of promises kept and prophecies fulfilled. During Advent, we hear Isaiah's prophecy of a Savior who would be sent from God. During Christmastime, at home and at church, we hear the good news of the birth of that Savior, Jesus of Nazareth.

It is hard for us to remember that it is not gifts under the tree that make Christmas so important. If the presents were all we looked forward to, then when the presents were opened, Christmas would be over for us.

But Christmastime is not just one day. It is a season of almost three weeks after December 25. Many good days come during Christmastime. There are the feasts of the Holy Family, Saint John, and the Holy Innocents. On January 1 we celebrate the solemnity of Mary, the Mother of God. The solemnity of the Epiphany, the Sunday after January 1, is a key time of celebration in the annual cycle of the church year. Epiphany celebrations usually last for a week or so, until the Baptism of the Lord brings the season to a close.

Many of these days are spent at home during the school break. But after school reopens, there is still at least a week of Christmastime left to enjoy. We can talk to one another about the events of the time away from school. We can balance the prayers of preparation that we shared during Advent with the prayers of celebration we will share during this joyful time. We can keep the season from ending too soon.

Put a candle in the prayer center and light it for prayer. You may want to add Christmas decorations as well. A fresh wreath, evergreens, and bright red and gold ribbons can be used. Of course, the stable will now be blessed and have all its statues added.

Try to wait until after Christmastime is over to take down any decorations. See if you can keep the classroom looking cheerful all through the winter. The end of the Christmas season should not be sad. In fact, some people leave their Christmas stable up until February 2, the feast of the Presentation of the Lord, or Candlemas, as it is also called.

Meal Prayer for Christmastime

Music options: Joy to the World (15) or another familiar Christmas carol

♩ begin or end with a song

LEADER   Let us offer God praise and thanksgiving.

⠇ all make the sign of the cross

LEADER   Rise up in splendor, Jerusalem!
ALL   **The glory of the Lord shines upon you.**

LEADER   God's holy day has dawned for us at last.
ALL   **Come, all you people, and adore the Lord.**
               Bless us, O Lord, and these your gifts
               which we are about to receive
               from your goodness.
               Through Christ our Lord. Amen.

⠇ all make the sign of the cross

Blessing of the Stable at Christmas

FIRST DAY OF CLASSES AFTER CHRISTMAS

Preparation: Use this blessing at your first meeting after the Christmas break. The stable itself may have been set up and blessed during Advent (see page 44). You may have added figures of Mary and Joseph during a celebration of *las posadas* (see page 50). In any case, students carrying all of the figures (except the magi) should be ready to come at the end of the procession and place them in or around the stable during the blessing. The placing of figures in the stable occurs in two places during the readings.

Keep the Wise Men and their camels hidden until they have their own entrance at Epiphany, or place them at some distance from the stable, as though they were on the road to Bethlehem. Move them a bit closer each day until Epiphany. (See page 85 or 87.)

Place a dish of holy water and an evergreen branch for sprinkling near the stable. Select a leader and two readers.

Music options: Joy to the World (15), O Come, Let Us Adore Him refrain, Glorias, or other familiar carols

LEADER   God's holy day has dawned for us at last.

ALL   Come, all you people, and adore the Lord.

 all move in procession to the stable singing
O Come, Let Us Adore Him or another appropriate Christmas carol

light a candle

LEADER   My friends, let us be silent for a moment to prepare ourselves to hear the good news.

allow a minute or two of silence

READER ONE   Listen to the words of the holy Gospel according to Luke   2:5–16

Mary was engaged to Joseph and traveled with him to Bethlehem. She was soon going to have a baby, and while they were there, she gave birth to her first-born son. She dressed him in baby clothes and laid him on a bed of hay because there was no room for them in the inn.

The stable, or crèche, is a visual proclamation of the Christmas Gospel. In some European countries, figures of typical townspeople in contemporary clothing join the traditional shepherds and magi in worshiping the newborn King. Instead of a shepherd's crook or containers of gold, frankincense, and myrrh, they bring the tools of other trades: stethoscopes and ballet slippers, mixing bowls and computers. In this way we remember that the coming of God's Messiah is timeless, and those who love him in every age and nation come to adore. It is today that we are asked to make him welcome. It is today that we bring our hearts and our lives for his blessing.

those carrying Mary and Joseph and the donkey and cow place them in the stable; Jesus is placed in the manger last and the reading continues

READER TWO   That night in the fields near Bethlehem some shepherds were guarding their sheep. All at once an angel came down to them from the Lord, and the brightness of the Lord's glory flashed around them. The shepherds were frightened. But the angel said, "Don't be afraid! I have good news for you, which will make everyone happy. This very day in King David's hometown a Savior was born for you. He is Christ the Lord. You will know who he is because you will find him dressed in baby clothes and lying in a manger."

Suddenly many other angels came down from heaven and joined in praising God. They said: "Praise God in heaven! Peace on earth to everyone who pleases God."

After the angels had left and gone back to heaven, the shepherds said to each other, "Let's go to Bethlehem and see what the Lord has told us about." They hurried off and found Mary and Joseph, and they saw the baby lying on a bed of hay.

The Gospel of the Lord.

ALL   **Praise to you, Lord Jesus Christ.**

place shepherds, sheep, and angels near the stable

LEADER   Saving God,
bless these images
that proclaim the good news
of the coming among us
of Jesus, our Lord and Messiah.

sprinkle the stable scene with holy water

LEADER   And bless us, Lord,
as we come to Bethlehem,
where animals and angels,

shepherds and seekers,
together behold your face.
Here snow becomes straw
and frost becomes flowers
as winter melts into everlasting spring.

sprinkle all who are assembled

LEADER In our holy Christmas,
in this festival of Christ,
give us the riches of your poverty
and show us the power
of your weakness
as we join the angels
in proclaiming your praise:
Glory in heaven and peace on earth,
now and for ever.
ALL **Amen.**

♩ *sing Gloria and other carols*

Blessing for Kwanzaa

DECEMBER 26 THROUGH JANUARY 1

Preparation: The following blessing prayer is written for a single event, but it may be divided and used as daily prayer on the seven days of the celebration. To do this, repeat the opening and closing prayers each day. To make this prayer shorter, omit the reflection questions and conversation after each reading.

Select seven leaders and seven readers.

Music options: One verse of We Are Marching (26), We Bring God's Holy Love (25), or another Christmas refrain can punctuate each section as a candle is lit

LEADER ONE Let us begin our prayer.

all make the sign of the cross

LEADER ONE Rise up in splendor, Jerusalem!
ALL **The glory of the Lord shines upon you.**

Since 1966, the seven-day celebration of Kwanzaa has provided an opportunity for African Americans to affirm their heritage, culture, and unity. The name Kwanzaa is

LEADER ONE	Let us reflect on the principle of *Umoja* [oo-mo-jah], which is unity.

light the central black candle

LEADER ONE	From unity comes our peace.
	From solidarity comes our strength as a people.

READER ONE	Listen to the word of the apostle Paul	
	to the Ephesians	4:3–4

Try your best to let God's Spirit keep your hearts united. Do this by living at peace. All of you are part of the same body. There is only one Spirit of God, just as you were given one hope when you were chosen to be God's people.

The word of the Lord.

ALL	**Thanks be to God.**

wait a few moments in silence, then discuss the reflection questions

LEADER ONE	How do we express our unity? How can we strengthen our feelings of solidarity?

after the discussion, conclude with the following prayer

LEADER ONE	Strengthen us, O Lord,
	for the day when all your children
	will live as one.
	Bless us now and for ever.
ALL	**Amen.**

♩ sing a verse of We Are Marching or another song

LEADER TWO	Let us reflect on the principle of *Kujichagulia* [koo-jee-cha-goo-lee-yah], which is self-determination.

light the red candle closest to the center

LEADER TWO	From our own voice comes wisdom; from self-knowledge, strength.

derived from the Swahili *matunda ya kwanza,* which means "first fruits of the harvest." From December 26 through January 1, harvest time in most of Africa, the black community gathers to celebrate their collective and individual efforts throughout the past year, to give thanks, to assess their accomplishments and contributions to the family and community, and to set goals for the new year.

The celebration is based on seven principles or values called *Nguzo Saba* [en-goo-zoe SAH-bah]. The principles are:

• *Umoja* [oo-mo-jah] (unity), December 26

• *Kujichagulia* [koo-jee-cha-goo-lee-yah] (self determination), December 27

• *Ujima* [oo-jee-mah] (collective work and responsibility), December 28

• *Ujamma* [oo-jah-mah] (cooperative economics), December 29

• *Nia* [nee-yah] (purpose), December 30

• *Kuumba* [koo-oom-bah] (creativity), December 31

• *Imani* [ee-mah-nee] (faith), January 1

Each day a candle is lighted and one principle is the focus of reflection, conversation, and commitment. The visual focus of the celebration is a holder with seven candles (three green candles on the left, a middle black candle, and three red candles on the right) placed on a mat of straw or African cloth. An arrangement of fruits and vegetables is added, in keeping with the theme of harvest. In the home, an ear of corn is included for each child of the family. In larger communities, a kernel of corn representing each child can be added to a bowl. A unity cup is placed among the decorations. The cup contains water, which may be passed to all those present. Or it may be used for a libation cup from which a few drops of water are poured onto the floor in honor of the ancestors.

Because Kwanzaa falls during the Christmas or winter break for most students, it is seldom celebrated in the classroom. However, many schools send a newsletter home with the children, suggesting ways for a family to integrate the celebration of Kwanzaa into their keeping of the Christmas season. In addition, some parishes and religious education groups plan an event during the time of Kwanzaa. Elements of Kwanzaa are sometimes incorporated into the celebration of the feast of the Holy Family on the Sunday after Christmas (or on December 30, if Christmas itself falls on a Sunday). The two festivals suggest many complementary themes.

A Kwanzaa program traditionally includes elements of welcoming, remembering, reassessment, recommitment, and rejoicing. It ends with a farewell calling for greater unity. Small handmade gifts (in keeping with the principle of *kuumba*

READER TWO   Listen to the words of the Psalmist   Psalm 139:1, 13–14

> You have looked deep
> into my heart, Lord,
> and you know all about me.
> You are the one
> who put me together
> inside my mother's body,
> and I praise you because of
> the wonderful way
> you created me.
> Everything you do is marvelous!
> Of this I have no doubt.
>
> The word of the Lord.

ALL   **Thanks be to God.**

wait a few moments in silence, then discuss the reflection questions

LEADER TWO   How do I take responsibility for myself? How do I name myself? Do we respect the name each person gives for himself or herself?

after the discussion, conclude with the following prayer

LEADER TWO   Strengthen us, O Lord,
for the day when all your children
will live as one.
Bless us now and for ever.

ALL   **Amen.**

♩ *sing a verse of We Are Marching or another song*

LEADER THREE   Let us reflect on the principle of *Ujima* [oo-jee-mah], which is our responsibility for one another.

light the green candle closest to the center

LEADER THREE When we live as one, we struggle as one.
We build our community together.

READER THREE Listen to the words of the apostle Paul
to the Galatians   5:13–14

My friends, you were chosen to be free. So don't
use your freedom as an excuse to do anything you
want. Use it as an opportunity to serve each other
with love. All that the Law says can be summed
up in the command to love others as much as you
love yourself.

The word of the Lord.

ALL **Thanks be to God.**

wait a few moments in silence, then discuss the reflection questions

LEADER THREE How can we work together to solve problems in our
families? In our school? In our community?

after the discussion, conclude with the following prayer

LEADER THREE Strengthen us, O Lord,
for the day when all your children
will live as one.
Bless us now and for ever.

ALL **Amen.**

♩ *sing a verse of We Are Marching or another song*

LEADER FOUR Let us reflect on the principle of *Ujamma* [oo-jah-
mah], which is the sharing of resources.

light the next red candle

LEADER FOUR As God is generous with sunshine and with rain,
so are we to be generous with our brothers and
sisters.

or creativity) may be distributed. Planners will note
that the celebration takes
place when New Year's
resolutions are traditionally
made, suggesting that a
review of the past year
and decisions for the future
might be given prominence.
Kwanzaa gatherings are
enhanced with additional
African decorations, songs,
and drums, as a way to
strengthen the community's
consciousness of their
cultural heritage.

READER FOUR   Listen to the words of the Acts of the Apostles   4:32–34

The group of followers all felt the same way about everything. None of them claimed that their possessions were their own, and they shared everything they had with each other. In a powerful way the apostles told everyone that the Lord Jesus was now alive. God greatly blessed his followers, and no one went in need of anything.

The word of the Lord.

ALL   **Thanks be to God.**

wait a few moments in silence, then discuss the reflection questions

LEADER FOUR   How can I contribute to the success of my family?
How do we conserve the resources of our school?
of our neighborhood?

after the discussion, conclude with the following prayer

LEADER FOUR   Strengthen us, O Lord,
for the day when all your children
will live as one.
Bless us now and for ever.

ALL   **Amen.**

♩ sing a verse of We Are Marching or another song

LEADER FIVE   Let us reflect on the principle of *Nia* [nee-yah], which is the sense of purpose.

light the next green candle

LEADER FIVE   Clear goals will direct our steps.
Like stars, they will guide our journey.

READER FIVE   Listen to the words of the apostle Paul
to the Ephesians   3:16–17, 19–21

God is wonderful and glorious. I pray that his Spirit
will make you become strong followers and that
Christ will live in your hearts because of your faith.
Stand firm and be deeply rooted in his love.

     I pray that Christ Jesus and the church will forever
bring praise to God. His power at work in us can do
far more than we dare ask or imagine. Amen.

The word of the Lord.

ALL   **Thanks be to God.**

wait a few moments in silence, then discuss the reflection questions

LEADER FIVE   What are our common goals? How do we further
the goals of the community? What effects have
my choices and decisions over the past year had
on the lives of those around me?

after the discussion, conclude with the following prayer

LEADER FIVE   Strengthen us, O Lord,
for the day when all your children
will live as one.
Bless us now and for ever.

ALL   **Amen.**

♩ *sing a verse of We Are Marching or another song*

LEADER SIX   Let us reflect on the principle of *Kuumba* (koo-oom-
bah), which is creativity.

light the last red candle

LEADER SIX   With our joy and talents, we bring beauty and music
to our community.

READER SIX Listen to the word of the prophet Joel 2:28–30

The Lord said:
Later, I will give my Spirit to everyone.
Your sons and daughters will prophesy.
Your old men will have dreams,
and your young men will see visions.
In those days I will even give
my Spirit to my servants, both men and women.
I will work wonders
in the sky above and on the earth below.

The word of the Lord.

ALL **Thanks be to God.**

wait a few moments in silence, then discuss the reflection question

LEADER SIX How have my family and my community been made better through the use I have made of my talents and gifts?

after the discussion conclude with the following prayer

LEADER SIX Strengthen us, O Lord,
for the day when all your children
will live as one.
Bless us now and for ever.

ALL **Amen.**

♩ *sing a verse of We Are Marching or another song*

LEADER SEVEN Let us reflect on the principle of *Imani* [ee-mah-nee], which is faith.

light the last green candle

LEADER SEVEN Faith in the Lord, and trust in those who have gone before us in the struggle will strengthen us to endure.

| READER
SEVEN | Listen to the words of the book of Revelation | 2:19 |

I am the Son of God! My eyes are like flames of fire, and my feet are like bronze. Listen to what I say.

I know everything about you, including your love, your faith, your service, and how you have endured. I know that you are doing more now than you have ever done before.

The word of the Lord.

ALL **Thanks be to God.**

wait a few moments in silence, then discuss the reflection questions

LEADER
SEVEN What faith guides my family? In what strong traditions am I rooted? What is the heart of my faith, and how deep is my commitment?

after the discussion, conclude with the following prayer

LEADER
SEVEN Strengthen us, O Lord,
for the day when all your children
will live as one.
Bless us now and for ever.

ALL **Amen.**

LEADER
SEVEN We praise you, God of Abraham and Sarah,
for calling us to take possession of the land
in which we live.
We thank you, God of Moses and Miriam,
for calling us to serve you in freedom.
We bless you for sending your Son, Jesus,
to be our Savior and strength,
our discipline, our joy and our peace.
All praise and glory to you
now and for ever.

ALL **Amen.**

 conclude with We Are Marching

put out the candles

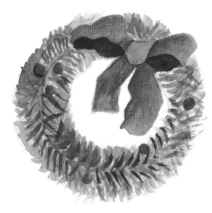

Blessing of New Year's Resolutions

JANUARY 1, OR ANY DAY IN EARLY JANUARY

Preparation: Present traditional New Year's resolutions to the safekeeping of God. After some time for reflection, ask each member of the class to write one specific promise on a small slip of paper. The papers should be brought to the prayer area where they can be collected in a basket, or in an envelope that can be sealed for privacy. During the prayer, the promises will be placed near the stable.

Gather near the stable. Select two leaders.

Music options: Joy to the World (15); Glory to God in the Highest may be spoken or sung.

light a candle

LEADER ONE Glory to God in the highest.

ALL **And peace to God's people on earth.**

all make the sign of the cross

LEADER ONE God of time and of eternity,
with Christmas joy we praise you
for the year gone by
and for the year we have begun.
Your Son comes among us
to bring glad tidings to the poor,
to proclaim a year of grace
for all the world.
We bring you these promises
as signs of our love.
Strengthen us to follow
you more closely
during the coming year.

the promises are collected and placed near the stable

LEADER ONE Let us bow our heads and pray.

Loving God,
Bless these promises and let them draw us closer to
you during the coming year.

We prayed, we prepared, and the promised Messiah has come. God's own Word has been spoken to us—not just in Bethlehem long ago, but today, in the stable of our hearts. Everything ordinary is now filled with blessing and promise. Everything created reflects the glory of God, because God has taken on our own nature, "the Word has become flesh."

In the midst of our Christmas festival we stop to look at ourselves and at our world, and to make some decisions about the way we live. It is the beginning of a new year, a second beginning in the middle of the school year, a priceless gift of time, and an opportunity for growth. How will each of us try during the coming year to reflect more perfectly the loving kindness of our God? How will this class show that we are a holy people called to follow a holy God?

LEADER TWO   Father of Jesus, our Lord,

                  fill this new year with mercy

                  and compassion,

                  and with good gifts

                  for all the world.

                  Unite us in your Spirit

                  as we join the angels

                  in proclaiming your praise:

ALL   **Glory to God in the highest**

                  and peace to God's people on earth.

LEADER TWO   Let us bless the Lord,

                  now and forever.

ALL   **Amen.**

 end with a song

put out the candle

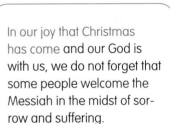

Blessing of New Year's Petitions

Preparation: With the help of newspapers or other sources of information, have a conversation about the needs of people around the world as the new year begins. Together, compose petitions for those needs. Write them on slips of paper or ribbons that will be placed near the stable.

Everyone will need a copy of the psalm. Divide students into groups to read the Side A and Side B parts, and gather near the stable. Select students to read the petitions.

Music options: Hear Us, O God/Óyenos, Señor (10) may be sung in response to each petition; Joy to the World (15); Glory to God in the Highest may be spoken or sung

light a candle

LEADER   Glory to God in the highest.

ALL   **And peace to God's people on earth.**

all make the sign of the cross

In our joy that Christmas has come and our God is with us, we do not forget that some people welcome the Messiah in the midst of sorrow and suffering.

Even as we greet the source of our salvation, we know that there is work still to be done. Sin has not yet been banished. Hatred and greed are not yet destroyed. The poor are still struggling, the homeless are still shivering in doorways.

Will the new year be a time of blessing for them? What are our hopes for the world? What are our prayers for the planet?

LEADER	There is an appointed time for everything,
ALL	**A time for every purpose under the heavens.**

SIDE A	A time to be born and a time to die;
	A time to dance and a time to cry.
	A time for winter and a time for spring;
	A time for study and a time to sing.

SIDE B	A time to wonder and a time to know;
	A time to love and a time to grow.
	A time to keep and a time to share;
	A time for work and a time for prayer.

SIDE A	A time to join and a time to part;

SIDE B	A time to end a thing and a time to start.

LEADER	There is an appointed time for everything,
ALL	**A time for every purpose under the heavens.**

LEADER	God's holy day has dawned for us at last.
ALL	**Come, all you peoples, and adore the Lord.**
	Glory to the Father, and to the Son,
	and to the Holy Spirit:
	as it was in the beginning, is now,
	and will be for ever. Amen. Alleluia.

LEADER	As we reflect on God's saving mercy,
	and look forward to the coming months of this year,
	let us remember these intentions.
	Please respond to each petition,
	Lord, show mercy to your people.

students announce each petition, then place the written copy near the stable

LEADER	Let us raise our hands and pray.
	God of wisdom and mercy,
	hear and answer the prayers
	of your children gathered here.

Strengthen us with your saving power
now and for ever.

ALL **Amen.**

LEADER Loving God,
bless, guide, and protect your people,
and when time is ended
bring us all into the glory of your kingdom.
We ask this through Christ our Lord.

ALL **Amen.**

LEADER Let us pray with the words that Jesus taught us.

ALL **Our Father . . .**

 end with a song

put out the candle

Epiphany Journey with the Magi
(con parranda)

SUNDAY AFTER JANUARY 1,
ALSO THE PERIOD BETWEEN EPIPHANY
AND THE BAPTISM OF THE LORD

Preparation: Practice Christmas carols; prepare copies of the words if you need them. Choose someone (the youngest, perhaps) to lead the singers, carrying a bright star on a pole. Others (the oldest perhaps) are chosen to carry figures of the magi from the stable. All might wear crowns or costumes and bring small gifts (such as gum drops or hand-made cards) for those who open their doors in welcome.

Your class might want to be prepared in case any "strangers" come knocking at your own door. Be sure to give them a warm welcome and applause for their singing. You might even offer them something good to eat before they continue on their journey.

Select several students to take turns speaking to those who answer their doors and someone in each room to greet "the strangers."

Music options: Joy to the World (15), We Three Kings, and other Christmas carols

form your procession, move to another classroom,
knock on the door, and when someone answers, say

It was once a widespread custom in Europe for groups of carol singers to hold an evening procession led by someone carrying a lantern shaped like a star. These singers might be dressed in costumes associated with the wise men, with crowns of gold paper and royal robes. Some might dress as other people in the Christmas Gospel. In many Hispanic countries, the custom of the *parrandas* or neighborhood caroling continues, and there is great devotion surrounding the *Tres Reyes Magos.*

Caroling seems to have begun in the Middle Ages, when troupes of costumed Christmas players went from village to village presenting pageants. They helped to spread the message of Christmas at a time when few people could read and fewer still could own a book. They were warmly welcomed for their songs and for the blessing they were thought to bring to those who opened their doors in hospitality.

Music has always formed an important part of Christmas celebrations. At first the songs were in Latin and were solemnly chanted. But from the time of Saint Francis of Assisi, lighter, happier carols were composed in the people's languages. The custom passed from Italy to France and Spain, to Germany, and then to England. Christmas carols have kept their simplicity, joy, and devotion.

SPEAKER Where is the child born to be king of the Jews? We saw his star in the east and have come to worship him.

GREETER Yes, the Savior is born. Come and let us welcome him together.

enter the "house"
admire their decorations
place the figures of your wise men beside theirs, near the stable
serenade the infant Jesus and all those in the room with Christmas carols
share the gifts you have brought or they have offered
thank the people for welcoming you
wish them well during the coming year
retrieve your figures of the magi

SPEAKER During this year of grace, 20__ (name the year) may the Lord bless you and keep you. May God's face shine upon you and bring you peace.

ALL **Amen.**

continue your journey, moving to another classroom or school office, or return to your own country singing carols, and place the figures of the magi in the stable

Epiphany Blessing of a Gathering Space

Preparation: Gather chalk, a stepladder to stand on, a bowl of holy water, and a small evergreen branch for a sprinkler.

Select a reader, two leaders, and four different speakers to say the prayer for each corner of the room.

Music option: We Three Kings

✚ all make the sign of the cross

LEADER ONE   It is the time of Epiphany. We honor the wise men who followed a star. God still leads those who want to find the Savior. God's glory will be shown to all who seek Him.

READER   Listen to the words of the holy Gospel according to Matthew   2:1–2, 4–7, 8–12

When Jesus was born in the village of Bethlehem in Judea, Herod was king. During this time some wise men from the east came to Jerusalem and said, "Where is the child born to be king of the Jews? We saw his star in the east and have come to worship him."

Herod brought together the chief priests and the teachers of the Law of Moses and asked them, "Where will the Messiah be born?"

They told him, "He will be born in Bethlehem, just as the prophet wrote,

'Bethlehem in the land of Judea,
you are very important among the towns of Judea.
From your town will come a leader,
who will be like a shepherd for my people Israel.'"

Herod secretly called in the wise men and told them, "Go to Bethlehem and search carefully for the child. As soon as you find him, let me know. I want to go and worship him too."

The wise men listened to what the king said and then left. And the star they had seen in the east went on ahead of them until it stopped over the place

> The word January, the first month of the new year, comes from the Latin word *janua*. It means "doorway." January is the year's doorway, an entrance into a bright new beginning!
>
> It is an old custom to bless doorways at Epiphany, and this custom can be celebrated in your school or classroom. As a blessing and a reminder to welcome the stranger and the traveler during the coming year, write the date in chalk above your door, along with the letters C, M, and B. These are the initials of the traditional names for the wise men: Caspar, Melchior, and Balthasar.

where the child was. They were thrilled and excited to see the star.

When the men went into the house and saw the child with Mary, his mother, they knelt down and worshiped him. They took out their gifts of gold, frankincense, and myrrh, and gave them to him. Later they were warned in a dream not to return to Herod, and they went back home by another road.

The Gospel of the Lord.

ALL   **Praise to you, Lord Jesus Christ.**

♩ sing a verse of We Three Kings

figures of the magi may be added to the stable

LEADER TWO   mark above the door with chalk: 20 + C + M + B + (the last two digits of the year)

LEADER TWO   Lord God,
fill this room (school, church)
with kindness for one another
and with respect for guests.
Teach us to welcome everyone
without judgment or prejudice
but with Christian joy.
Fill us with true wisdom
which is to seek Jesus always,
now and for ever.

ALL   **Amen.**

move to each corner of the room and sprinkle it with holy water

SPEAKERS   in turn, each speaker says

Lord God, fill every corner of our world
with safety, peace, and love.
Guide us to the glory of Jesus our Savior.
We ask this through Christ our Lord.

ALL   **Amen.**

WINTER
January and February

Christmastime is over. Now things get back to normal. In the language of prayer, normal is called Ordinary Time.

The term "ordinary" comes from "ordinal," meaning "counted." The Church keeps time by counting the Sundays of the year: the First Sunday, the Tenth Sunday, the Thirteenth Sunday, and so on.

But "ordinary" is not the same as "unimportant." We do not disappear between holidays. We do not stop eating or studying or growing. We do not stop praying or caring about one another. And we do not stop being God's dearest children.

During Ordinary Time we have a chance to enjoy the feasts and festivals that occur in January and February. The time between the feast of the Baptism of the Lord and Ash Wednesday is also called Carnival. It begins with readings and prayers that carry on the Christmas-Epiphany proclamation of Jesus as the light of the world. This prepares us for the blessing of candles on the feast of the Presentation of the Lord, also called Candlemas, on February 2. After that we begin to move toward Lent. This period before Lent may be long or short, depending upon the date of Easter. The festival of delicious food and good fun becomes more intense as the Monday and Tuesday (Mardi Gras) before Ash Wednesday draw near.

During the winter, nature can be harsh. For some of us the winter can feel long. For many people, however, winter is not just long. It is the hardest time of the year. We want to remember that hungry and homeless people need our help, Our help may be a matter of life and death to them.

People need the most help after Christmastime, especially if the weather turns bad for a long time. Unfortunately, many people seem exhausted by Christmas-giving and turn their eyes away from the poor. Our parishes and schools are always looking for ways to help people in trouble. There may be something we can do to support that work.

Meal Prayer for Wintertime

Music options: Bless Us, O Lord (3), We Bring God's Holy Love (25)

LEADER   Let us offer God praise and thanksgiving.

⁘ all make the sign of the cross

LEADER   We thank you, God, for the gift of life.
          And we thank you for all that helps us grow.
          Lord, we hunger for bread,
          and we hunger for justice.
ALL   **Lord, have mercy.**

LEADER   Christ, we hunger for freedom,
          and we hunger for peace.
ALL   **Christ, have mercy.**

LEADER   Lord, we hunger for your love,
          and we hunger for your kingdom.
ALL   **Lord, have mercy.**
          Bless us, O Lord, and these your gifts
          which we are about to receive
          from your goodness.
          Through Christ our Lord. Amen.

⁘ all make the sign of the cross

♩ end with a song

Prayer of Thanksgiving during the Winter Season

ANY TIME DURING THE WINTER WHEN YOU ARE IN THE MOOD

Preparation: Take turns leading the acclamations. Allow others to add more.

LEADER   Heaven and earth, bless the Lord.
ALL   **Praise and glorify God for ever.**

LEADER   Sparkling ice and mountains of snow, bless the Lord.
ALL   **Praise and glorify God for ever.**

LEADER   Warm fires and crispy marshmallows, bless the Lord.
ALL   **Praise and glorify God for ever.**

LEADER   Cold winds and rattling windows, bless the Lord.
ALL   **Praise and glorify God for ever.**

LEADER   Frozen ponds and runny noses, bless the Lord.
ALL   **Praise and glorify God for ever.**

LEADER   Snow forts and toboggan hills, bless the Lord.
ALL   **Praise and glorify God for ever.**

LEADER   Thick socks and soggy mittens, bless the Lord.
ALL   **Praise and glorify God for ever.**

let everyone add their words of praise; then say

LEADER   Let the earth and its people,
    its animals and its seasons,
    give grateful praise to their Creator
    now and for ever.
ALL   **Amen.**

continue to enjoy winter games until time to go indoors

> This prayer is suitable for moments of particular beauty or discovery, such as a new snowfall, a sparkling ice-covered tree, or the discovery of a bright red cardinal perched on black branches in a snow-white land-scape. Make snow angels (if there is snow in your schoolyard), put out some birdseed, and offer this prayer of thanksgiving while you are still outdoors.
>
> Many more acclamations can be added by the group.

Prayer on Martin Luther King Day

THIRD MONDAY IN JANUARY

Preparation: If the prayer is for the whole school, ask a representative from each class to meet and write intercessions. If the prayer is for the class, the petitions can be written together.

    Select a reader.

Music options: Shalom, My Friends (20), We Are Marching (26), All Will Be Well (1), We Bring God's Holy Love (25)

LEADER   Let us begin our prayer.

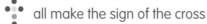 all make the sign of the cross

LEADER   Lord our God,
       see how oppression and violence
       are our sad inheritance,
       one generation to the next.
       We look for you where the lowly are raised up,
       where the mighty are brought down.
       We find you there in your servants,
       and we give you thanks this day
       for your preacher and witness,
       Dr. Martin Luther King, Jr.
       Fill us with your spirit.
       Where our human community is divided by racism,
       torn by repression,
       saddened by fear and ignorance,
       may we give ourselves to your work of healing.
       Grant this through Christ our Lord.

ALL   **Amen.**

READER   Listen to the words of the first letter of John   4: 16–21

God is love. If we keep on loving others, we will stay one in our hearts with God, and he will stay one with us. If we truly love others and live as Christ did in this world, we won't be worried about the day of judgment. A real love for others will chase those worries away. The thought of being punished is what makes us afraid. It shows that we have not really learned to love.

Martin Luther King, Jr. led African Americans in their struggle for civil rights. He preached Christian love and peacefulness. He sought justice without the use of violence.

    Martin Luther King was born January 15, 1929, when black Americans were subject to unjust laws and hateful attitudes. Like his father and the great reformer for whom he had been named, Martin studied for the ministry. He was the new pastor of the Dexter Street Baptist Church in Montgomery, Alabama, when Rosa Parks was arrested for refusing to give up her seat on a city bus to a white passenger. The boycott of the bus line, which Dr. King led, brought the struggle of African Americans to the attention of the country, and the United States Supreme Court ruled that segregation on city buses was illegal.

    Martin Luther King was a powerful preacher. His speeches and sermons awakened both black and

We love because God loved us first. But if we say we love God and don't love each other, we are liars. We cannot see God. So how can we love God, if we don't love the people we can see? The commandment that God has given us is: "Love God and love each other!"

The word of the Lord.

ALL **Thanks be to God.**

LEADER Let us reflect in silence.

pause briefly after each question

Do I have friends who belong to different ethnic groups or different neighborhoods?
Do I ever make fun of people who are not like me?
What have I done to promote good feelings and understanding between my friends and people from other groups?

pause for a few moments of silence

Let us remember these intentions.

students offer the petitions they have prepared

LEADER God of all nations and Creator of all peoples,
heal all that divides us.
Teach us to live together in peace.
As our world is one, so our future is one.
Give us one heart and one vision.
Make us one body in Christ Jesus,
and fill us with the joy of your Holy Spirit.
We ask this through Christ our Lord.

ALL **Amen.**

LEADER Let us pray with the words that Jesus taught us.
ALL **Our Father . . .**

♩ end with a song

white Americans to the injustice of segregation and prejudice. The most famous of his speeches was given in 1963, in front of the Lincoln Memorial in Washington. It included the stirring words, "I have a dream." By that time people across the country shared his dream and were working together to end these practices.

In 1964, Dr. King received the Nobel Peace Prize. In that same year important civil rights laws were passed to ensure a more just society.

His life was ended in 1968, when he was killed by an assassin, but his struggle for racial justice still remains to be completed. The best way we can honor his memory is by continuing to expect for ourselves, and to see that others receive, equal respect, equal opportunity, and equal welcome.

Prayer for Christian Unity

JANUARY 18 THROUGH JANUARY 25,
WEEK OF PRAYER FOR UNITY

Preparation: In this prayer the intercessions name Christians of many different churches who are witnesses of Gospel values. Before the prayer, share the stories of these important people with the class. Other names may be substituted, and additional petitions may be added. An adult may want to give a reflection or homily during the prayer.

Gather around the baptismal font or a bowl of holy water. Bring a branch for sprinkling.

Select a leader (or a leader for each of the six petitions) and a reader.

Music options: Come, Let Us Sing with Joy (6), Send Forth Your Spirit, O Lord (19), We Bring God's Holy Love (25)

LEADER   Let us begin our prayer.

• all make the sign of the cross

LEADER   All who are baptized in Jesus Christ become members of the Body of Christ. We all share the light of Christ, and we all honor the Bible as God's word spoken to each of us.

Although we now see many churches, all who live in Christ are called to unity through the Holy Spirit.

READER   Listen to the words of the apostle Paul
to the Ephesians   4:1–6

I beg you to live in a way that is worthy of the people God has chosen to be his own. Always be humble and gentle. Patiently put up with each other and love each other. Try your best to let God's Spirit keep your hearts united. Do this by living at peace. All of you are part of the same body. There is only one Spirit of God, just as you were given one hope when you were chosen to be God's people. We have only one Lord, one faith, and one baptism. There is one God who is the Father of all people.

The word of the Lord.

ALL   **Thanks be to God.**

From the beginning, the followers of Jesus did not always get along together without arguments. In time, the community became broken into many separate churches. In some cases there have been anger, jealousy, and even warfare between groups of people who are trying to remain faithful to Jesus, the one Lord of all. Yet there has always been a desire to be reunited and live more clearly as the one Body of Christ.

Pope John XXIII invited the leaders of all the Christian churches to visit him in the Vatican. This was a historic occasion, and it showed that the time had come to put aside differences and prejudices. In 1964, the Vatican Council urged Catholics to join in the annual observance of the week of prayer for Christian unity. Today, members of the churches work to love and respect one another, they share in works of justice and charity, and each January they spend a week praying for better ways of living out their unity in

LEADER	Our response to the psalm is "Listen and rejoice."
	Listen to God's voice today!
ALL	**Listen and rejoice!**

Christ. Every school and parish can do its part to build Christian respect, under-standing, and unity.

LEADER	The Lord is our God,
	and we are his people,
	the sheep he takes care of
	in his own pasture.
	Listen to God's voice today!
ALL	**Listen and rejoice!**

Psalm 95:7

LEADER	Let us pray for the unity of the Church and the needs of Christians everywhere. Please respond to each intercession, "Lord, hear our prayer."
	For prayerful Christians like Catherine of Siena and Jonathan Edwards, who renew in us a spirit of devotion, let us pray:
ALL	**Lord, hear our prayer.**

LEADER	For generous Christians, like Mother Teresa and Doctor Albert Schweitzer, who care for the sick and suffering, let us pray:
ALL	**Lord, hear our prayer.**

LEADER	For brave Christians, like Maxmilian Kolbe and Dietrich Bonhoeffer, who accept death for the sake of the gospel, let us pray:
ALL	**Lord, hear our prayer.**

LEADER	For talented Christians, like Michelangelo and Johann Sebastian Bach, who praise God through art and music, let us pray:
ALL	**Lord, hear our prayer.**

LEADER   For visionary Christians,
              like Francis of Assisi and Harriet Tubman,
              who work for peace and justice in the world,
              let us pray:

ALL   **Lord, hear our prayer.**

LEADER   For Christians of learning,
              like Thomas Aquinas and Reinhold Niebuhr,
              who share their vision of God's love
              with the churches,
              let us pray:

ALL   **Lord, hear our prayer.**

move to the water

LEADER   Let us pray.

              Gracious Father,
              you give us new birth
              in the waters of Baptism,
              and speak to our hearts
              through the scriptures.
              Heal and renew your Church,
              overcome all that divides it,
              so that Christians may soon gather at one altar,
              to proclaim your saving love
              to the ends of the earth.
              We ask this through Christ our Lord.

ALL   **Amen.**

LEADER   *sprinkle the community with water from the font*

♩ *all sing a song*

LEADER   Let us pray with the words that Jesus taught us.

ALL   **Our Father . . .**

⠃ *all make the sign of the cross*

Blessing of Candles

FEBRUARY 2, FEAST OF THE PRESENTATION OF THE LORD, ALSO CALLED CANDLEMAS

Preparation: Candles used in the prayer center may be blessed, along with any candles that students bring from home. The candles are gathered in one place, such as on a table or desk covered with a beautiful cloth. One large candle is placed in a holder, ready to be lighted at the beginning of the blessing.

Two forms of blessing are given below. The first is suitable for a whole school or for many children in a classroom or chapel. It calls for two readers. For a shorter blessing, omit the reading.

The second blessing is suitable for older children, a smaller group of children, or for groups with enough adults to help the children light the candles without danger. Place a basket on the table. In it, place enough tapers or votives for each participant and the same number of empty candle holders to receive them when they are lighted. A dish of sand or a piece (or pieces) of wood with holes drilled in it can hold tapers. Glass or other dishes can hold votives.

Select a leader and two readers for a large group, and a leader and one reader for a small group.

Music options: The refrain, The Lord Is My Light and My Salvation . . . , can be sung. Begin and end the blessing with a Christmas carol, such as Joy to the World (15), or We Are Marching (26).

Blessing of Candles for a Large Group

♩ begin and end with a song

LEADER   Let us begin our celebration.

⁘ all make the sign of the cross

LEADER   Jesus Christ is the light of the world,
           a light no darkness can overpower!

       light the large candle

LEADER   Let us all say (or sing):
           The Lord is my light and my salvation;
           of whom should I be afraid?

ALL   **The Lord is my light and my salvation;**
           of whom should I be afraid?

This feast has been celebrated in the West since at least the sixth century. It is based on the story told in Luke 2:22–40. In accordance with Mosaic law, Mary and Joseph brought their eight-day-old son, Jesus, to the Temple for circumcision. Jesus, the light of the world, was brought by Mary and Joseph to be offered to God. So this day is a feast of light. Candles for use in the church throughout the entire year are solemnly blessed. Often a procession of the faithful carries the wondrous light of newly blessed candles to every corner of the church.

The Gospel reading from Luke describes how Jesus is recognized as the long awaited Messiah by the prophets Simeon and Anna. The words of Simeon are one of the canticles or prayer-songs used in the daily prayer of the church. In it Simeon calls Jesus a "light for all nations" that will bring "honor to your people Israel."

Candles are a simple and powerful sign of the light of Christ, and they have been used in Christian churches and homes since earliest times. They remind us that we have been given the light. We are not asleep, nor are we blind. Through the coming of Christ, we can see beneath the surface of things. Like Simeon and Anna, we can see in the ordinary looking baby the appearance of Emmanuel, God-with-us.

It is an old custom on Candlemas to put a few spring flowers near the statue of the Christ child from the nativity set and to bless candles that will be used during the coming year. At the end of the day, the stable and its set of figures is put away for another year.

EMMANUEL

READER ONE   Listen to the words of the holy Gospel
according to Luke   2:25–32, 36, 36–38

At this time a man named Simeon was living in Jerusalem. Simeon was a good man. He loved God and was waiting for God to save the people of Israel. God's Spirit came to him and told him that he would not die until he had seen Christ the Lord.

When Mary and Joseph brought Jesus to the temple to do what the Law of Moses says should be done for a new baby, the Spirit told Simeon to go into the temple. Simeon took the baby Jesus in his arms and praised God,
"Lord, I am your servant,
and now I can die in peace,
because you have kept
your promise to me.
With my own eyes I have seen
what you have done
to save your people,
and foreign nations
will also see this.
Your mighty power is a light
for all nations,
and it will bring honor to your people Israel."

READER TWO   The prophet Anna was also there in the temple. In her youth she had been married for seven years, but her husband died. And now she was eighty-four years old. Night and day she served God in the temple by praying and often going without eating.

At that time Anna came in and praised God. She spoke about the child Jesus to everyone who hoped for Jerusalem to be set free.

The Gospel of the Lord.

ALL   **Praise to you, Lord Jesus Christ.**

LEADER   On the day of our Baptism, we were given a lighted candle with these words: "Walk always as children of the light, and keep the flame of faith alive in your hearts."

Let us now renew that faith by holding up our candles
asking God to bless these candles. They are a sign
of Christ, who is light and life to us.

God our Creator and Redeemer,
bless these candles
as signs of your presence
and signs of our faith.

In the beauty of your holy light,
keep us in quiet and in peace.
Turn our hearts to you
that we may be light for our world.

All praise be yours through Christ,
the light of nations,
the glory of Israel,
for ever and ever.

ALL   **Amen.**

all make the sign of the cross

Blessing of Candles for a Small Group

begin and end with a song

LEADER   Let us begin our prayer.

all make the sign of the cross

LEADER   Jesus Christ is the light of the world,
               a light no darkness can overpower!

light the large candle

LEADER   Let us all say (or sing):
               The Lord is my light and my salvation;
               of whom should I be afraid?

ALL   **The Lord is my light and my salvation;**
               of whom should I be afraid?

LEADER   To each of us today Jesus says, "Come, follow me, walk in my light!" As a sign that we are awake and attentive, and that we desire to walk in the light of Christ, we will each light a small candle from the large one, and place it on the table.

the leader calls each person by name (For example, "Bridget, come, follow Christ." "Jose, come, follow Christ.")
when called, each person lights a candle and places it in a holder

READER   Listen to the words of the holy Gospel
according to Matthew   5: 14–16

You are like light for the whole world. A city built on top of a hill cannot be hidden, and no one would light a lamp and put it under a clay pot. A lamp is placed on a lamp stand, where it can give light to everyone in the house. Make your light shine, so that others will see the good that you do and will praise your father in heaven.

The Gospel of the Lord.

ALL   **Praise to you, Lord Jesus Christ.**

all keep a few moments of silence

LEADER   Let us pray.

God our Creator and Redeemer,
bless these candles
as signs of your presence
and signs of our faith.

In the beauty of your holy light,
keep us in quiet and in peace.
Keep us safe and turn our hearts to you
that we may be light for our world.

All praise be yours through Christ,
the light of nations,
the glory of Israel,
for ever and ever.

ALL   **Amen.**

 all make the sign of the cross

Blessing of Throats

FEBRUARY 3, COMMEMORATION OF SAINT BLASE

Preparation: Two candles are tied together in the form of a cross. The ribbon tie is usually red, perhaps in recognition of the fact that Bishop Blase died a martyr.

Students may want to adapt or rewrite the intercessions, perhaps including the names of friends and family members who are ill.

For a shorter prayer, use only the introductory antiphon, the reading, and the blessing prayer.

Select a leader and a reader.

Music options: All Will Be Well (1), We Sing of the Saints (27)

LEADER   Let us begin our prayer.

all make the sign of the cross

LEADER   Our help is the name of the Lord.

ALL   **Who made heaven and earth.**

LEADER   On this feast of Saint Blase, patron of the sick,
we pray for God's protection
from illnesses of the throat
and other diseases.
We pray for freedom from colds and sore throats
during the rest of this winter season.
The blessing of throats is a sign of our faith
in God's love and care for us
and for all the sick.

READER   Listen to the words of the holy Gospel
according to Matthew   8:14 – 17

Jesus entered the house of Peter, and saw Peter's mother-in-law lying in bed with a fever. Jesus touched her hand, the fever left her, and she rose and waited on him.

When it was evening, people brought Jesus many who were possessed by demons, and he drove out

Saint Blase was a doctor as well as a bishop in Armenia during the fourth century. It is believed that Blase once healed a boy who was choking on a fish bone. Because of that, he is the patron of the sick, especially people with illnesses of the throat.

It is an ancient custom to pray for good health with a blessing of throats on his feast day. A priest or deacon touches the throat of each person in the assembly with candles that were blessed on February 2, the feast of the Presentation of the Lord, and makes the sign of the cross during the blessing prayer. A lay minister also uses the candles but does not make the sign of the cross during the prayer of blessing.

the spirits by a word and cured all the sick, to fulfill what had been said by Isaiah the prophet:

He took away our infirmities
and bore our diseases.

The Gospel of the Lord.

ALL **Praise to you, Lord Jesus Christ.**

LEADER Let us all say:
Put your hope in the Lord;
take courage and be strong.

ALL **Put your hope in the Lord;**
take courage and be strong.

LEADER To each intention, let us respond,
Lord, have mercy.
For the healing of the sick, we pray:

ALL **Lord, have mercy.**

LEADER For the strength of those who suffer, we pray:

ALL **Lord, have mercy.**

LEADER For the comfort of those who are mentally and physically disabled, we pray:

ALL **Lord, have mercy.**

LEADER For the wisdom of doctors and nurses, we pray:

ALL **Lord, have mercy.**

LEADER For the steadfastness of those whose friends are sick, we pray:

ALL **Lord, have mercy.**

LEADER For the compassion of those who care for the sick, we pray:

ALL **Lord, have mercy.**

LEADER For the success of those who search for cures, we pray:

ALL **Lord, have mercy.**

LEADER	That all who seek the help of Saint Blase today may be protected from illnesses of the throat and other forms of sickness, we pray:
ALL	**Lord, have mercy.**

LEADER	Let us pray with the words that Jesus taught us.
ALL	**Our Father . . .**

MINISTER	holding crossed candles to the throat of each person, without making the sign of the cross, repeat

Through the intercession of Saint Blase,
   bishop and martyr,
may God deliver you from every disease of the throat
and from every other illness:
In the name of the Father, and of the Son,
   and of the Holy Spirit.

each person responds in turn

ALL	**Amen.**

♩ end with a song

Prayer for Our Lady of Lourdes

FEBRUARY 11

Preparation: Place flowers or a lighted candle before an image of Mary. Use a picture of Our Lady of Lourdes or an Immaculate Mary statue if one is available. Select a leader and a reader.

Music options: Sing of Mary (21), We Sing of the Saints (27), with verse for feasts of Mary, or a familiar hymn to Mary such as Immaculate Mary

♩ begin and end with a song

LEADER	Long ago, Our Blessed Mother brought to Saint Bernadette a message of healing and peace. On this feast day, let us remember all those who are in pain, and all those who care for them.

⋮ all make the sign of the cross

On this day Catholics remember the appearance of the Blessed Virgin Mary to a 14-year-old girl named Bernadette in Lourdes, France, in 1858. Mary told Bernadette to wash in water from the spring. The girl saw no spring nearby, so she began to dig in the earth to find water. The people with her thought she was crazy and dragged her away. That night, water bubbled up just where Bernadette had dug. Now, pilgrims from all over the world come to wash in the water of that spring and to pray for healing at the shrine of Lourdes.

Bernadette's visions occurred just four years after the immaculate conception of Mary was proclaimed a doctrine of the Church. When Bernadette asked the "beautiful lady" what her name was, she said, "I am the Immaculate Conception." A religious medal portrays Mary as Bernadette described her and includes the words of her title. For more information, read the entry for December 8 in this book, page 46.

In 1993, the Pope named this feast the World Day of the Sick. He asked that Catholics pray on this day in solidarity with the sick and suffering throughout the world, think about the role of suffering in God's plan, and thank God for Catholic healthcare workers. He also asks us to respond to the suffering of people around the world.

| READER | Listen to the words of the holy Gospel according to Matthew 11:28–30 |
| | |

If you are tired from carrying heavy burdens, come to me and I will give you rest. Take the yoke I give you. Put it on your shoulders and learn from me. I am gentle and humble, and you will find rest. This yoke is easy to bear, and this burden is light.

The Gospel of the Lord.

ALL **Praise to you, Lord Jesus Christ.**

LEADER Let us take a moment to remember those we know who are sick or troubled, and in need of our prayers today.

pause so that children may mention people by name, or remember them silently

LEADER Let us ask Mary our Mother to pray with us. The response to our petitions is, "Holy Mary, pray for them." That the sick, injured or disabled may receive healing, we pray:

ALL **Holy Mary, pray for them.**

LEADER That the fearful may receive courage, we pray:

ALL **Holy Mary, pray for them.**

LEADER That the anxious may receive comfort, we pray:

ALL **Holy Mary, pray for them.**

LEADER That the dying may receive peace, we pray:

ALL **Holy Mary, pray for them.**

LEADER That those who care for the sick may receive gentleness, we pray:

ALL **Holy Mary, pray for them.**

LEADER That all who suffer may be joined to the sacrifice of Jesus, we pray:

ALL **Holy Mary, pray for them.**

LEADER	Mary our mother,
	you stood with Jesus during his suffering on the cross,
	and so we ask you to be with all your children who
	are sick and troubled.
	Comfort them and bring their prayers
	to the merciful heart of God.
	We ask this through Christ our Lord.
ALL	**Amen.**

LEADER	Those who trust in the Lord
	are like a great mountain
	that cannot be shaken
	and will last forever.
	Trusting in God's wisdom,
	let us pray with the words that Jesus taught us.
ALL	**Our Father . . .**

Prayer for a Valentine's Day Celebration

Preparation: Valentines, heart-shaped decorations, posters for the classroom or home, or a plate of Saint Valentine's Day cookies could be blessed. Students stand or sit in a circle. Valentines can be held or placed on the floor or table in front of their owners. Any containers of food should be in the center.

The celebration should be more restrained in years when the feast occurs during Lent. Select a leader and a reader.

Music option: We Bring God's Holy Love (25)

LEADER	Let us begin our prayer.

all make the sign of the cross

LEADER	The love of Christ has gathered us together.
	Let us all say:
	Let us rejoice and be glad.
ALL	**Let us rejoice and be glad.**

Saint Valentine was a third-century bishop who bravely died for his faith. The name Valentine means "valiant" or brave. This day seems to have been connected to love before it became Valentine's feast day. There is an old legend that birds choose their mates on February 14, and the mating of birds is a clear signal that spring will be coming soon. A saint who died for the sake of God is certainly a fine patron of love and lovers, and a day that calls to mind the springtime resurrection of the earth is a good day for a saint's feast.

For hundreds of years, secret letters of love and friendship sent on this day have been called Saint Valentine's notes, or valentines.

This is a day to give cards, kisses, or hugs to the people whose love makes our lives better.

READER   Listen to the words of the first letter of John   4:11–12, 16

Dear friends, since God loved us this much, we must love each other. No one has ever seen God. But if we love each other, God lives in us, and his love is truly in our hearts.

God is love. If we keep on loving others, we will stay one in our hearts with God, and he will stay one with us.

The word of the Lord.

ALL   **Thanks be to God.**

LEADER   We are children of a loving God.
We carry God's own love in our hearts.
Let us never be afraid to show friendship,
appreciation, and love.

Let us pray.

God our Creator,
bless the love that brings people together
and grows ever stronger in our hearts.
May all the messages that carry the name
of your holy Bishop Valentine
be sent in good joy
and received in delight.
We ask this through Christ our Lord.

ALL   **Amen.**

all make the sign of the cross

LEADER   Let us offer each other a sign of friendship.

Early Spring
March

March is said to "come in like a lion and go out like a lamb." In most of the northern hemisphere, weather is blustery and wet, with the remnants of snow turning to slush. It is a month of transition, when the hours of daylight catch up to the hours of darkness and finally become equal. The day when all is in balance, the vernal equinox, is the first day of spring. March, when light struggles against darkness and warmth begins to fight off the chill of winter, was fittingly named by the ancient Romans for Mars, their god of war.

Lent often begins during March, and there are several interesting holy days to brighten the month. There is Saint Patrick's Day (March 17), which is often observed with parades, Irish songs, and "the wearing of the green." Saint Joseph's Day (March 19) belongs to all nations, but it is especially loved by Italian Catholics, who traditionally celebrate with a parish dinner where food is offered to all the hungry of the neighborhood.

On March 25, we celebrate the Annunciation of the Lord, one of the major feasts of the year called a solemnity. It reminds us of the coming of the angel Gabriel to Mary, with words of importance for the whole world. She was invited by God to be the mother of the Redeemer. Her reply, "Be it done to me according to your word," changed the course of history. The Son of God became an infant in Mary's womb; God took on a human nature just like ours; the prayers and hopes of God's people were fulfilled. We joyfully celebrate the Lord's birth nine months later, on Christmas, but the mystery of the Incarnation really begins with the Annunciation. It is not a day to skip over, but to celebrate with songs and flowers (if we can find any in the March landscape).

For many centuries March 25 was New Year's day, and the celebrations lasted until April 1. In the late sixteenth century, the start of the new year was moved to January 1, but some people refused to accept the new date. They continued to observe the old customs and partied up to the first of April. They became known as "April Fools."

March is a good month to learn more about calendars and to think about our use of the time God gives us.

Meal Prayer for Early Spring

Music options: Bless Us, O Lord (3), Come, Let Us Sing with Joy (6)

LEADER   Let us offer God praise and thanksgiving.

 all make the sign of the cross

LEADER   Shout praises to the Lord!
                With all that I am, I will shout God's praises.
ALL   **I will sing and praise the Lord God**
                for as long as I live.

LEADER   Blessed are you, Lord.
                You have fed us from our earliest days.
                You give food to every living creature.
                Fill our hearts with joy and delight.
                Let us always have enough
                and something to spare
                for works of mercy
                in honor of Christ Jesus, our Lord.
                Through Christ may glory, honor, and power
                be yours for ever and ever.
ALL   **Amen.**

 all make the sign of the cross

♩ end with a song

Prayers for Saint Patrick's Day

MARCH 17

Preparation: Any of the following prayers for Saint Patrick's day can be said aloud, or one might be made into a prayer card and given to the children on Saint Patrick's day.

Music options: This Day God Gives Me (24), We Sing of the Saints (27), with verse for March 17: Saint Patrick

Opening Prayer for Saint Patrick's Mass

LEADER   God our Father,
you sent Saint Patrick
to preach your glory to the people
   of Ireland.
By the help of his prayers
may all Christians proclaim your
   love to all.
Grant this through our Lord
   Jesus Christ, your Son,
who lives and reigns with you and
   the Holy Spirit,
one God, for ever and ever.

ALL   **Amen.**

The Breastplate (or Lorica) of Saint Patrick

LEADER   Today I put on
God's strength to steer me,
God's power to uphold me,
God's wisdom to guide me,
God's eye for my vision,
God's ear for my hearing,
God's word for my speech,
God's hand to protect me,
God's pathway before me,
God's shield for my shelter.
I thank God who is with me,
through Christ our Lord.

ALL   **Amen.**

Saint Patrick was an unusual missionary. No one else succeeded so greatly in spreading the Gospel in a pagan land. When he first arrived in Ireland, most of its people were either unaware of Christianity or thought of it as an alien faith. But by the generation after his death, most of the people had embraced the Christian faith.

Patrick was born in what is now Wales, the son of a deacon and grandson of a priest. Nevertheless, he said later that his love for the faith was weak when he was a boy. All that changed when Patrick was kidnapped and taken to Ireland as a slave. For seven long years he remained in captivity, tending livestock. In his loneliness, he learned to put his life in God's hands. Finally, Patrick escaped, returned home, and became a priest. After studying in Rome, he returned to Ireland as a missionary and bishop. He died in 461.

The Irish people love Patrick dearly and tell many stories about him. He used the shamrock, they say, as a meditation on the Trinity of three divine Persons (three "leaflets") in one God (a single "leaf"). He was a wonder-worker who was able to get people's attention by outshining the Druid priests. In one contest he was able, they say, to rid Ireland of all its snakes.

The Irish people brought their devotion to Saint Patrick with them to America. In the nineteenth century, a great many Irish people emigrated because of poverty and famine in that country. Hundreds of thousands of them settled in the United States and built churches and schools with their first earnings in their new homeland. To this day you will find churches all over the country dedicated to Patrick as a way of showing gratitude for their saint's protection and pride in their Irish heritage.

Patrick wrote prayers. Some are called "Lorica," which means the piece of armor worn to protect the chest. A prayer called a lorica declares a person's faith that God alone is all the protection we need. Loricae were a common form of prayer in Ireland long before Patrick arrived. Patrick used a form of prayer that the Irish people were already accustomed to and easy for people to remember. That's one of the things that made him such an excellent missionary and bishop.

Loricae are good prayers to memorize. Then they can be said in one's heart at any time during the day.

Four More Prayers of Saint Patrick

Preparation: These brief prayers can be copied by the students and can easily be memorized.

Christ beside me,
Christ before me,
Christ behind me,
Christ within me,
Christ beneath me,
Christ above me.

Christ on my right hand,
Christ on my left.

Christ where I lie,
Christ where I sit,
Christ where I rise.

Christ in the hearts of all who think of me.
Christ in the mouths of all who speak to me.
Christ in every eye that sees me.
Christ in every ear that hears me.

Prayers for Saint Joseph's Day

MARCH 19, FEAST OF SAINT JOSEPH, HUSBAND OF MARY

MAY 1, FEAST OF SAINT JOSEPH THE WORKER

Meal Prayer for Saint Joseph's Day

Music options: Bless Us, O Lord (3), We Sing of the Saints (27), with verse for feasts of Joseph

LEADER   Let us begin our prayer.

all make the sign of the cross

LEADER   We remember Saint Joseph, the good man who made a home for Jesus, the Messiah. Joseph was named for the hero who saved Israel during the time of famine and forgave the brothers who had betrayed him.

Let us pray.

wait a minute or two, then continue

LEADER   Almighty God,
in your wisdom and love
you chose Joseph to be the husband of Mary,
the mother of your Son.
As Jesus relied on his protection on earth
may we have the help of his prayers in heaven.
We ask this through Christ our Lord.

ALL   **Amen.**

LEADER   Let us thank God for the food that is before us.

ALL   **Bless us, O Lord, and these your gifts
which we are about to receive from your goodness.
Through Christ our Lord. Amen.**

LEADER   Good Saint Joseph, patron of those
who need fathering, food,
or forgiveness, pray for us.

ALL   **Amen.**

Saint Joseph was the husband of Mary and the foster father of Jesus. Joseph was a descendant of the royal family of King David, but he was not rich. He worked as a carpenter in the small town of Nazareth. The Gospel of Matthew calls Joseph a "good man." He is the patron of parents, workers, and carpenters, and he is the protector of the universal Church. He is also the patron of a happy death, because it is likely that he died with Mary and Jesus beside him.

The Italian people have a special love for Saint Joseph, and they have many customs to celebrate his feast day. Some parishes and even some families prepare a "Saint Joseph's table," which is often a potluck supper. Everyone brings something to give to the poor. Fish but not meat is part of the feast, because good fish is plentiful in Italy, and because the holy day usually falls during Lent. A statue of Saint Joseph is used as the centerpiece of the table. Sometimes a place is set at the table for the saint.

The link between Saint Joseph and food for the poor may have come about because the people of Sicily appealed to him during a time of famine, and they were saved. Joseph was named for a great hero of the Old Testament, the son of Jacob, who also supplied food to people during a famine. His story is told in Genesis 37–45.

and to protect its fragile beauty.
We ask this through Christ our Lord.

ALL   **Amen.**

LEADER   Let us pray with the words that Jesus taught us.
ALL   **Our Father . . .**

♩ end with a song

Prayers for the Solemnity of the Annunciation

MARCH 25

Liturgy of the Word for the Annunciation

Preparation: Bring flowers to put before an icon or beautiful picture of the Annunciation.

  Select a leader and a reader.

Music options: Sing of Mary (21), We Sing of the Saints (27), with verse for feasts of Mary, If Today You Hear the Voice of God (11)

♩ begin and end with a song

LEADER   Let us begin our prayer.

 all make the sign of the cross

LEADER   The Lord's promise has come true. As the prophet
said, "A virgin will have a baby boy, and he will
be called Immanuel." Let us say:
Blessed be the name of the Lord.

ALL   **Blessed be the name of the Lord.**

On this feast we celebrate the mystery of the incarnation, when the Son of God became a human being. On March 25, nine months before celebrating the birth of Jesus, we celebrate his conception in the womb of Mary, his mother.

In the Gospel of Luke we read of the coming of the angel Gabriel to Mary at her home in Nazareth. Gabriel told Mary of God's plan that the Savior would be her child. Mary answered, "I am the Lord's servant! Let it happen as you have said." With that acceptance, Mary became the Mother of God. We rejoice that God loved us enough to become one of us. We are happy that Mary first, and then many others, accepted Jesus.

It is a happy thing to celebrate the pregnancy of Mary in the spring, when nature itself reminds us that God's love brings new life to all creation. We can scatter crumbs to welcome the birds, busy about their job of nest-building. We can plant seeds, which, like Jesus, grow in darkness before they are "born." The feast of the

READER   Listen to the words of the holy Gospel
according to Luke   1:26–35, 38

God sent the angel Gabriel to the town of Nazareth in Galilee with a message for a virgin named Mary. She was engaged to Joseph from the family of King David. The angel greeted Mary and said, "You are truly blessed! The Lord is with you."

Mary was confused by the angel's words and wondered what they meant. Then the angel told Mary, "Don't be afraid! God is pleased with you, and you will have a son. His name will be Jesus. He will be great and will be called the Son of God Most High. The Lord God will make him king, as his ancestor David was. He will rule the people of Israel forever, and his kingdom will never end."

Mary asked the angel, "How can this happen? I am not married!"

The angel answered, "The Holy Spirit will come down to you, and God's power will come over you. So your child will be called the holy Son of God."

Mary said, "I am the Lord's servant! Let it happen as you have said." And the angel left her.

The Gospel of the Lord.

ALL   **Praise to you, Lord Jesus Christ.**

allow a few moments of silence to ponder the following questions

LEADER   Mary was willing to do whatever God asked of her. Am I willing to do what God asks of me? What have we done this year to become more faithful to God?

LEADER   Loving God,
you give us your finest grace,
your greatest blessing.
You give us yourself.
In Christ, you share our life.
In Christ, you share our suffering and our joy.
All glory to you, now and for ever.

ALL   **Amen.**

Annunciation is one of the three days in Lent when flowers are allowed in the church. We can place flowers near the statue or icon of Mary where we gather to pray.

People in the Philippines and in Greece fly kites and sail their boats on this day to celebrate the Holy Spirit, who filled Mary with God's life-giving breath. In Sweden, light, airy waffles are eaten. Long ago Swedes called the feast of the Annunciation *"Varfrudagen,"* which means "Our Lady's Day." Over the years, people became care-less with their pronunciation, calling it *"Vafferdagen,"* and then *"Vaffeldagen,"* which means "Waffle Day." This explains the Swedish custom of making heart-shaped waffles on March 25 to celebrate the heart of the Virgin Mary.

LEADER	
Let us pray with the words that Jesus taught us.	
ALL	**Our Father . . .**

LEADER	Let us all say:
ALL	**Hail Mary, full of grace,**
	the Lord is with you!
	Blessed are you among women
	and blessed is the fruit of your womb, Jesus.
	Holy Mary, mother of God,
	pray for us sinners,
	now and at the hour of our death. Amen.

all make the sign of the cross

Litany for the Annunciation

LEADER   We are glad that Mary said "yes" to the plan of God, and Jesus became a child in her womb. Mary became his mother and the mother of all who would follow him. Let us honor her in prayer.

all make the sign of the cross

LEADER	ALL
Lord, have mercy.	**Lord, have mercy.**
Christ, have mercy.	**Christ, have mercy.**
Lord, have mercy.	**Lord, have mercy.**
Holy Mary,	**pray for us.**
Holy Mother of God,	**pray for us.**
Sinless Mother,	**pray for us.**
Ark of the covenant,	**pray for us.**
Health of the sick,	**pray for us.**
Refuge of sinners,	**pray for us.**
Comfort of the troubled,	**pray for us.**
Help of Christians,	**pray for us.**
Queen of all saints,	**pray for us.**
Queen of peace,	**pray for us.**

LEADER	Pray for us, holy Mother of God.
ALL	**That we may become worthy of the promises of Christ.**

LEADER	Eternal God, through the prayers of Mary our Mother, give us a work to do in your plan of salvation. We ask this through Christ our Lord.
ALL	**Amen.**

⁘ all make the sign of the cross

The Angelus

LEADER	Let us begin our prayer.

⁘ all make the sign of the cross

LEADER	The angel spoke God's message to Mary,
ALL	**and she conceived of the Holy Spirit.** **Hail Mary . . .**

LEADER	"I am the lowly servant of the Lord:
ALL	**let it be done to me according to your word."** **Hail Mary . . .**

LEADER	And the Word became flesh
ALL	**and lived among us.** **Hail Mary . . .**

LEADER	Pray for us, holy Mother of God:
ALL	**That we may become worthy of the promises of Christ.**

> The mystery of the incarnation of the Lord is expressed in the Angelus prayer, which retells the story of Gabriel's announcement to Mary. It is an old tradition to ring church bells each day to remind Christians to pray the Angelus in the morning, at noon, and in the evening. Some people still keep this custom.

LEADER   Let us pray.
             Lord, fill our hearts with your grace:
             once, through the message of an angel
             you revealed to us the incarnation of your Son;
             now, through his suffering and death
             lead us to the glory of his resurrection.
             We ask this through Christ our Lord.
ALL   **Amen.**

all make the sign of the cross

Prayer at Carnival and Mardi Gras

CARNIVAL, FROM THE BAPTISM OF THE LORD
TO ASH WEDNESDAY (ESPECIALLY THE LAST TWO WEEKS
BEFORE ASH WEDNESDAY)

MARDI GRAS (ALSO CALLED SHROVE TUESDAY),
DAY BEFORE ASH WEDNESDAY

Preparation: Bring the spirit of carnival into the school or classroom by decorating with crepe paper streamers. Invite students to tell jokes and play games, or make music with simple instruments, such as triangles, drums or anything else you can find or make. Be sure to have something delicious to eat.

Music options: Jubilate Servite (14), Celtic Alleluia (4), and any alleluias you know

LEADER   Blessed are you, Lord our God,
             Ruler of the universe
             for giving us this season
             of grace and happiness.
             Let us all say, "Blessed be God for ever."
ALL   **Blessed be God for ever.**

The days before Ash Wednesday are the time of carnival. In many cities of the world, there are parades with elaborate floats, gaudy street decorations in gold, green, and purple, and crazy costumes. Carnival is a time to be playful. It is a burst of color, energy, and enjoyment before the serious business of Lent begins.

People often wear brightly decorated masks as a way to show that Lent will be a time to put aside our ways of hiding who we are and what we really think. It may be difficult to stop pretending, so before Lent begins we relax and poke fun at ourselves with silly masks and practical jokes.

In the past, adults gave up eating meat for the whole of Lent. The word "carnival" means "good-bye to meat" in Latin. So Carnival, especially the last day before Ash Wednesday, was an opportunity to finish off your supply of good meat and gravy and rich pastries.

LEADER   Loving God,

          we thank you for the promise

          that springtime will follow

          these last days of winter.

          We thank you for the promise

          that Easter will follow the hard work of Lent.

          We thank you for Carnival (or Mardi Gras)

          and the chance to rejoice together.

          We thank you through Christ our Lord.

ALL   **Amen.**

♩ sing many "Alleluias" with all your might

Farewell to the Alleluia

THE LAST GATHERING BEFORE ASH WEDNESDAY

Preparation: Make a beautiful banner or scroll with the word "alleluia" on it. If the group is large, the banner should also be large and colorful—or ask each student to decorate a small banner. Find a box to fit it (or them) and a dry place to bury the box or lock it away. The "tomb" can be a cupboard that can be locked, a trunk or chest, or an actual hole in the ground. Gather bells, noisemakers, horns, and other instruments.

When you are ready to begin, form a procession. Carry the bells and other instruments, the shovel or lock and key, the box, and the banner(s).

Music options: Jubilate Servite (14), Celtic Alleluia (4), and any alleluias you know

♩ begin and end with a song

LEADER   Let us go forth to bury our song of joy.

          Let us go forth with strong voices and happy hearts.

go in procession to the place of burial singing joyfully all the Alleluias you know and waving the banner(s); at the place, keep singing, open the cupboard or dig a hole, raise the alleluia banner(s) so all can see, end the song, ring bells and noisemakers, or play the instruments for a minute

Carnival ends with Mardi Gras. These are the French words for "Fat Tuesday," a day when many people eat pancakes running with butter and syrup. In Russia they are called *blini,* and are often covered with sour cream and caviar. Doughnuts are also a favorite, especially in Poland where they are called *pączki* (poonch-key), and are filled with jelly or custard. Hot cross buns and pretzels are also traditional foods for Mardi Gras.

Before Lent, we say good-bye to the alleluia. The word, always sung with joy and energy, means "praise God" in the Hebrew language. The Church does not sing this song of joy during Lent, a season of penance and simplicity. Putting it aside gives greater delight to its return, when we sing many beautiful alleluias on Easter.

During the Middle Ages, many churches sang hymns praising the alleluia and wishing it well on its last day before Lent began. Then it was "buried" for forty days. The school or an individual class can do the same. A ceremony for welcoming the return of the alleluia at Easter is on page 142.

the leader gives a signal for silence
someone collects the noisemakers to keep them quiet
the banner or banners are put in their box and buried or locked away

LEADER   Lord of joyful noise,
God of solemn silence,
today we bury this word of praise
so that we can turn our thoughts
to the sadness of sin in this world
and the suffering that it causes.
You are a loving Father to us,
a forgiving Savior,
a guiding Spirit,
always ready to turn our steps
toward goodness and peace.
Give us a good and holy Lent.
In forty days,
when Lent is finished
bring us back to this place
to claim our right to Easter joy.
We ask this through Christ our Lord.

ALL   Amen.

in perfect silence return to your customary place

Lent

The Forty Days between Ash Wednesday and Holy Thursday

In some ways, Lent is the most famous of all the Church's seasons. Perhaps that is because of its many traditions, or because it is so long. The six weeks of Lent take us from the end of winter to the beginning of spring.

During Lent we put away the joyful "alleluia." We will not sing it again until Easter, when we rejoice in the resurrection of Jesus.

We also clear away unneeded decorations and give our homes and classrooms a good spring cleaning.

Lent is not an unhappy time, but it is a serious time. It is an opportunity to think about how much the Gospel means to us and how well we are living up to God's law of love. We watch and pray with Christ. We choose actions that help us become more prayerful, help us live more simply, and teach us to share what we have with those who are in need. That is the purpose of Lenten sacrifices.

On Ash Wednesday and each Friday of Lent, adults and children over the age of seven abstain from eating meat. Fasting reminds us of the goodness of God, the strength it takes to control our desires, and our unity with the hungry people of the world. Children can participate in the spirit of Lenten fasting by not wasting food, by eating the healthful foods that are prepared by their families, or by eating fewer sweets. Helping to make meals pleasant for everyone is also a fine Lenten practice. Children should talk over their ideas with their parents before changing their eating habits.

Lent is a time to turn back to those we have hurt or offended, and to apologize, ask pardon, and restore peace between us. We turn our thoughts inward and try to recognize the ways we have refused to obey God's laws or failed to live up to God's call that we lead a holy life. The sacrament of penance helps us in this task. A way of celebrating that sacrament is given on page 128.

In addition to the prayers in this section, a number of prayers of forgiveness, peace, and reconciliation suitable for Lent are on pages 211–213 of this book.

Meal Prayer for Lent

LEADER	Let us offer God praise and thanksgiving.

all make the sign of the cross

LEADER	Behold! Now is the acceptable time!
ALL	**Now is the day of salvation!**

LEADER	I was hungry: *(Matthew 25:35–36)*
ALL	**And you gave me food.**

LEADER	I was thirsty:
ALL	**And you gave me drink.**

LEADER	I was a stranger:
ALL	**And you welcomed me.**

LEADER	I was naked:
ALL	**And you clothed me.**

LEADER	I was ill:
ALL	**And you cared for me.**

LEADER	I was in jail:
ALL	**And you visited me.**

LEADER	Lord Jesus Christ, be with all those who are in need. Bless us, and bless the food we eat today. Help our families, our school, and our parish keep a good and holy Lent. And bring us quickly to the glory of Easter. We ask this through Christ our Lord.
ALL	**Amen.**

The Preparation of Ashes

Preparation: Bring palms saved from last year's Palm Sunday celebration to an outdoor place away from the wind. Place foil in the bottom of a barbecue grill. Bring a lighter, a poker to stir the fire, a kitchen strainer, a big spoon, a box or crock large enough to hold the ashes, and a cover for the box or crock. If the palms are too long to fit into the barbecue grill, cut them into smaller pieces.

After the fire is out, pour the ashes from the foil into the strainer, then use the spoon to stir them through the strainer into the box or crock. Cover the box or crock to keep the ashes from spilling.

If the blessing and giving of ashes will take place after this preparation, you will also need holy water, a sacramentary or the *Book of Blessings,* and song books or other participation materials. A deacon or priest blesses the ashes, but any adult can help to distribute them.

Select a leader and a reader.

Music option: From Ashes to the Living Font (7)

LEADER	Let us begin our prayer.

⋮ all make the sign of the cross

LEADER	Praised be the God of grace, mercy, and peace. Let us all say: Blessed be God for ever!
ALL	**Blessed be God for ever!**
LEADER	A year ago we held these palms and sang "Hosanna" to Jesus our Messiah. We marched in procession to show that we would follow him. Today we burn these palms and renew our promise to follow Christ our Lord.
READER	Listen to the words of the prophet Joel 2:12, 13, 15, 16, 17

The Lord said, "It isn't too late.
You can still return to me with all your heart.
Turn back to me with broken hearts.
I am merciful, kind, and caring.

Ash Wednesday is the first day of Lent. On that day many Christians receive a cross of ashes on their foreheads. This powerful sign has been used by God's people for hundreds of years. The cross of ashes tells friends and neighbors that we know we are not perfect. We do not always love God as we should, and we do not always act with love and care toward those around us. On Ash Wednesday we own up to that and begin a six-week period of prayer, reflection, and almsgiving.

The cross is a sign of suffering, but suffering that can strengthen and redeem. Ashes are a sign of death, the event that will someday bring each of us face to face with our loving and forgiving God.

Sound the trumpet on Zion!
Call the people together.
Bring adults, children, babies,
and even bring newlyweds from their festivities.
Offer this prayer near the altar:
'Save your people, Lord God!'"

The word of the Lord.

ALL   **Thanks be to God.**

light the fire
wait in silence or sing a song until the fire burns out
when cool strain the ashes into a box or crock and cover it

LEADER   Merciful God,
you called us forth from the dust of the earth;
you claimed us for Christ in the waters of baptism.
Look upon us as we enter these Forty Days
bearing the mark of ashes,
and bless our journey through the desert of Lent
to the font of rebirth.
May our fasting be a hunger for justice;
our alms, a making of peace;
our prayer, the chant of humble and grateful hearts.
All that we do and pray is in the name of Jesus,
for in his cross you proclaim your love
now and for ever.

ALL   **Amen.**

all make the sign of the cross

Prayer for Ash Wednesday

Preparation: Select a leader and a reader.

LEADER   Let us begin our prayer.

all make the sign of the cross

LEADER   Praised be the God of grace, mercy, and peace.
Let us all say: Blessed be God for ever!

ALL   **Blessed be God for ever!**

READER   Listen to the words of the book of Daniel   9:3–5, 9

To show my sorrow, I, Daniel, went without eating
and dressed in sackcloth and sat in ashes. I
confessed my sins and earnestly prayed to the Lord
my God:
    "Our Lord, you are a great and fearsome God, and
you faithfully keep your agreement with those who
love and obey you. But we have sinned terribly
by rebelling against you and rejecting your laws and
teachings. Lord God, you are merciful and forgiving."

The word of the Lord.

ALL   **Thanks be to God.**

LEADER   Merciful God,
you called us forth from the dust of the earth;
you claimed us for Christ
in the waters of Baptism.
Look upon us as we enter these Forty Days
bearing the mark of ashes,
and bless our journey through the desert of Lent
to the font of rebirth.
May our fasting be a hunger for justice;
our alms, a making of peace;

In ancient times people showed sorrow by wearing humble clothes made of sackcloth, which is plain, inexpensive cloth used for grain sacks, like burlap or pillow ticking. They also put ashes on their heads. On Ash Wednesday Christians still use ashes as a sign of sorrow for offending God through their selfish acts. On this day we begin Lent, the time to make peace with God and with one another.

our prayer, the chant of humble and grateful hearts.
All that we do and pray is in the name of Jesus,
for in his cross you proclaim your love
for ever and ever.

ALL   **Amen.**

LEADER   Let us pray with the words that Jesus taught us.
ALL   **Our Father . . .**

Blessing of the Lenten Prayer Center

Preparation: Put something in the prayer center as a reminder of Lent. The table or shelf can be covered with a purple cloth, the traditional color for Lent. Add a cross made of twigs, or the classroom crucifix. A bowl of ashes reminds us of Ash Wednesday, the beginning of Lent. An empty, dry bowl might remind us that we are waiting for the water of Baptism at Easter. A bowl planted with flower bulbs or seeds, or a vase of bare branches can remind us that Lent is a time of growth and preparation for the flowering of Easter joy. The class can talk this over and agree on the signs they want to use. Perhaps they can be changed from week to week.

A container for the alms that we collect and for our promises to do good might also be placed in the prayer center.

Music options: For Your Gracious Blessing (8), Lent songs, p. viii

gather around the prayer corner

LEADER   Let us begin our prayer.

all make the sign of the cross

LEADER   To you, O Lord, I lift up my soul.
ALL   **In you, my God, I put my trust.**

READER   Listen to the words of the Acts of the Apostles   17:24, 25, 27

God made the world and everything in it.
He is Lord of heaven and earth.
He gives life, breath, and everything else to all people.

It is a Lenten custom to clear away unneeded decorations and clutter so that our physical spaces become as uncluttered as our spirits. This helps us to reflect on the things that are important and valuable in our lives and to pray without distractions. This makes it easier to give the classroom a good spring cleaning.

It is an important part of our tradition to collect alms during Lent. The word "alms" comes from the Greek word for "compassion." Compassion is the ability to feel what someone else is feeling. We give part of our allowance or baby-sitting money to help the poor. We bring in canned goods or

God has done all this so that we will look for him
and reach out and find him.
He isn't far from any of us.

The word of the Lord.

ALL **Thanks be to God.**

LEADER   My brothers and sisters,
let us bow our heads as we bless this prayer center.

Loving God,
bless these Lenten signs
that will remind us
to reach out and find you.
Bless our efforts to grow in our love for you,
in our generosity toward others,
and in our willingness to live as true followers
of Jesus, your Son,
in whose name we pray.

ALL **Amen.**

♩ end with a song

clothes. Sometimes money is collected by the Saint Vincent de Paul Society in the parish, or for an international charity, such as Catholic Relief Services, Operation Rice Bowl, or the Heifer Project.

Another way to show compassion is to do good things for people who need a little help. We might shovel the sidewalk for someone or help them with spring cleaning. Even doing our regular chores without delay or complaint can be a wonderful gift to the family.

A Penitential Service

LENT, ADVENT, OR OTHER TIMES OF THE YEAR

Preparation: Read through the whole service, adapting it for your students. Change or add more petitions. Adapt the ritual if your group is too large to stand in a circle. Prepare the church or room with symbols of the season. This is especially important during Advent and Lent.

It is probably best that an adult take the part of Leader (omitting the prayers designated PRIEST). This will allow all the students to put their attention on the self-examination that is necessary for prayers of penance.

If the sacrament of Reconciliation is offered during this service, the priest may read all of the LEADER parts, as well as those marked PRIEST. Show this service to the priest early, so that he can join in the preparation and make changes if necessary.

Select a reader.

You may want to change the reading each time you use this service. Adapt the prayers according to the reading you choose. Some good readings are:

- Jesus cures a blind man, John 9:1–12, 35–38
- Jesus cures a paraplegic, Luke 5:17–26
- The Beatitudes, Luke 6:20–26
- The New Covenant, Jeremiah 31:31–34
- The Ten Commandments, Exodus 20:1–17
- Zacchaeus, Luke 19:1–10
- The Merciful Father, Luke 15:11–32
- The Last Judgment, Matthew 25:31–46

Music options: Shalom, My Friends (20), Closing songs: In the Lord I'll Be Ever Thankful (12,) Lent songs, p. viii

In Lent, the springtime of the Church's year, we take time to think about ways we can grow and become better. It is our tradition to join in prayers of penance at this time and sometimes to celebrate the sacrament of Reconciliation. This sacrament is a way of admitting that we sometimes act in mean or selfish ways, doing harm to others and not doing the good we are capable of. We ask God's forgiveness and grace.

This penitential service can be used by a class or several classes together and may include the sacrament of Reconciliation. It can be shortened or adapted in other ways and is useful for Lent and other times of the year as well.

LEADER	Let us begin our prayer.

 all make the sign of the cross

PRIEST	Grace and peace be with you from God the Father and Christ Jesus our Savior.
ALL	**And also with you.**
LEADER	God is filled with love for us. God wants us to be filled with love also. But we are not always loving. Sometimes we are selfish and sinful. Today we will think about this.

We will listen to God's word. We will pray. We will
ask for God's forgiveness. We will give thanks, because
we know that God has promised to forgive us whenever we ask from our hearts.

Let us pray.

wait a few moments in silence

LEADER   Lord,
hear the prayers of those who call on you,
forgive the sins of those who confess to you.
In your merciful love
give us your pardon and your peace.
We ask this through Christ our Lord.

ALL   **Amen.**

READER   Listen to the words of the holy Gospel
according to Luke   10:25–28

An expert in the Law of Moses stood up and asked
Jesus a question to see what he would say. "Teacher,"
he asked, "What must I do to have eternal life?"

Jesus answered, "What is written in the
Scriptures? How do you understand them?"

The man replied, "The Scriptures say, 'Love the
Lord your God with all your heart, soul, strength, and
mind.' They also say, 'Love your neighbors as much
as you love yourself.'"

Jesus said, "You have given the right answer. If you
do this, you will have eternal life."

The Gospel of the Lord.

ALL   **Praise to you, Lord Jesus Christ.**

the teacher or priest may wish to speak to the group

LEADER   We are children of a God who is holy and loving.
But we do not always do the good that we want to do,
and we sometimes do wrong things that we are sorry

about. As we open our hearts to God's mercy, let us respond to each petition, "Lord, bless and forgive us."

Let us pray.

Merciful God,
we sometimes fail to love you as we should.
For speaking your name in anger, we pray:

ALL **Lord, bless and forgive us.**

LEADER For failing to thank you for all your gifts, we pray:
ALL **Lord, bless and forgive us.**

LEADER For failing to pray with attention, we pray:
ALL **Lord, bless and forgive us.**

LEADER For failing to care for your creation, we pray:
ALL **Lord, bless and forgive us.**

more petitions concerning God may be added

LEADER Merciful God,
we sometimes fail to love other people as we should.
For showing disrespect to parents, we pray:
ALL **Lord, bless and forgive us.**

LEADER For talking about other people unkindly, we pray:
ALL **Lord, bless and forgive us.**

LEADER For refusing to share with others, we pray:
ALL **Lord, bless and forgive us.**

LEADER For failing to help when we are needed, we pray:
ALL **Lord, bless and forgive us.**

more petitions concerning other people may be added

LEADER Let us take a few minutes now
and in silence promise God
to become better in some practical way.

wait a few moments in silence

LEADER   Let us bow our heads and pray.

ALL   **I confess to almighty God,**
and to you, my brothers and sisters,
that I have sinned through my own fault
in my thoughts and in my words,
in what I have done,
and in what I have failed to do;
and I ask blessed Mary, ever virgin,
all the angels and saints,
and you, my brothers and sisters,
to pray for me to the Lord our God. Amen.

LEADER   Let us form a circle and join our hands as a sign
of our desire to forgive one another as God forgives
us and to help one another become worthy children
of a holy and loving God.

when all have joined hands, continue

LEADER   Lord our God,
we want to be more generous
in loving you and our neighbors.
Hear our prayers
and help us to turn away from sin.
Help us to become more loving.
Help us to keep the promises we made today.
We ask this through Christ our Lord.

ALL   **Amen.**

LEADER   Let us pray with the words that Jesus taught us.

ALL   **Our Father . . .**

LEADER   May the almighty and merciful God
bless and protect us.

all make the sign of the cross

at this time, if a priest is available, those who wish may go to individual confession; when all have finished, continue:

PRIEST Loving God,
        you have shown us your mercy
        and restored us in the image of your Son.
        We praise and bless you in his name,
        now and for ever.
ALL   **Amen.**

PRIEST May almighty God bless you,
        the Father, and the Son, and the Holy Spirit.
ALL   **Amen.**

PRIEST The Lord has freed you from your sins.
ALL   **Thanks be to God.**

♩ end with a song

Prayer for Placing Palm Branches in the Prayer Center

MONDAY AFTER PALM SUNDAY OF THE LORD'S PASSION

Preparation: Gather palm branches into an arrangement for the prayer corner. Select a leader and a reader.

LEADER Let us begin our prayer.

 all make the sign of the cross

LEADER Hosanna in the highest!
        Blessed is he who comes in the name of the Lord.
ALL   **Hosanna in the highest!**

LEADER We have come to the last days of Lent. The story of Christ's suffering will be in our thoughts as we move toward Holy Thursday and the Three Days, when we celebrate the passing of Jesus through suffering and death to life at God's right hand.

The branches we receive on Palm Sunday remind us of the willingness with which Jesus went to Jerusalem, even though it meant death for him. We join those who followed him into Jerusalem with joy, not knowing what being his disciple would cost.

When we place some branches in the classroom, near the cross and the

132

READER   Listen to the words of the first letter of Saint Paul to the Corinthians   4:13–14

We speak because we know that God raised the Lord Jesus to life. And just as God raised Jesus, he will also raise us to life. Then he will bring us into his presence.

The word of the Lord.

ALL   **Thanks be to God.**

LEADER   Let us bow our heads and pray.

Lord our God,
let these branches
remind us of Christ's triumph.
May they teach us
to rejoice in his cross
and praise you in his resurrection.
We ask this through Christ our Lord.

ALL   **Amen.**

scriptures, they are a sign that we are willing to pay the price of following him. And we have been following him all during Lent. The last week of Lent will speed by, bringing us to the sacred three days of the Triduum. Then the Church around the world remembers the dying and rising of Jesus our Savior.

Blessing before Easter Break

Preparation: Shortly before dismissal, the students gather so that the teacher will be able to bless each one.

Music options: Go Now In Peace (9), Lent songs, p. viii

TEACHER   Let us begin our prayer.

all make the sign of the cross

TEACHER   May the Lord's face shine on us,
and may the Lord guide our feet
into the way of peace.
Blessed be the name of the Lord,
now and for ever.

ALL   **Amen.**

The days of Lent are almost over. We have kept the long weeks of prayer and good deeds. We have contributed to the almsgiving that is asked of every Christian. Because of our gifts, others may be able to celebrate the great festival of Christ's resurrection with joy.

Now we are ready to join our families in celebrating the Triduum, the three holiest days of the Christian calendar. During this time we will again become part of the dying and rising of Christ our Savior. A ritual of blessing will bring Lent to a satisfying end.

TEACHER   Let us put ourselves into the hands of the Lord,
           and pray that God will bless us and our families
           during the coming holy days when the Church
           celebrates the mystery of the dying and rising of
           Jesus our Savior.

           May all of us help to make our homes
           places of joy, love, peace, and safety.
           May we be generous and considerate,
           helping others keep the celebration
           of the dying and rising
           of our Lord and Savior, Jesus Christ.

           Please respond "Amen" as I bless each of you.

the teacher goes to each student in turn,
traces the sign of the cross on the student's forehead, and says

TEACHER   N____, go with God.
STUDENT   Amen.

when the individual blessings are completed, prayer continues

TEACHER   My dear friends and students,
           may almighty God give you light and joy.
           And until we gather here again,
           may God bless all of us.

 all make the sign of the cross

 end with a song

Prayers for the Triduum

Holy Thursday

Preparation: This prayer can be used in a parish gathering for children on Holy Thursday, or could be put on a prayer card and taken home. The prayer may be shortened by omitting the reading. Select a leader and a reader.

Music option: Lent songs, p. viii

> On Holy Thursday we remember that Jesus washed the feet of his disciples as a sign of loving service. He told his followers to remember his actions and care for others as he did.
>
> At that same Passover meal Jesus gave us the sacrament of his body and blood. With great joy the parish community will celebrate the Eucharist on the evening of Holy Thursday.

LEADER	As we keep these Three Days, let us all say: Holy God!
ALL	**Holy God!**
LEADER	Holy mighty One!
ALL	**Holy mighty One!**
LEADER	Holy immortal One, have mercy on us!
ALL	**Holy immortal One, have mercy on us!**
READER	Listen to the words of the holy Gospel according to Matthew 26:26–28

During the meal Jesus took some bread in his hands. He blessed the bread and broke it. Then he gave it to his disciples and said, "Take this and eat it. This is my body."

Jesus picked up a cup of wine and gave thanks to God. He then gave it to his disciples and said, "Take this and drink it. This is my blood, and with it God makes his agreement with you. It will be poured out, so that many people will have their sins forgiven."

The Gospel of the Lord.

ALL	**Praise to you, Lord Jesus Christ.**
LEADER	Saving God, we thank you for the sacred meal of bread and wine

which Jesus gave the Church
on the eve of his passion.
May the food of the Eucharist
strengthen us for the work of justice and peace.
We ask this through Christ our Lord.

ALL   **Amen.**

LEADER   We adore you, O Christ, and we bless you.
ALL   **Because by your holy cross**
you have redeemed the world.

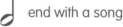 end with a song

Good Friday

Preparation: This prayer can be used in a parish gathering for children on Good Friday, or it could be put on a prayer card and taken home.
    The prayer may be shortened by omitting the reading. Gather around a crucifix. Select a leader and reader.

Music option: Lent songs, p. viii

LEADER   As we keep these Three Days, let us all say:
Holy God
ALL   **Holy God!**

LEADER   Holy mighty One!
ALL   **Holy mighty One!**

LEADER   Holy immortal One, have mercy on us!
ALL   **Holy immortal One, have mercy on us!**

READER   Listen to the words of the holy Gospel
according to Luke   23:44–46

Around noon the sky turned dark and stayed that way until the middle of the afternoon. The sun stopped shining, and the curtain in the temple split down the middle. Jesus shouted, "Father, I put myself in your hands!" Then he died.

The Gospel of the Lord
ALL   **Praise to you, Lord Jesus Christ.**

Good Friday is the day of Christ's suffering and death. We celebrate with the parish community and keep a spirit of quiet and prayer. This is a day for adults to fast and for everyone to abstain from meat. A Blessing of the Cross is on page 9.

LEADER   We glory in the cross of our Lord Jesus Christ,
for he is our salvation,
our life, and our resurrection;
through him we are saved and made free.
By his holy and glorious wounds
may Christ our Lord
awaken our compassion
for all who are suffering,
now and for ever.

ALL   **Amen.**

LEADER   We adore you, O Christ, and we bless you:

ALL   **Because by your holy cross
you have redeemed the world.**

 end with song

Holy Saturday

Preparation: This prayer can be used in a parish gathering for children on Holy Saturday, or it could be put on a prayer card for the students to take home. The prayer may be shortened by omitting the reading.

    Select a leader and a reader.

Music option: Lent songs, p. viii

LEADER   As we keep these Three Days, let us all say:
Holy God!

ALL   **Holy God!**

LEADER   Holy mighty One!

ALL   **Holy mighty One!**

LEADER   Holy immortal One, have mercy on us!

ALL   **Holy immortal One, have mercy on us!**

Christ is hidden in the tomb. His followers long for his return. As we wait and make final preparations for the glorious day of resurrection, we remember and renew our baptismal faith.

READER   Listen to the words of the holy Gospel
according to Luke   23:55–56

The women who had come with Jesus from Galilee
followed Joseph [of Arimathea] and watched how
Jesus' body was placed in the tomb. Then they went
to prepare some sweet-smelling spices for his burial.
But on the Sabbath they rested, as the Law of Moses
commands.

The Gospel of the Lord.

ALL   **Praise to you, Lord Jesus Christ.**

LEADER   Lord Jesus Christ,
even as you once died, we shall die.
Even as you rested in the grave,
we shall rest in the grave.
Remember us now as you come into your kingdom.
Bless all who wait
and prepare for your coming,
now and for ever.

ALL   **Amen.**

LEADER   We adore you, O Christ, and we bless you:

ALL   **Because by your holy cross
you have redeemed the world.**

♩ end with a song

Easter Sunday

Christ our Lord has risen today! The parish church and the family home are made festive with brightly colored eggs and with flowers from a world made beautiful in springtime. We embrace; we share a feast; we rejoice with many alleluias!

Preparation: Decorate the prayer space with flowers, Easter baskets and colored eggs. Have a candle ready to light. This prayer can be used in a parish gathering for children on Easter morning, or it could be put on a prayer card for the students to take home. The prayer may be shortened by omitting the reading.
    Select a leader and a reader.

Music options: Oh, How Good Is Jesus Christ!/¡Oh, Que Bueno Es Jesús! (18), or a familiar Easter hymn such as Jesus Christ Is Risen Today, and many alleluias

LEADER   This is the day the Lord has made;

ALL   **Let us rejoice and be glad in it.**

light a candle

READER   Listen to the words of the holy Gospel
          according to Luke   24:1–4, 5–6

          Very early on Sunday morning the women went
          to the tomb, carrying the spices that they had
          prepared. When they found the stone rolled away
          from the entrance, they went in. But they did
          not find the body of the Lord Jesus, and they did
          not know what to think.

             Suddenly two men in shining white clothes stood
          beside them. The men said, "Why are you looking in
          the place of the dead for someone who is alive? Jesus
          isn't here! He has been raised from death."

          The Gospel of the Lord.
ALL   **Praise to you, Lord Jesus Christ.**

LEADER   Jesus Christ is the light of the world, alleluia!
ALL   **A light no darkness can overpower, alleluia!**

♩ all sing a verse of an Easter hymn such as the following:

              Jesus Christ is risen today, Alleluia!
              Our triumphant holy day, Alleluia!
              Who did once upon the cross, Alleluia!
              Suffer to redeem our loss. Alleluia!

LEADER   This is the day the Lord has made;
ALL   **Let us rejoice and be glad in it.**
          Amen. Alleluia!

Eastertime

Easter Sunday through Pentecost Sunday

Christ is risen! Alleluia! The simplicity and sacrifice of Lent are over. We turn our eyes to the glory of Jesus and the joy he has given us in the resurrection. The natural world reflects this joy, as springtime causes the earth to burst with new life. We reclaim the joyful music of our alleluias. For fifty days we will keep the season of glory that completes our Lenten season of penance and discipline.

Eastertime is about new life, and the signs of new life are all around us. There are eggs, rabbits, chicks, flowers, green grass, and butterflies. We rejoice that new members of our parish entered the life of our church when they were baptized and confirmed and brought into full communion at the Easter Vigil. All of us nourish the life of God when we share in the Easter sacrament of the Eucharist. And so we sing over and over, "alleluia," "praise God!"

Light is a sign of grace, peace, and life. During Advent we lit candles on the wreath to show that the Savior brings God's light into the world's darkness. During Christmastime we recalled the words of Simeon, who called Jesus the "light of revelation." We put lights on trees and in windows, remembering the light of the star that led the wise men to the stable. Now, during Eastertime, we celebrate Jesus again with symbols of light. The paschal candle, the giant candle that is lighted during this season whenever we celebrate in the church, shows that Jesus lives. His light was not put out with death but shines now because of his resurrection.

The sun rises each morning, bright and strong. It too is a sign of the resurrection of Jesus. The sun has always been recognized as a sign of God's warmth, love, and life-giving power. What would we do without it? Let us think about this as we enjoy the longer and warmer days and as we see the plants and flowers that the sun seems to be calling out of the earth.

Meal Prayer for Eastertime

Music options: Bless Us, O Lord (3), Eastertime songs, p. viii, or any alleluias you know

LEADER   Let us begin our prayer.

 all make the sign of the cross

LEADER   This is the day the Lord has made;
ALL   **Let us rejoice and be glad in it.**

LEADER   Christ is risen, alleluia!
ALL   **Christ is truly risen, alleluia!**

LEADER   Joyfully do we praise you, Lord Jesus Christ.
       Risen from the grave,
       you appeared to your disciples
       in the breaking of bread.
       Remain here with us
       as we share these gifts.
       May we receive you as a guest
       in all our brothers and sisters
       and be welcomed by you
       to share the feast of your Spirit,
       for you live and reign
       for ever and ever.
ALL   **Amen. Alleluia.**

all make the sign of the cross

♩ end with a song

Welcoming the Alleluia

FIRST GATHERING AFTER EASTER BREAK

Preparation: Make sure the banner(s) is/are still where you put it/them forty days ago. Decorate the place with flowers, pennants, and other signs of Easter. Bells, noisemakers, and instruments should be there as well.

Everyone first gathers in the classroom. Select a leader and two readers.

Music options: Jubilate Servite (14), Celtic Alleluia (4), or any alleluias you know

LEADER	Let us begin our celebration.

 all make the sign of the cross

LEADER	Let us say: Blessed are you, God of Israel, so rich in love and mercy.
ALL	**Blessed are you, God of Israel,** **so rich in love and mercy.**
READER ONE	Listen to the words of the holy Gospel according to Matthew 27:57–60

That evening a rich disciple named Joseph went and asked for Jesus' body. Pilate gave orders for it to be given to Joseph, who took the body and wrapped it in a clean linen cloth. Then Joseph put the body in his own tomb that had been cut into solid rock and had never been used. He rolled a big stone against the entrance to the tomb and went away.

The Gospel of the Lord.

ALL	**Praise to you, Lord Jesus Christ.**
LEADER	Let us go forth in silence and in peace.

move silently in procession from the gathering place to the burial place; bring shovel, key, or whatever is needed to open the box; then stop and listen to the second reading

The first thing to do after Easter break is to restore the alleluia to your prayers! For classes that "buried the alleluia" with a ritual of bells and song, here is another ritual to raise it from its "tomb." (The ritual of burial is described on page 119.) Even if you did not put away the alleluia, you can still welcome it back with joy and lots of music.

Reclaim the alleluia early in the morning on the day you return to class after Easter break, before prayer and before using any Easter songs or greetings.

READER TWO Listen to the words of the holy Gospel
according to Matthew   28:1–7

It was almost daybreak on Sunday when Mary
Magdalene and the other Mary went to see the tomb.
Suddenly a strong earthquake struck, and the Lord's
angel came down from heaven. He rolled away
the stone and sat on it. The angel looked as bright
as lightning, and his clothes were white as snow.
The guards shook from fear and fell down, as though
they were dead.

The angel said to the women, "Don't be afraid!
I know you are looking for Jesus, who was nailed to
a cross. He is not here! God has raised him to life,
just as Jesus said he would. Come, see the place
where his body was lying. Now hurry! Tell his disciples
that he has been raised to life and is on his way to
Galilee. Go there, and you will see him."

The Gospel of the Lord.

ALL   **Praise to you, Lord Jesus Christ.**

dig up or unlock the box
hold up the alleluia banner(s)
everyone shout alleluia!
clap, cheer, ring bells, and make a joyful noise

♩ sing an Easter song with lots of alleluias and move to the place where
the banner(s) will be hung; return to the place where you began,
singing and ringing bells all the time

143

Blessing of the Easter Prayer Center

Two important Easter symbols are water and light. The paschal candle was blessed during the Easter Vigil. It represents the light of the risen Christ shining out for all believers to see. The markings are a cross and the four digits of the year. At the top of this image is the Greek letter alpha (A) and at the bottom is the Greek letter omega (Ω). They are the first and last letters of the Greek alphabet. They recall the words of the book of Revelation 1:8, "The Lord God says, 'I am the Alpha and Omega, the one who is and was and is coming. I am God All-Powerful.'"

There are many other symbols of resurrection and new life, such as brightly colored eggs, flowers (especially lilies), flowering branches, and butterflies.

Preparation: Together the class can prepare Easter signs for the prayer center and keep them refreshed during the fifty days of the joyful season. This can include an "alleluia" banner, flowers, candles, and a bowl of fresh water.

Select a leader and reader.

Music options: Oh, How Good Is Jesus Christ!/¡Oh, Que Bueno Es Jesús! (18), Celtic Alleluia (4), and other familiar Easter hymns

LEADER   Christ is risen like the sun, alleluia!

ALL   **The light of Christ shines
over the whole world, alleluia!**

READER   Listen to the words of the Acts of the
Apostles   2:24–25, 27–28

God set Jesus free from death and raised him to life.
Death could not hold him in its power. What David
said are really the words of Jesus,
"The Lord won't leave me in the grave.
I am his holy one,
and he won't let my body decay.
He has shown me the path to life,
and he makes me glad by being near me."

The word of the Lord.

ALL   **Thanks be to God.**

LEADER   My brothers and sisters, let us bow our heads
and pray.

Loving God, we have gathered signs
of springtime beauty, joy, and rebirth.
We ask you to bless these Easter signs
that will remind us that Jesus is risen
and is with us as he promised,
sharing his life with us
and filling our hearts with joy.

For this we thank you
through Christ our Lord.

ALL   **Amen.**

♩ sing an Easter song with many alleluias

Blessing of the Newly Initiated

AFTER BAPTISM, CONFIRMATION, OR FIRST COMMUNION

Preparation: A large candle should be in a central place. The newly initiated or received gather near it. One or more of them prepares the announcement, such as, "At the Easter Vigil I was initiated into the Church through Baptism, Confirmation, and First Communion." Or, "Last Sunday, we celebrated the sacrament of Confirmation."
  Select a leader and a reader.

Music options: Jubilate Servite (14), Send Forth Your Spirit, O Lord (19), In the Lord I'll Be Ever Thankful (12), For Your Gracious Blessing (8)

LEADER   Christ is risen like the sun, alleluia!

ALL   **The light of Christ shines over the whole world, alleluia!**

light the candle

NEWLY INITIATED/ RECEIVED   Friends and classmates, I (we) bring you good news and invite you to share in my (our) joy.
This is my (our) announcement:

announce your good news

all may clap as a sign of good wishes

READER   Listen to the words of the apostle Paul to the Ephesians
                        3:19–21

I want you to know all about Christ's love, although it is too wonderful to be measured. Then your lives will be filled with all that God is.

> This blessing is for students, family members, or friends initiated or received into the Catholic Church at the Easter Vigil or during the Easter season. It is also appropriate after Confirmation or First Communion whenever those sacraments are celebrated during the year.

I pray that Christ Jesus and the church will forever bring praise to God. His power at work in us can do far more than we dare ask or imagine.

The word of the Lord.

ALL   **Thanks be to God.**

LEADER   Let us pray for our friends,
whom God has richly blessed.

May God bless and strengthen you.
May God fill you with love
so that you may live faithfully
your new life in Christ.
We ask this through Christ our Lord.

ALL   **Amen.**

♩ end with a song

Blessing of Seeds, Seedlings, Sprouts, or Blossoms

ROGATION DAYS: MONDAY, TUESDAY, AND WEDNESDAY BEFORE ASCENSION THURSDAY

ANY SUITABLE DAY DURING THE PLANTING AND GROWING SEASONS

Preparation: This blessing can be held in the classroom or outdoors. Place seeds or seedlings in a basket or other container. Bring digging tools if you will plant them in a garden, or pots and soil if you will plant them in containers for the classroom. Be sure to ask an experienced gardener for advice on your choice of seeds and the care of your plants so that your garden will be healthy and colorful.

If you will bless plants already sprouted, weed the garden plot to "dress it up" for the ceremony. You might put "alleluia" signs on twigs and stick them in the ground or in your pots to make the occasion more festive.

You will need a container of water—enough to give the newly planted seeds or newly sprouted flowers a good watering.

Select a leader and reader.

Music options: For Your Gracious Blessing (8), Sing Out, Earth and Skies (22)

LEADER   Let us praise God,
who gives us the seeds and calls us to the harvest.

Help the earth rejoice by planting or tending a garden. The three days leading to Ascension Thursday were once called "rogation days." That word means "to ask." During these days people would walk in procession through their newly planted or newly

Let us all say, "Blessed be God for ever."

ALL   **Blessed be God for ever.**

LEADER   Today we seek God's blessing on these seeds (plants, flowers, this garden). They remind us that God is the source of the rain and sun and soil that invite our plants to blossom. As these plants grow and are cared for, may they be signs of the new life that comes from God.

READER   Listen to the words of the book of Genesis   1:11–13

God said, "I command the earth to produce all kinds of plants, including fruit trees and grain." And that's what happened. The earth produced all kinds of vegetation. God looked at what he had done, and it was good. Evening came and then morning—that was the third day.

The word of the Lord.

ALL   **Thanks be to God.**

LEADER   Let us call upon God our Creator.
For rain to water the earth, we pray:

ALL   **Lord, hear our prayer.**

LEADER   For sunshine to warm the earth, we pray:

ALL   **Lord, hear our prayer.**

LEADER   For time to enjoy our plants, we pray:

ALL   **Lord, hear our prayer.**

LEADER   For the happiness of knowing that you are present in our work, we pray:

ALL   **Lord, hear our prayer.**

LEADER   Let us lift up our hands and pray.

Lord of the harvest,
you place the gifts of creation in our hands
and call us to till the earth and make it fruitful.
We ask your blessing
as we prepare to place these seeds in the earth

sprouting fields, praying fervently and asking God to bless their crops. Those who tend gardens, fields, and animals know that spring is an important time for growth and fruitfulness. We too can ask God to bless our gardens during this season.

If we planted small containers of rye grass or wheat berries before Easter and they are now sprouting, we can bless them. If we planted bulbs for the feast of angels last fall, we can bless the colorful bed of tulips, daffodils, or crocuses that is now growing like an earthly alleluia.

147

(or care for these plants).
May the care we show
remind us of your tender love for your people.
We ask this through Christ our Lord.

ALL   **Amen. Alleluia!**

sprinkle water on the seeds or seedlings, then put them in the earth; when everything is planted soak the plants well with the remaining water; when all is finished gather everyone once more and say

LEADER   May God nourish us and care for us,
now and for ever.

ALL   **Amen. Alleluia!**

♩ end with a song

Prayer for Gardens and Growing Plants

Music options: For Your Gracious Blessing (8), Sing Out, Earth and Skies (22)

LEADER   Blessed are you, Lord our God,
Creator of the universe,
for you bring forth plants in abundance
for our food
and for our pleasure.

ALL   **Blessed be God for ever.**

LEADER   O God, from the beginning
the earth has produced plants of every kind.
During this growing season,
give us seeds and soil, sunshine and rain,
so that there may be food for us
and for all your creatures.
We ask this through Christ our Lord.

ALL   **Amen.**

LEADER   Let us pray with the words that Jesus taught us.

ALL   **Our Father . . .**

♩ end with a song

It is not too late to plant some early blooming flowers such as cosmos, cleome, morning glory, nasturtium, lavatera, four o'clocks, and zinnia. They will help us to celebrate Earth Day (April 22), the feast of Saint George (April 23), and the feast of the Spanish farm couple, Saints Isidore and Maria Torribia (May 15).

Saint George, whose name means "earth worker" in Greek, is a patron of gardeners, farmers, ranchers, and all who live close to the land.

Saints Isidore and Maria are also patrons of farmers. Celebrations and blessings of farmers and farmlands are held on their day.

Prayer for the Solemnity of the Ascension

IN SOME DIOCESES OF THE UNITED STATES, THURSDAY, THE FORTIETH DAY OF EASTERTIME

IN OTHER AREAS OF THE UNITED STATES AND IN CANADA, THE SEVENTH SUNDAY OF EASTER

Preparation: Gather near the prayer center or outdoors where you can feel the gentle breeze and gaze up at the sky as the disciples did. Have a candle and matches for lighting it.

For a shorter prayer, omit the reading. Select a leader and a reader.

Music options: Oh, How Good Is Jesus Christ!/¡Oh, Que Bueno Es Jesús! (18), Shalom, My Friends (20), Celtic Alleluia (4)

LEADER	Christ is risen like the sun, alleluia!
ALL	**The light of Christ shines over the whole world, alleluia!**

light a candle

READER	Listen to the words of the Acts of the Apostles 1:3–4, 5, 8–11

For forty days after Jesus had suffered and died, he proved in many ways that he had been raised from death. He appeared to his apostles and spoke to them about God's kingdom.

While he was still with them, he said: "John baptized with water, but in a few days you will be baptized with the Holy Spirit.

"The Holy Spirit will come upon you and give you power. Then you will tell everyone about me in Jerusalem, in all Judea, in Samaria, and everywhere in the world." After Jesus had said this and while they were watching, he was taken up into a cloud. They could not see him, but as he went up, they kept looking up into the sky.

Suddenly two men dressed in white clothes were standing there beside them. They said, "Why are you standing here and looking up into the sky? Jesus has

This feast reminds us that Jesus lives now in glory with his Father, while at the same time he lives with and in his people on earth. The gospels of Matthew, Mark, and Luke, and the Acts of the Apostles contain accounts of the way Jesus disappeared from the sight of his disciples. But first Jesus reminded them to carry on his work by preaching his good news to the whole world and baptizing all who believe in him. He promised that he would be with them always, and he promised to send the Holy Spirit to strengthen and guide them.

Now we see Christ in the faces of those around us. We see him hungry and homeless; we see him lonely, bullied, and teased. We see him in all those who need our help. We also see him in those who love us and care for us, and in those who teach, coach, heal, and help us. We see him in the faces of our brothers, sisters, and friends. This feast reminds us to keep our eyes open. Jesus is indeed risen, and he is very close to us.

been taken to heaven. But he will come back in the same way that you have seen him go."

The word of the Lord.

ALL   **Thanks be to God.**

LEADER   Jesus is taken up to heaven!
May he come again to rule over us,
now and for ever.

ALL   **Amen.**

LEADER   Jesus sits at God's right hand!
May he watch over his people with love,
now and for ever.

ALL   **Amen.**

LEADER   Jesus gives us his gospel and his mission!
May he give us a share in his glory,
now and for ever.

ALL   **Amen.**

LEADER   May we live in the light of Christ.

ALL   **Amen.**

♩ end with a song

put out the candle

Prayers for the Pentecost Novena

NINE DAYS BETWEEN ASCENSION THURSDAY AND
PENTECOST

Preparation: Students will be in class no more than six of the nine days of the Pentecost novena. Therefore only six prayers are suggested. Each day, begin with the opening prayer, follow with the reading and the prayer for the day and end with the closing prayer.

Religious education classes might choose any of the six prayers they like best. Students might add to the petitions for each prayer those virtues they think are needed in the Church today.

For shorter prayers, omit the readings. Have a candle ready and matches for lighting it.

Select a leader and a reader for each day.

Music option: Send Forth Your Spirit, O Lord (19), We Bring God's Holy Love (25)

Opening Prayer for Each Day

LEADER   Christ is risen like the sun, alleluia!

**ALL   The light of Christ shines
over the whole world, alleluia!**

light a candle

LEADER   Blessed are you, holy and saving God
for the strengthening gift of your Spirit.

ALL   Blessed be God for ever.

Day One   Knowledge, Wisdom, and Understanding

begin with the Opening Prayer

READER   Listen to the words of the apostle Paul
to the Ephesians   1:17–18

I ask the glorious Father and God of our Lord Jesus Christ to give you his Spirit. The Spirit will make you wise and let you understand what it means to know

The risen Jesus told his disciples to wait prayerfully for the coming of the Holy Spirit, who would strengthen and guide them. They were waiting in Jerusalem when the Spirit came with signs of wind and fire. The Spirit brought them energy for a new mission and formed them into a people of love and courage. They immediately began preaching on the street corner, excited to share their story of Jesus.

People from many countries and languages were able to understand the words of their preaching. The miracle is a sign that the Gospel is for every land and people. It is a sign of the power of the Spirit helping those who share the good news of Jesus. Because of this we say that the Church was born on Pentecost.

These things happened on the Jewish feast of Shavuot, which falls seven weeks and one day after Passover (which makes fifty days altogether). For this reason we celebrate the coming of the Spirit seven weeks and a day after the Easter passover of Jesus, and we call it "Pentecost," which means "fiftieth" day.

Pentecost is our annual celebration of the Holy Spirit, who is the life and unity of the Church, the source of its holiness, dedication, and wisdom. Pentecost is a solemnity, which means a feast that deserves special notice and preparation. The "novena" or nine days between Ascension Thursday and Pentecost Sunday are a time of reflection on the presence of the Holy Spirit among us and prayer for the gifts that the Holy Spirit brings. It helps us prepare a place in our lives for a new coming of the Spirit.

During the Pentecost novena we can pray for the good of the Church and for the strength of our parish, as well as for a deepening devotion we have for the God who made us, who saves us and who is with us at every moment.

Red is the color of Pentecost decorations. Red and red-orange remind us of the flames that signaled the coming of the Holy Spirit at the first Pentecost in Jerusalem.

Red flowers can be brought to the prayer corner. We can also use doves, clouds, and wind as Spirit symbols. Prayer can take place outdoors, where we can feel the breeze or wind for ourselves. Wind chimes or streamers of fabric or paper that flutter in the breeze remind us of the quiet way the Spirit of God moves in us and in the world. Many small candles can be lighted.

God. My prayer is that light will flood your hearts and that you will understand the hope that was given to you when God chose you.

The word of the Lord.

ALL   **Thanks be to God.**

LEADER   Let us pray for gifts of knowledge, wisdom, and understanding. Please respond to each petition, "Come, Holy Spirit."

Spirit of God, help us to learn more about the meaning of your holy scriptures, we pray:

ALL   **Come, Holy Spirit.**

LEADER   Spirit of God, make us wise in all our decisions, we pray:

ALL   **Come, Holy Spirit.**

LEADER   Spirit of God, rid our minds of hatred and envy, we pray:

ALL   **Come, Holy Spirit.**

more petitions may be added

end with the closing prayer

Day Two   Wonder, Joy, and Reverence

begin with the Opening Prayer

READER   Listen to the words of the apostle Paul to the Romans   8:14–16

Those people who are led by God's Spirit are his children. God's Spirit doesn't make us slaves who are afraid of him. Instead, we become his children and call him our Father. God's Spirit makes us sure that we are his children.

The word of the Lord.

ALL   **Thanks be to God.**

LEADER	Let us pray for gifts of wonder, joy, and reverence before God. Please respond to each petition, "Come, Holy Spirit."
	Spirit of God, teach us to speak your name lovingly, we pray:
ALL	**Come, Holy Spirit.**
LEADER	Spirit of God, fill us with wonder at the signs of your presence, we pray:
ALL	**Come, Holy Spirit.**
LEADER	Spirit of God, make your Church a source of joy in the world, we pray:
ALL	**Come, Holy Spirit.**

more petitions may be added

end with the closing prayer

Day Three   Courage

begin with the Opening Prayer

READER	Listen to the words of the Acts of the Apostles 20:22, 22–24
	Paul said, "I don't know what will happen to me in Jerusalem, but I must obey God's Spirit and go there. In every city I visit, the Holy Spirit tells me I will be put in jail and will be in trouble in Jerusalem. But I don't care what happens to me, as long as I finish the work that the Lord Jesus gave me to do."
	The word of the Lord.
ALL	**Thanks be to God**
LEADER	Let us pray for gift of courage. Please respond to each petition, "Come, Holy Spirit."
	Spirit of God, give us courage to do what is right, we pray:
ALL	**Come, Holy Spirit.**

Prayers for the days of the Pentecost novena focus our attention on "the seven gifts of the Holy Spirit." Those gifts are promised to all who join in doing the work of God. In addition, Saint Paul writes that the Holy Spirit makes us "loving, happy, peaceful, patient, kind, good, faithful, gentle, and self-controlled." These virtues, along with modesty, continence, and chastity, have been called "fruits of the Spirit." The gifts and fruits of the Holy Spirit are the focus of the petitions in the novena prayers. The class can compose additional petitions.

LEADER	Spirit of God, Give us courage to forgive one another, we pray:
ALL	**Come, Holy Spirit.**
LEADER	Spirit of God, give courage to those who are suffering, we pray:
ALL	**Come, Holy Spirit.**

more petitions may be added

end with the closing prayer

Day Four   Right Judgment, Self-control, Peace

begin with the Opening Prayer

READER	Listen to the words of the apostle Paul to the Romans 8:5, 6
	People who are ruled by their desires think only of themselves. Everyone who is ruled by the Holy Spirit thinks about spiritual things. If our minds are ruled by the Spirit, we will have life and peace.
	The word of the Lord.
ALL	**Thanks be to God.**
LEADER	Let us pray for gifts of right judgment, self-control, and peace. Please respond to each petition, "Come, Holy Spirit."
	Spirit of God, guide us to right decisions and loving actions, we pray:
ALL	**Come, Holy Spirit.**
LEADER	Spirit of God, make your Church a source of kindness and peace in the world, we pray:
ALL	**Come, Holy Spirit.**

LEADER	Spirit of God, teach us to be patient and gentle with those who are weaker than we are, we pray:
ALL	**Come, Holy Spirit.**

more petitions may be added

end with the closing prayer

Day Five   Wonder, Awe

begin with the Opening Prayer

READER	Listen to the words of the prophet Joel 2:28–29

The Lord said:
I will give my Spirit to everyone.
Your sons and daughters will prophesy.
Your old men will have dreams,
and your young men will see visions.
In those days I will even give
my Spirit to my servants, both men and women.

The word of the Lord.

ALL	**Thanks be to God.**

| LEADER | Let us pray for gifts of wonder and awe. Please respond to each petition, "Come, Holy Spirit."

Spirit of God, show us your vision of a world where everyone is kind and loving, we pray: |
|---|---|
| ALL | **Come, Holy Spirit.** |

LEADER	Spirit of God, fill us with joy and wonder at your love for us, we pray:
ALL	**Come, Holy Spirit.**

LEADER	Spirit of God, teach us awe and respect for the beauty of your earth, we pray:
ALL	**Come, Holy Spirit.**

more petitions may be added

end with the closing prayer

Day Six   Unity, Mercy, Justice

begin with the Opening Prayer

READER

Listen to the words of the first letter of Paul to the Corinthians

12: 7–11

The Spirit has given each of us a special way of serving others. Some of us can speak with wisdom, while others can speak with knowledge, but these gifts come from the same Spirit. To others the Spirit has given great faith or the power to heal the sick or the power to work mighty miracles. Some of us are prophets, and some of us recognize when God's Spirit is present. Others can speak different kinds of languages, and still others can tell what these languages mean. But it is the Spirit who does all this and decides which gifts to give to each of us.

The word of the Lord.

ALL

Thanks be to God.

LEADER

Let us pray for gifts of unity, mercy, and justice. Please respond to each petition, "Come, Holy Spirit."

Spirit of God, strengthen your Church to speak for the poor and the helpless, we pray:

ALL

Come, Holy Spirit.

LEADER

Spirit of God, bring peace and unity to all nations, we pray:

ALL

Come, Holy Spirit.

LEADER

Spirit of God, show us how to use our talents generously in the service of others, we pray:

ALL

Come, Holy Spirit.

more petitions may be added

end with the closing prayer

Closing Prayer for Each Day

LEADER   Come, Holy Spirit,
                fill the hearts of your faithful,

ALL   **And kindle in them the fire of your love.**

LEADER   Send forth your Spirit
                and they shall be created,

ALL   **And you will renew the face of the earth.**

LEADER   Lord, by the light of the Holy Spirit
                you have taught the hearts of your faithful.
                In the same Spirit
                help us to relish what is right
                and always rejoice in your consolation.

ALL   **Amen.**

♩ end with a song

Prayer for the Gifts of the Holy Spirit

LEADER   Loving God,
                by water and the Holy Spirit
                you freed us from sin
                and gave us new life.
                Send your Holy Spirit upon us
                to be our Helper and Guide.
                Give us the spirit of wisdom and understanding,
                the spirit of right judgment and courage,
                the spirit of knowledge and reverence.
                Fill us with the spirit of wonder and awe
                in your presence.
                We ask this through Christ our Lord.

ALL   **Amen.**

This short prayer asks for the traditional gifts based on Isaiah 11:1–3. The Hebrew version of that passage lists wisdom, understanding, counsel, fortitude, knowledge, and fear of the Lord. The Greek or Septugint version adds piety, bringing the number to seven.

Late Spring
April and May

April is a happy month. April First is a day for jokes and good-hearted tricks. At one time April began the year, and when that date was changed to the first of January, many people kept celebrating in April anyway. They were called April Fools, and customs of silliness and teasing grew up around the day.

During April the sun strengthens, and the day lengthens. The generous weather brings out colorful tulips, crocus, hyacinth, daffodils, and azalea. Flowering trees such as forsythia, dogwood, apple, and cherry carry clouds of pale blossoms.

April seems to turn everyone into a poet. Perhaps time outdoors will inspire us to write a few poems. It will put us in the right mood for a hearty celebration of Earth Day (April 22). The poet Charles O'Donnell wrote, "I have never been able to school my eyes / against young April's blue surprise." What do you think he was talking about? And we all know that "April showers bring May flowers." This wisdom helps us to make the best of the rainy weather in the spring. We know that there will be plenty of flowers for our May altars because of it.

In many countries people look forward to creating a May altar in their homes and classrooms. A statue or picture of Mary is placed on a shelf or table that has been decorated with blue and white cloths, ribbons and lace, and candles. Fresh flowers are kept on the altar during the entire month. Families often gather around their altar each day to say the rosary or other Marian prayers. The custom reminds us that the whole month of May is dedicated to Mary. Our prayers during this time acclaim Mary with such titles as Mother of God, Mother of the Church, Blessed Mother, Mother of good counsel, Mirror of holiness, and Ark of the covenant. Perhaps during May we can try our own hands at prayerful poetry.

We might also look for images and prayers to Mary from around the world. They can remind us of the universal respect that is shown for the quiet woman of Nazareth.

It is fortunate to live in the northern hemisphere, where Eastertime, the festival of new life, is celebrated in April and May, when the earth itself is bursting with life. A little poetry and a lot of flowers will help us celebrate all of the feasts and special occasions that occur in these months.

Meal Prayer for Late Spring

Music options: Bless Us, O Lord (3), or the hymn below

LEADER   Let us offer God praise and thanksgiving.

⁘ all make the sign of the cross

LEADER   Let us pray.

pray silently for a minute or two

> Lord, lover of life,
> you feed the birds of the skies
> and dress the lilies of the field.
> We bless you for all your creatures
> and for the food we are about to receive.
> We humbly pray that in your goodness
> you will provide
> for our brothers and sisters
> who are hungry.
> We ask this through Christ our Lord.

ALL   **Amen.**

♩ end with a song; the following words can be sung to the melody for Praise God from Whom All Blessings Flow

> Be present at our table, Lord.
> Be here and everywhere adored.
> Thy creatures bless and grant that we
> May feast in Paradise with thee. Amen.

⁘ all make the sign of the cross

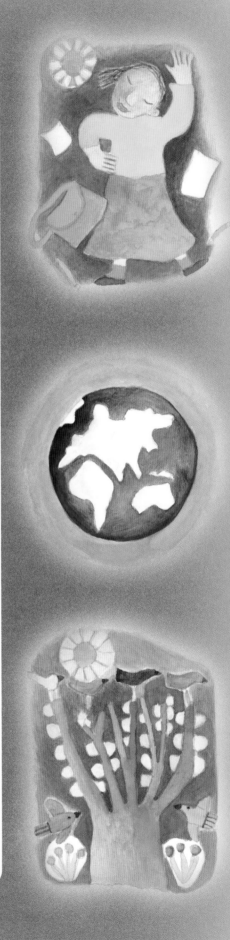

159

Prayer for the Earth on Earth Day

APRIL 22

Preparation: The prayer can be used by a class or by a whole school. Clean or weed a place where you can pray and then perhaps enjoy a picnic or snack. Write some petitions appropriate for the day. Carry pennants on sticks that can be stuck in the ground, or streamers and wind chimes that can be hung from trees to mark your prayer space. Bring holy water for a blessing. If you will eat something, be sure to bring bags for your trash.

Select a leader and five readers.

Music options: Sing Out, Earth and Skies (22), Jubilate Servite (14), Come, Let Us Sing with Joy (6), Sing to God with the Tambourine (23), or other familiar hymns such as Praise God from Whom All Blessings Flow

Earth Day has been celebrated since 1970, when astronauts showed us pictures of our planet from space. It looks fragile and very beautiful. Today we can think about how we are taking care of this planet. We can make some plans to do even better. Perhaps we can enjoy a picnic or a snack in the school garden or a visit to the park.

move in procession to the spot you have chosen, carrying ribbons, streamers, pennants, wind chimes, holy water, and the written petitions

♩ sing a verse or more of the song you have chosen

LEADER   We gather to show our respect for the earth and
           to thank the loving God who has made it our
           home planet.

           Let us all say:
           All that is living sing praise!

ALL   **All that is living sing praise!**

LEADER   The place where God meets with us
           is holy ground, a sacred space.
           Truly, the entire earth is holy.
           Let us mark the place where we
           will worship God this morning,
           and celebrate its holiness.

plant the pennants; hang the streamers, ribbons, and wind chimes; settle yourselves for the prayer

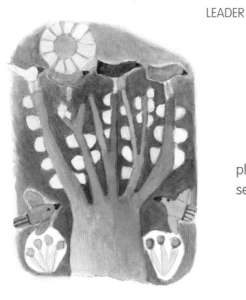

LEADER	After each prayer, let us say:
	All that is living sing praise!
ALL	**All that is living sing praise!**

LEADER	God's greatness and goodness fill the world.
ALL	**All that is living sing praise!**

LEADER	Let the earth, awesome in beauty, sing praise!
ALL	**All that is living sing praise!**

LEADER	Let the earth, solid under our feet, sing praise!
ALL	**All that is living sing praise!**

LEADER	Let the earth, inspiration of poets, sing praise!
ALL	**All that is living sing praise!**

LEADER	Let the earth, generous to builders, sing praise!
ALL	**All that is living sing praise!**

LEADER	Let the earth, offering seed to farmers, sing praise!
ALL	**All that is living sing praise!**

LEADER	Let the earth, giving food for the hungry,
	sing praise!
ALL	**All that is living sing praise!**

LEADER	Let the earth, filled with surprises, sing praise!
ALL	**All that is living sing praise!**

LEADER	Let the earth, and all who dwell on it,
	praise and glorify God now and for ever.
ALL	**Amen. Alleluia!**

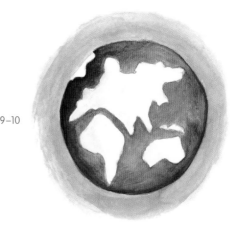

READER ONE	Let us listen to the story of the creation from the book of Genesis 1:9–10
	God said, "I command the water under the sky to come together in one place, so there will be dry ground."

And that's what happened. God named the dry ground "Land," and he named the water "Ocean." God looked at what he had done and saw that it was good.

READER TWO God said, "I command the earth to produce all kinds of plants, including fruit trees and grain."

And that's what happened. The earth produced all kinds of vegetation. God looked at what he had done, and it was good. Evening came and then morning—that was the third day.

READER THREE God said, "I command the ocean to be full   1:20–23
of living creatures, and I command birds to fly above the earth." So God made the giant sea monsters and all the living creatures that swim in the ocean. He also made every kind of bird.

God looked at what he had done, and it was good. Evening came and then morning—that was the fifth day.

READER FOUR God said, "I command the earth to give life   1:24–25
to all kinds of tame animals, wild animals, and reptiles."

And that's what happened. God made every one of them. Then he looked at what he had done, and it was good.

READER FIVE God said, "Now we will make humans, and   1:26—27
they will be like us. We will let them rule the fish, the birds, and all other living creatures."

So God created humans to be like himself; he made men and women.

God looked at what he had done. All of it was very good! Evening came and then morning—that was the sixth day.

READER ONE	So the heavens and the earth and everything else were created.	2:1

	The word of the Lord.
ALL	**Thanks be to God.**
LEADER	Our response to each petition is "Lord, hear our prayer."

members of the class read the petitions they have prepared

when all have finished, continue

LEADER	Blessed are you, Lord our God, Creator of the universe.

sprinkle the four corners of the prayer space with holy water, saying

LEADER	Bless this space dedicated to you through the prayers of your people. You fill the whole world with your glory, and give it to us as a home. Teach us to recognize its wonders, to treasure its variety, and to protect its fragile beauty. We ask this through Christ our Lord.
ALL	**Amen. Alleluia!**

♩ *end with a song*

163

May Procession with a Crowning of an Image of Mary

ANY DAY IN MAY

In former times, it was the custom in many countries of Europe and America for Catholics to walk in procession through town on feast days of Mary. They carried flowers, banners, candles, and a statue of the Mother of God, decorated and crowned with ribbons and flowers. The children wore the white clothes used for their first communion, confirmation, or graduation, sometimes with satin capes. The youngest child often scattered flower petals along the street in front of the statue of the Virgin.

In the United States, the processions were often limited to the parish property or inside the church, and only the students of the parochial school did the marching. In recent years the celebrations have become simpler, so that their purpose, to honor the Mother of God during the season of resurrection and life, can be clear.

Preparation: Plan a ceremony to honor Mary. Select elements that are convenient for your class or school. Some of the possibilities are: procession, decoration of the statue or the area where it is located, crowning of the statue or icon, Marian hymns, Bible readings that mention Mary. If the ceremony is a parish rather than a school event, decide whether it is best held at the time of regular religion classes, on Saturday, or Sunday after one of the Masses.

The event can be simple or elaborate, but it should always be festive and theologically appropriate. The purpose of this, as for all the rituals recommended in this book, is to give children opportunities to pray with the church and to express their religious devotion, never to create a pleasing show for adults of the parish. It also is important to plan a ceremony that will not outshine or distract from the liturgical celebrations of Easter, Ascension, and Pentecost.

• Decide on the degree of festivity you want. The service can be as simple as students putting a vase of flowers on the prayer table where a picture of Mary has been placed. Or it can include all of the elements mentioned in the above description.

• Select the statue or icon you will use. A crown of flowers can be prepared to fit the image. If the image is of Mary with the infant Jesus in her arms, crowns should be prepared for both figures. (The figure of Jesus is always crowned before that of the Madonna.) If the image is a large statue or a stained-glass window, the crown might be placed on a pillow, altar, or table nearby. If the image is an icon or painting, consider hanging a flower garland around the frame instead of using a crown.

• Plan the movement of the event. The blessing can begin in one spot (such as a classroom) and move to another (such as the church), or it can be a procession within a classroom. It can also be done by simply gathering a small group of the children around the image.

• Plan the building of the shrine. Students might carry drawings, banners, streamers, pennants, or flowers. Candles can be carried by older children, perhaps in unbreakable vigil-sized containers. Depending upon the degree of formality, you might need the processional cross, a bowl of holy water, or perhaps a container with charcoal for incense.

Decide ahead of time where the offerings will be put when the procession arrives at the ceremonial space. Vases of water should be ready to receive flowers. A container of sand for lighted tapers also should be ready. Pennants and banners will need holders or hangers. If someone will be reaching across a pedestal or altar to crown the statue(s), see that any ladders are safe and that lighted candles are out of the way. Never allow children in communion veils near lighted candles.

If several class groups will have ceremonies at different times, divide the duties and decorations among them.

• Choose the ministers and prepare them. Select a leader and a reader. In addition, you might need altar servers with a processional cross, candlebearers, a thurifer with incense, or a bowl with holy water. Select the person(s) to carry the crown(s) and place it (them) on the image.

Music options: Sing of Mary (21), We Sing of the Saints (27), with verse for feasts of Mary, and other familiar hymns to Mary

LEADER   Christ is risen, alleluia!

ALL   **Christ is truly risen, alleluia!**

LEADER   Lord God, you have given us life
and guided us on our journey.
Be with us as we honor Mary
in song and prayer.

♩ all sing a song about Mary and walk in procession to the image;
when all have arrived and found their places, say

LEADER   My brothers and sisters,
we gather this day
to honor the blessed Virgin Mary
who shows us how to trust God's word,
and how to follow Jesus with love.
Let us pray.

wait a few minutes so that everyone can become still and prayerful

LEADER   Loving God, you give us Mary
as our mother, our model, and our queen.
Let our love for her bring us closer to you.
We ask this through Christ our Lord.

ALL   **Amen.**

READER   Listen to the words of the book of Revelation   12:1, 5

Something important appeared in the sky. It was a woman whose clothes were the sun. The moon was under her feet, and a crown made of twelve stars was on her head.

The woman gave birth to a son, who would rule all the nations with an iron rod. He was taken to God and placed on his throne.

The word of the Lord.

ALL   **Thanks be to God.**

LEADER   My friends,
         today we bless God
         and we honor the Mother of God.
         I invite you now
         to bow your head and pray.

         Loving God,
         in Mary you have given your Church
         a sign of the glory to come.
         May those who honor Mary
         look to her as a model of holiness
         for all your people.
         We ask this through Christ our Lord.
ALL   **Amen.**

sprinkle the crown(s) with holy water or wave incense over it (them)

crown the image or honor it with flowers

LEADER   We turn to you for protection,
         holy Mother of God.
         Listen to our prayers
         and help us in our needs.
         Save us from every danger,
         glorious and blessed Virgin.

♩ move toward the place where the procession ends, singing joyfully

Blessing of Mother's Day Gifts

SECOND SUNDAY IN MAY

Preparation: *Make pictures, small gifts, or greeting cards for women you wish to honor on Mother's Day. These can include natural and adoptive mothers, stepmothers, foster mothers, grandmothers, godmothers, den mothers, friends' mothers, aunts, and other women who are important to you. If any of these persons have died, write a prayer for them. Assemble these gifts and remembrances at the prayer corner. Instead of gifts or greeting cards, you can simply write each woman's name on a card, bend the card in half so that it stands up, and place it on the table in the prayer center.*

LEADER   Let us begin our prayer.

all make the sign of the cross

LEADER   Loving God,
you give us life and you feed us
just as a mother gives life to her children
and gives them good things to eat.
Bless our mothers, stepmothers, grandmothers,
aunts, friends, and other women
who have helped to mother us.
Teach us to respect and honor them always.
We ask this through Christ our Lord.

ALL   **Amen.**

LEADER   Let us pray.

Loving God,
bless these gifts we have prepared.
Let them be a sign of our love
and our gratitude
to the loving women
who have cared for us.
Fill our mothers' hearts with joy
now and for ever.

ALL   **Amen.**

Mother's Day is an important joyful time in the United States. Children often take time from their school work to make cards or gifts for their mothers. These can be blessed, and mothers can be remembered in prayer on the last day of classes before Mother's Day.

Julia Ward Howe is best remembered as the poet who wrote the words of the "Battle Hymn of the Republic." But she also organized the first Mother's Day in Boston. In 1872, she planned the Mother's Day for Peace, when women gathered to mourn for their sons and husbands who died in the Civil War and to discuss strategies to maintain peace.

Thirty-five years later, when Anna Jarvis of Philadelphia asked her church to plan a service in memory of all mothers who had died, her idea became popular around the country. The meaning of Mother's Day changed from mothers working for peace to children remembering their mothers.

In 1914, President Woodrow Wilson proclaimed the second Sunday of May Mother's Day.

Prayer for Memorial Day

Last Monday in May

Preparation: The actual day of remembrance is a holiday, so class prayers should be offered during the week preceding. If the idea of war seems remote to the students, or even romantic, take time during the week to discuss it. Invite a veteran or military chaplain to talk about it; visit your town's war memorial and learn about those it commemorates; study library books or videos on warfare and peacemaking. The point is not to become anxious about violence or fascinated by it, but to develop a sense of the seriousness and costs of war, the reality of suffering and death, and the stake we all have in developing strategies for peace.

For the prayer you will need the names of people to be remembered. Prepare a list of members of the military who have died. Perhaps the students will wish to include people still living. Start the list with some general categories, such as "all those who died at Pearl Harbor," or "all those who served in Desert Storm." The students may know some names from history, such as Casimir Pulaski or Chief Tecumseh. Children can ask at home for the names and perhaps pictures of relatives who served or are serving in the armed forces. The names and pictures can be placed in the prayer corner during the weeks before and after Memorial Day. The prayer for the dead and for the protection of the living can be said for them daily.

If the students have a sense that all uniformed personnel should be honored on Memorial Day, police officers and fire fighters might be included, and the wording of the prayers adapted. It is good to remember those who put their lives at risk for the sake of others, especially those who died in the line of duty.

Assign the students who will read the lists of the names of the dead and of those now serving in the armed forces.

Select a leader and two readers.

Music options: Come, All You Blessed Ones (5), Jesus Remember Me/Cristo Recuérdame (13), We Bring God's Holy Love (25)

LEADER   Let us begin our prayer.

⁙ all make the sign of the cross

LEADER   God of mercy,
            lead all families
            and all nations of the world
            to support one another
            and to live in peace.
            We ask this through Christ our Lord.
ALL   **Amen.**

Memorial Day is a day to pray for members of the armed forces who died while serving their country. Since 1868, people of the United States have taken this day to honor those who died and to pray for peace and reconciliation.

This day is also called Decoration Day because many people place flowers, wreaths, and flags on the graves of people who died in war. Flowers are also placed at public memorials in towns across the country. The President will place a wreath at the Tomb of the Unknown in Arlington National Cemetery. That tomb honors service men and women who died far from home and lie in unknown graves around the world.

Each year, the President proclaims Memorial Day a day of prayer for permanent peace. As we pray for world peace, let us look forward to the day when all nations are willing to settle disputes without war.

In our prayer let us also remember the civilians around the world who have been killed in wars, or who

LEADER   In preparation for Memorial Day let us remember those who have died in the service of their country.

READER ONE   read the names of the dead

allow a minute or two of silence, then continue

LEADER   Eternal rest grant unto them, O Lord,
and let perpetual light shine upon them.
May they rest in peace.

ALL   **Amen.**

LEADER   May their souls
and the souls of all the faithful departed,
through the mercy of God, rest in peace.

ALL   **Amen.**

LEADER   Let us remember the names of those who are now serving in the armed forces.

READER TWO   read the names of the living

allow a minute or two of silence, then continue

LEADER   Merciful God,
watch over our friends
and fellow citizens.
Protect them from danger.
Teach them the right use of power.
And let their service be useful
in bringing peace to the world.
We ask this through Christ our Lord.

ALL   **Amen.**

LEADER   Let us pray with the words that Jesus taught us.

ALL   **Our Father . . .**

♩ *end with a song*

are homeless or starving because of it. There are also many thousands of children whose parents have been killed in war. Let us pray for them all.

Blessing before Summer Vacation

Preparation: The teacher is the leader of this prayer.

Music option: Go Now in Peace (9), For Your Gracious Blessing (8)

TEACHER   Let us begin our prayer.

⋰ all make the sign of the cross

TEACHER   May the Lord's face shine on us,
and may the Lord guide our feet
into the way of peace.
Blessed be the name of the Lord,
now and for ever.

ALL   **Amen.**

TEACHER   Let us put ourselves into the hands of the Lord,
and pray that God will bless us
and our families
during the wonderful months of summer.
May all of us help to make our homes
places of relaxation, joy, love,
peace, and safety.
May we be generous and considerate,
not thinking only about ourselves
but helping others enjoy the blessings
of the summertime.

Please respond "Amen" as I bless each of you.

the teacher goes to each student in turn,
traces a cross on the student's head, and says

TEACHER   N____, go with God.
STUDENT   **Amen.**

when the individual blessings are completed, prayer continues

It is good to end the year in a ceremonial way. After a few days or hours of preparation, the time will finally come when lockers and desks have been cleaned out, the last prizes awarded, summer plans and addresses exchanged, small tokens of gratitude for a wonderful year given and received, and perhaps a final party with treats and songs enjoyed. That is the time for the teacher to make sure everyone is ready for the final dismissal bell. Then gather and quiet the students so that you can bless each of them.

TEACHER   Lord God,

this class has shared many things this year.
We were linked by common tasks
and time together.
Those ties are broken now.
We say good-bye and end our year.
Lord, bless each of these,
my students and friends,
especially those I will not see again.
Keep each of us in your care
during the coming summer
and throughout our lives.
Guide our steps and strengthen our hearts
until we gather once again in your kingdom.
We ask this through Christ our Lord.

ALL   **Amen.**

TEACHER   Let us end this year as we began it,
with the sign of the cross.

 all make the sign of the cross

end with a song

> Recall that the classroom is a sacred space, made so by the life and growth it has sheltered. When the last book is boxed and the last desk is scrubbed, take a few minutes to bless the classroom and to take leave of it.

Blessing and Farewell to the Classroom

THE TEACHER'S LAST VISIT TO THE EMPTY CLASSROOM

Preparation: This prayer is for the teacher to pray at the end of the year. As you prepare to leave, have the names of the children ready and prepare some incense or a bowl of holy water.

TEACHER   begin with the sign of the cross

Lord, open my lips.
And my mouth will proclaim your praise.
O God,
you call me to be a teacher,
sharing in children's wonder at your world
and at the power of your love.
The children are gone now,
and my job is finished.

be quiet for a minute or two

Merciful God,
you know the expectations of August
and the reality of June.
You know my regret and contrition
for hopes not realized,
things not done,
needs not met,
errors, angers, and injuries.

be quiet for a minute or two

Redeeming God,
in your mercy, forgive and cleanse me.
Let this incense (holy water)
be a sign of release and purification.

Bless and renew this room
as you bless and renew
all who have worked here.
Make it a safe and nurturing shelter
for students and teachers yet to come.

bless the room with incense or holy water

Loving God,
I thank you for the bright spirits
of my students.
They have taught me much.
Surround them with safety and love.
Be with them on their journey.
Let the memory of the months spent in
this room always bring them joy.

read the list of your students, commending each to God

Gracious God,
be forgiving of my failure!
Be glorified in my success!
Turn my face toward the future,
and renew my energy for what is yet to be.

pray with the words of Paul to the Philippians   3:12

"I have not yet reached my goal,
and I am not perfect.
But Christ has taken hold of me.
So I keep on running and struggling
to take hold of the prize."

In the name of the Father, and of the Son,
and of the Holy Spirit. Amen. Alleluia!

Summertime

With the passing of the great solemnity of Pentecost, we are ready for summertime. With the last day of school we begin to celebrate this amazing season with bare feet, bright sunshine, summer sports, trips to the library and visits with relatives and friends. The world is rich, green and colorful, filled with adventures and surprises.

The Church welcomes with green vestments this season called "Ordinary Time." The term *ordinary* comes from *ordinal* meaning "counted." The Church keeps time by counting the Sundays of the year: the first Sunday, the tenth Sunday, the fourteenth Sunday, and so on. The Easter Sundays end with Pentecost, so the "Sundays of Ordinary Time" will bring us through the entire summer and fall.

Even in ordinary language, *ordinary* does not mean "dull." Ordinary food can be very nourishing. Ordinary clothes are usually the most comfortable. Ordinary jobs can be very important. And ordinary people make our world a very good place in which to live. Ordinary people and ordinary things, in other words, can usually be counted on.

With the coming of June, many parish routines are changed. Religious education classes end, parochial schools close, choirs take time off, and liturgy committees hang out the "Gone Fishing" sign.

Nevertheless, in many parishes there are a few occasions during the summer when children and their families are invited to celebrate in a special way. They are opportunities for children to experience the parish as a year-round, lifelong environment of celebration and worship. Too often a parish equates festivity only with the labor intensive celebrations surrounding Christmas and Easter, missing other feast days during the year that invite spontaneous bursts of wonder, joy, reflection, and praise. Those days are invitations to our creativity, our community spirit, and our sensitivity for the riches of the liturgy. In that spirit, we offer a few ideas in this final section of Part One. Additional ideas and prayers can be found in *Children's Daily Prayer for Summer* (published by LTP).

Meal Prayer for Summer

Music options: Bless Us, O Lord (3), In the Lord I'll Be Ever Thankful (12)

♪ begin or end with a song

LEADER   Let us offer God praise and thanksgiving.

 all make the sign of the cross

ALL   **In the name of the Father, and of the Son,
and of the Holy Spirit.**

LEADER   Loving God
We give you thanks
for this food we are about to eat.
Teach us to be grateful
for your many gifts to us,
and help us to share
what we have with others.

ALL   **Amen.**

 all make the sign of the cross

LEADER   Loving God, keep us close to you always,
          and make us a source of blessing
          to our families and friends.
          Strengthen us for the events of this summer,
          fill us with delight in your creation,
          and awaken us to the needs of others,
          now and forever.

ALL   **Amen.**

♩ end with a song(s)

Blessing for Father's Day

THIRD SUNDAY IN JUNE

Preparation: With school closed for the season, there is probably no way to help the children make cards or simple gifts for their fathers. If they are encouraged to bring something made at home, those who forget will be left empty handed. Therefore, whatever is done to recognize the fathers will probably be done entirely at the Sunday gathering on that day.

Plan a simple shrine of recognition. As they enter the vestibule or the church, invite all parishioners to write the names of their fathers on cards and tape them to small candle holders. The candles can be lighted and arranged near a statue of Saint Joseph, on a side altar, or on a decorated table in the entry area of the church.

If the community is too large for candles to be a practical option, ask everyone to write the names on sticky notes and place them on an area of the wall that you have defined with a banner proclaiming "A Celebration of Fathers!"

Before the dismissal and closing hymn, the priest can bless all the fathers named, and all the fathers in the church.

PRIEST   Loving God,
          you give us life.
          You nurture and guide us
          and ask us to call you Father.
          Bless our fathers, stepfathers, grandfathers,
          uncles, priests, friends,
          and other men who have helped to father us,
          modeling their care
          on your own unchanging love and protection.
          Teach us to respect and honor them always.
          We ask this through Christ our Lord.

ALL   **Amen.**

Surprisingly, the idea of Father's Day was born on Mother's Day. In 1909, Sonora Dodd listened to a sermon about mothers in her Spokane, Washington, church, and reflected on the fact that she had been raised almost entirely by her caring and generous father, because her mother died when Sonora was very young. The following year she organized a day to honor fathers on June 19, her father's birthday. The custom soon spread to the entire state of Washington, and then to other states. It was not proclaimed as a national celebration, however, until 55 years later, in 1966.

PRIEST   Loving God,

           bless these men, who stand beside us today.

           Let them be a sign to us of your own generous love.

           Fill their hearts with courage

           and with joy

           now and forever.

ALL   **Amen.**

A Celebration of Holy Men on Father's Day

Preparation: In preparation for one or more Masses on Father's Day, set aside 30 minutes to an hour for a celebration of holy men. It would be an enjoyable part of the parish picnic if you choose Father's Day for that event.

The planners should think through the logistics of the celebration, and make any adaptations that seem appropriate.

Place tables in the gathering space (outdoors if possible). On each table place a supply of inexpensive ribbon cut in random lengths (from 4 to 6 feet). Use ribbons in a variety of bright colors and varying widths (from 2 to 5 inches). Supply wide-tip markers that can be used to write on the ribbons, and thumb tacks or tape to attach the ribbons to the banner poles.

As the parishioners arrive, divide them into small groups (6 to 8 people) and give each group a tall, T-shaped banner pole, along with these instructions:

• Remember some of the men who have "fathered" you in your Christian life, sources of love, guidance, support, wisdom, and good example. They may be members of your family, people you have read about, men of the Bible, saints of the Church — the more the better!

• Share the stories of those men with others in your group.

• Write the name of each holy man in large letters on a ribbon, and also write what it is about him for which you are grateful. (Was he a "loving teacher," a "courageous leader," a "prayerful" mentor?)

• Attach the ribbons to your group's banner pole. Decide who will carry your group's pole in the procession.

Music option: We Are Marching (26)

form a procession; musicians take their places behind the server with the processional cross; the groups join the procession, walking with their banner, and the ministers and celebrant take their places at the end (If the parish owns a portable banner or statue, it would of course be part of the procession. If rhythm instruments are available they can be distributed to the children.)

The musicians lead the procession in song as it moves around the area, perhaps around the block, and finally into the church. Once there, the banners are brought forward for a blessing while everyone

Not all men, of course are fathers. Nevertheless, Father's Day can provide an opportunity for celebrating the contribution that men make to the parish and to the larger Church. All men are called at various times during their lives and in various ways, to offer their love, leadership, and support to dependent members of the community. Like God, whom we call Father, they are a source of the community's life and strength. (This celebration might be adapted for use on Saint Joseph's Day, the feast of an apostle or another saint.)

finds a seat. After the blessing the banners are put in buckets of sand (or other holders) artistically placed around the church, or taped to the ends of the pews farthest from the center aisle.

the priest or deacon blesses the banners, using holy water.

all make the sign of the cross

PRESIDER   Gracious God,
we rejoice on this holy day
that you have given us many good and holy men
as our models and our support in Christian growth.

We ask that you
bless these banners
that acclaim the many holy men
who have taught us the meaning of discipleship.

sprinkle the banners with holy water

PRESIDER   Those men whose names and virtues
we recall and honor this day
stand with us
as worthy guides on our earthly pilgrimage.
Bless and strengthen those still living.
Welcome those who have died
into the company of your saints.
And raise us all to eternal life,
as you have promised through Christ our Lord.

ALL   **Amen.**

if the liturgy follows, the priest adds

PRESIDER   In the presence of the holy men,
and with their spirit,
we prepare now to celebrate your holy mysteries.

 end with a song

Prayer for the Solemnity of John the Baptist

JUNE 24

Preparation: The vigil of the birth of John the Baptist is a good time for the parish picnic. In many countries, especially French-speaking lands, it is customary to have an evening cookout at the beach or riverside. There are games, bonfires, or fireworks "to honor this shining light who blazed the way for the Messiah."

The children of the parish could enjoy water events in honor of the Baptist, especially if the parish has a lawn or a nearby park. Wading pools, fountains, and plastic containers for pouring would be welcome. Children might also be invited to make paper boats, christen them with their own baptismal names, and launch them in a few wading pools. Floating tea lights would be appropriate and would be beautiful additions to the pools as the sun begins to set.

Any prayers and blessings that are customary for the parish picnic should conclude on this day with the song of Zechariah, John's father. Select a leader and divide the group into Side A and Side B. Provide copies of the canticle.

Music option: We Sing of the Saints (27), with verse for feasts of John the Baptist

Song Of Zechariah

Luke 1:68–79

LEADER
Praise the Lord, the God of Israel!
He has come to save his people.

SIDE A
Our God has given us a mighty Savior
from the family of David his servant.
Long ago the Lord promised
by the words of his holy prophets
to save us from our enemies
and from everyone who hates us.

SIDE B
God said he would be kind
to our people and keep
his sacred promise.
He told our ancestor Abraham
that he would rescue us
from our enemies.
Then we could serve him without fear,
by being holy and good as long as we live.

We learn from the gospel of Luke that Elizabeth, the mother of John the Baptist, was six months pregnant when Mary learned that she too would bear a child. Accordingly, our celebration of the birthday of John falls six months before the celebration of the birth of Jesus. Thus the two feasts embrace and balance our year, alternatively proclaiming the Gospel of preparation and fulfillment.

June 24 is midsummer day, a time near the summer solstice. On a day when ancient people celebrated the sun's gift of light and warmth with bonfires and offerings to the "spirits," Christians now honor John, who prepared the way for Jesus, the light of the world, who would bring the Holy Spirit.

John told his disciples (who worried that Jesus was drawing greater crowds than John), that "he must increase and I must decrease" (John 3:30). So with the turning of the year, the natural sunlight begins from this day to decrease in strength, until midwinter, when Jesus the light of the world is born again in our hearts, and the days begin to lengthen.

SIDE A

You, my son, will be called
a prophet of God in heaven above.
You will go ahead of the Lord
to get everything ready for him.
You will tell his people
that they can be saved
when their sins are forgiven.

ALL

God's love and kindness
will shine upon us
like the sun that rises in the sky.
On us who live
in the dark shadow of death
this light will shine
to guide us into a life of peace.
Amen.

Prayer to the Sacred Heart

SOLEMNITY OF THE MOST SACRED HEART OF JESUS

FRIDAY AFTER THE SECOND SUNDAY AFTER PENTECOST

While images of Jesus with an exposed heart, crowned by thorns, perhaps, or enveloped in flames are relatively modern, devotion to his Sacred Heart is an ancient tradition. Prayers for the feast focus on God's immense love which Jesus embodies and makes visible to us. The feast always falls on a Friday, the Church's weekly day of remembrance of the love with which Jesus sacrificed himself on the cross.

Preparation: The prayer might be printed in the parish bulletin or made available in the church, so that families with children can pray it on the feast day.

LEADER   Let us begin our prayer.

⋮ all make the sign of the cross

READER   Listen to the words of the apostle Paul
to the Romans: 8:35, 31–39

Can anything separate us from the love of Christ?
Can trouble, suffering, and hard times, or hunger
and nakedness, or danger and death?

In everything, we have won more than a victory
because of Christ who loves us. I am sure that

nothing can separate us from God's love—not life or death, not angels or spirits, not the present or the future, and not powers above or powers below. Nothing in all creation can separate us from God's love for us in Christ Jesus our Lord!

The word of the Lord.

ALL   **Thanks be to God.**

LEADER   Let us pray:
Lord, have mercy.

ALL   **Lord, have mercy.**

LEADER   Christ, have mercy.

ALL   **Christ, have mercy.**

LEADER   Lord, have mercy.

ALL   **Lord, have mercy.**

LEADER   Heart of Jesus, source of justice and love,

ALL   **have mercy on us.**

LEADER   Heart of Jesus, patient and merciful,

ALL   **have mercy on us.**

LEADER   Heart of Jesus, our life and resurrection,

ALL   **have mercy on us.**

LEADER   Heart of Jesus, our peace and reconciliation,

ALL   **have mercy on us.**

LEADER   Heart of Jesus, delight of all the saints,

ALL   **have mercy on us.**

LEADER   Heart of Jesus, worthy of all praise,

ALL   **have mercy on us.**

LEADER   Jesus, gentle and humble of heart,

ALL   **Touch our hearts
and make them like your own.
Amen.**

Prayer for Independence Day

JULY 4

On July 4, 1776, the Declaration of Independence was approved by Congress, and our nation officially began its journey toward freedom. Historically this event stands in the tradition of the exodus from Egypt and other movements to liberate people from every kind of slavery. The struggle of the Israelites did not end with their entry into the Promised Land, and in the same way, the American struggle did not end with the surrender of Cornwallis at Yorktown. External and internal freedom were still only partially won. Women could not vote. Catholics could not hold public office. Native Americans were considered savages. And of course, African Americans were still enslaved.

For over 200 years the struggle to realize our national dream has continued. There have been great successes. But there have also been enough failures to keep us from becoming complacent. Let this year's celebration be an opportunity to stand in solidarity with all of our citizens, to recognize and rejoice in the heroes and accomplishments of the nation, and to renew our commitment to the work of correction and nurturing.

Preparation: This is not a day to plan large events at the parish. Most families will be participating in civic events and family outings. But before moving to parades and picnics, before hanging the bunting and waving the flags, members of the parish might join in a well-planned liturgy held at a convenient hour so that they can pray for the authenticity, welfare, safety, and strength of the nation. At the end of the liturgy, cards with the following prayer can be given to the children and their families to use as a Catholic "pledge of allegiance."

LEADER   Merciful God
on this day of national celebration,
as we recall the lives and hopes
of our country's founders,
we pray that their vision
may inspire us anew
to protect the weak,
to comfort the fearful,
to defend the mistreated,
to welcome the stranger,
to provide for the needy,
to challenge the greedy and hate-filled,
to relieve the exploited,
to respect the rights and beliefs of others,
and to hold our nation to its pledge
of liberty and justice for all.
For this task we ask your blessing and strength
now and for ever.

ALL   **Amen.**

Prayers for the Solemnity of the Assumption
August 15

Harvest Blessing for the Assumption

Preparation: Invite each family to bring a basket of fresh fruit or produce to the church. If the items come from the gardens or fields of parishioners, so much the better. Bunches of summer flowers (especially wildflowers) and aromatic herbs (such as sage, mint, chives, and potpourri) can be brought as well. Ask the children to help arrange the gifts in a colorful display in the gathering space or around an image of Mary. Place the bread and wine for the liturgy with the other gifts. After the liturgy children can help package the food and flowers for people in nursing homes or families in need.

This gathering and blessing of gifts can take place before the vigil Mass (August 14) or before any of the Masses of the feast day itself. If many parishioners are not able to participate on a weekday, it might be used on the Sunday closest to the feast.

Before Mass the celebrant, servers, and lector process to the gifts, accompanied by the first verse of the opening hymn. The servers bring either incense or holy water for the blessing. The same hymn should open and close the blessing.

Select a reader.

Music options: Sing of Mary (21), Sing Out, Earth and Skies (22), For Your Gracious Blessing (8), or other familiar hymns to Mary

PRESIDER   Let us praise God who blesses us generously with the foods and flowers of the summer season. Let us all say, Blessed be God for ever.

ALL   **Blessed be God for ever.**

PRESIDER   The Lord's goodness is without measure.
Just as the body of our mother Mary
was taken from the earth
and raised up to the throne of God,
so in return God gives mother earth
these gifts for our nourishment,
healing and pleasure.

the presider incenses the food and flowers,
or sprinkles them with holy water

According to the ancient tradition on which the feast of the Assumption is based, Mary went to live in Ephesus after the death and resurrection of her son. When the time came for her to die, John, Bishop of Ephesus, sent word to the other apostles, who were by this time scattered around the Mediterranean area, and they hastened to her bedside. Thomas, who had to come all the way from India, was delayed and did not arrive until after her death and funeral. On opening the tomb to allow him to pay his respects, they were amazed to find in place of the body of their venerable "mother" and friend, an abundance of lilies. Her body had been "assumed" into heaven uncorrupted and reunited with her spirit.

In 1950, Pope Pius XII proclaimed as a binding teaching of the church that "the Immaculate Mother of God, Mary ever Virgin, when the course of her earthly life was finished, was taken up body and soul into the glory of heaven." The teaching strengthens our understanding of the value of our bodies as well as our souls, and God's pledge to raise us all in the power of Christ's resurrection.

The Assumption is a holy day of obligation in the United States, which means that Catholics celebrate the Eucharist on that day. Because it is a solemnity, a vigil Mass may be celebrated on the evening of August 14.

Legend also tells us that during the time between her death and the reopening of her tomb, all the flowers lost their scent and all the herbs lost their medicinal properties. In this way nature itself grieved the loss of Mary, who embodies the earth's own beauty and healing power. With the opening of the tomb, the fragrance of flowers was restored, along with the efficacy of medicinal herbs.

The oldest celebrations of this feast have a harvest character, since it falls in mid-August. In Belgium, for example, processions still wind from the churches to the fields where the new fruits and grains are blessed.

The feast of the Assumption is an excellent time for celebrating the dignity of women. God chose to honor Mary in this special way at a time in history when women were considered the property of male spouses or relatives.

READER   Listen to the words of the prophet Joel   2:21–23, 26

The Lord works wonders and does great things.
So tell the soil to celebrate
and wild animals to stop being afraid.
Grasslands are green again;
fruit trees and fig trees are loaded with fruit.
Grapevines are covered with grapes.
People of Zion,
celebrate in honor of the Lord your God!
He is generous and has sent
the autumn and spring rains in the proper seasons.
My people, you will eat until you are satisfied.
Then you will praise me
for the wonderful things I have done.

The word of the Lord.

ALL   **Thanks be to God.**

PRESIDER   Let us pray.

All-gracious God,
we appeal to your tender care
that even as you temper the winds and rains
to nurture the fruits of the earth
you will also send upon them the gentle shower
of your blessing.
Fill the hearts of your people with gratitude,
that from the earth's fertility
the hungry may be filled with good things
and the poor and needy proclaim the glory
of your name.
We ask this through Christ our Lord.

ALL   **Amen.**

all make the sign of the cross

more verses of the opening hymn are sung while the celebrant, servers and other ministers move in procession to the altar for the liturgy

A Celebration of Holy Women for Assumption Day

Preparation: When planning for the liturgy of the Assumption, set aside 30 minutes to an hour for a celebration of holy women. The event can take place before the vigil Mass (August 14) or before any of the Masses on the feast day itself. If many parishioners are not able to participate on a weekday, it might take place on the Sunday closest to the feast. The planners should think through the logistics of the celebration and make any adaptations that seem appropriate.

Place tables in the gathering space (outdoors if possible). On each table place a supply of inexpensive ribbon cut in random lengths (from 4 to 6 feet). Use ribbons in a variety of bright colors and varying widths (from 2 to 5 inches). Supply wide-tip markers that can be used to write on the ribbons, and thumb tacks or tape to attach the ribbons to the banner poles.

As the parishioners arrive, divide them into small groups (6 to 8 people) and give each group a tall, T-shaped banner pole, along with these instructions:

• Remember some of the women who, like Mary, have been models for you in your Christian life. They may be members of your family, people you have read about, women of the Bible, saints of the Church—the more the better!

• Share the stories of those women with others in your group.

• Write the name of each great woman in large letters on a ribbon, and also write what it is about her that you admire. (Was she a loving teacher, a courageous leader, a prayerful woman?)

• Attach the ribbons to your group's banner pole. Decide who will carry your group's pole in the procession.

Music options: Sing of Mary (21), We Are Marching (26), and other hymns to Mary

form a procession; musicians take their places behind the server with the processional cross; the groups join the procession, walking with their banner, and the ministers and celebrant take their places at the end (If the parish owns a Marian banner or transportable statue, it would of course be part of the procession. If rhythm instruments are available they can be distributed to the children.)

The musicians lead the procession in song as it moves around the area, perhaps around the block, and finally into the church. Once there, the banners are brought forward for a blessing while everyone finds a seat. After the blessing the banners are put in buckets of sand (or other holders) artistically placed around the church, or taped to the ends of the pews farthest from the center aisle.

the priest or deacon blesses the banners, using holy water

PRESIDER   **Let us continue our prayer.**

all make the sign of the cross

It is clear from the New Testament passages that relate to Mary that she is presented to the community as a model of discipleship. From her initial fiat to her supportive and prayerful presence at the time of Pentecost, Mary was one who gave herself without question to the plan of God. She brought the needs of the wedding party to her son's attention, she heard the word of God and kept it, and she remained steadfast at the foot of the cross.

PRESIDER   Gracious God,
we rejoice on this holy day
that you gave us Mary as our model
and that you have received her
into the glory of heaven.
We ask that you bless these banners
that acclaim the many holy women
who, with Mary, have taught us the meaning
of discipleship.

sprinkle the banners with holy water

PRESIDER   Those women whose names and virtues
we recall and honor this day
walk with us
as worthy guides on our earthly pilgrimage.
Bless and strengthen those still living.
Welcome those who have died
into the company of Mary and all your saints.
And raise us all to eternal life,
as you have promised through Christ our Lord.

ALL   **Amen.**

if the liturgy follows, the priest adds

PRESIDER   In the presence of these holy women,
and with their spirit,
we prepare now to celebrate your holy mysteries.

♩ *end with a song*

Part Two

Prayers for Special Times

| LEADER | May God, who saves you from all harm, give you peace. |
| ALL | **Amen.** |

⋮✚ all make the sign of the cross

♩ close with a song

Prayers for the Feast of a Patron Saint or Patron of the School or Parish

NOVEMBER 1: SOLEMNITY OF ALL SAINTS
OR ANY FEAST DAY OF A PATRON SAINT

Preparation: Some saints are well known, such as Saint Patrick, but others, like Saint Giles, are not. Some titles of Jesus and Mary also require study. If the patron is not well known, you will have to do some exploring. Your introduction can include something (not everything!) you have learned.

Some patron saints are honored with traditional customs, foods, and prayers. There may even be some suggestions for their day in Part One of this book. Others, however, have no ready-made customs and invite us to be creative in planning a celebration. The feast of a patron saint is an opportunity to make our prayer lively and to write some prayers from the heart.

When you prepare for your patron's feast, you can follow the sample given here, making the necessary changes to fit your patron saint. Be sure to set a focus for your prayer. It might be a virtue or insight of your saint or something that happened to him or her. Select a reading from the Bible that relates to this focus.

Be sure to prepare the leaders, readers, musicians, and all who will be participating in the prayer.

It is important to celebrate our favorite saints. These might include the founder of a religious order or the saints for which our school or parish is named. Those are our patrons, in whose protection we live. The Church believes that it is so important to form a strong bond with our patrons that the feast of that saint is a solemnity. That means it is a day like a Sunday, with the highest rank in the liturgical calendar.

Celebration begins at Evening Prayer on the night before the feast and lasts until sundown the following day.

Preparation: Decorate the prayer center with a Bible opened to Luke's Gospel. Marigolds are traditional for this feast.

Ask the students to make bookmarks for their personal or classroom Bibles. On it, they might want to write or draw a favorite saying or event from Luke's Gospel. The bookmarks can be cut from colored paper and perhaps laminated. They can be placed in a basket near the Bible and blessed during the prayer.

Music option: We Sing of the Saints (27), If Today You Hear the Voice of God (11)

♩ begin and end with a song

LEADER   Let us begin our celebration of the feast of Saint Luke.

⠿ all make the sign of the cross

LEADER   Today is the feast of the patron of our parish [school], Saint Luke the evangelist. We rejoice that Luke was such a good storyteller, and we thank God for leading him to write down for us a trustworthy account of the things that Jesus said and did.

READER   Listen to the words of the holy Gospel according to Luke   1:1–4

Many people have tried to give an orderly account of the events that happened among us. They have written down just what was told to them by the people who actually saw these events. Information also came from those who serve God by bringing the word to others.

I have carefully studied everything that happened, from the very first. I have decided to write an orderly account for you, Theophilus. Then you will see that what you have been taught is true.

The Gospel of the Lord.

ALL   **Praise to you, Lord Jesus Christ.**

Luke did not meet Jesus, but drew his faith from the Church, as we do. Legends tell us that Saint Luke was a doctor and an artist and that he traveled with Saint Paul on his missionary journeys.

Saint Luke wrote the third gospel to "give an orderly account" of the words and actions of Jesus as he moved from the hills of Galilee to the holy city of Jerusalem. Luke followed with the Acts of the Apostles showing the movement of the Church from Jerusalem to Rome. On every page Luke paints a picture of a gentle, healing Jesus, and a Spirit-filled, welcoming Church.

We have a great treasure in the writings of Saint Luke. His Gospel is the only place we learn of the angel's visit with Mary and her visit with Elizabeth, the coming of the shepherds to the stable, the argument of Mary and Martha, the gratitude of a man cured of leprosy, the parables of the prodigal son and the good Samaritan, and the appearance of Jesus on the road to Emmaus.

TEACHER   an adult may wish to lead a short reflection

LEADER   Wise and loving God,
you led Saint Luke
and other men and women
to write words
that would bring us closer to you.
Bless these markers that we have made
as a sign of our love for your holy word.
Let them remind us to study the Bible carefully
and respect the teachings that you
have prepared for us.
For the writings of Saint Luke, let us bless the Lord.
Let the Church gathered here respond,
Blessed be God for ever.

ALL   **Blessed be God for ever.**

LEADER   For the good news of Jesus,
which is known throughout the world,
let us bless the Lord.

ALL   **Blessed be God for ever.**

LEADER   For the Bibles in our classrooms and our homes,
that allow us all to study the word of God,
let us bless the Lord.

ALL   **Blessed be God for ever.**

LEADER   For good Saint Luke, patron of artists,
doctors, butchers, and this parish [school],
let us bless the Lord.

ALL   **Blessed be God for ever.**

LEADER   Lord God,

we thank you for the life and the work of Saint Luke.

Help us to understand the Gospel

better and better each day.

Let your word, like good seed,

take root in our hearts and bear fruit in our lives.

We ask this through Christ our Lord.

ALL   **Amen.**

LEADER   Let us pray with the words that Jesus taught us.

ALL   **Our Father . . .**

⠿   all make the sign of the cross

♩   end with a song

Blessing of New Students

Preparation: After the teacher introduces the new students to the class, the teacher assigns one or more buddies to help each new student become acquainted with the school and its activities. At least one buddy is with the new student at all times during the school day. When the new student knows at least six students by name and the buddies have learned as much as they can about him or her, they are ready for the blessing.

So that all the students can say the prayer together, write it on the board or provide each student with a copy.

Music option: For Your Gracious Blessing (8)

LEADER   Today we welcome N____. We have already learned some things about him (or her).

invite the buddies to take turns sharing something they have learned

LEADER   N____ has begun to know us too.

invite him/her to name several students

When new students enter school after the year has begun it may seem that everyone has already formed their friendships. Moving to a new school can be a painful experience, but it does not have to be that way. There are ways to make newcomers feel welcome. Once they feel welcome, they can relax and become friends. But first we must build a foundation for friendship.

LEADER   Let us now welcome N_____ by blessing him/her.
We begin our prayer.

 all make the sign of the cross

ALL   N_____, our friend,
may God bless and protect you always.
May God show you mercy
and kindness.
May God be good to you
and give you peace.
Amen.

Blessing of Graduating Students

Preparation: Part of the prayer service is a presentation by the graduating students of their memories of past years and their reflections on moving into a new phase of their lives. It might include pictures or poems or an original song. Let the students talk this over and plan it in advance.

The prayer gives the guests who have gathered an opportunity to ask the Holy Spirit to bless the graduates with specific gifts, mentioning the reason each gift is being requested. Supply index cards and pencils and ask everyone to follow the same form for their petitions. You can give examples that use this form: "For the gift of wisdom, in order to make good decisions, let us pray . . ." or "For the gift of compassion, that in a new school these graduates may notice other students who need friendship, let us pray. . . ." Encourage everyone to keep their prayers short, clear, and simple, and not to turn them into mini-homilies.

Collect the petitions and select as many as you will use. Put the rest in an offering basket and place it by the candle or icon in your prayer area.

Music options: Go Now in Peace (9), Shalom, My Friends (20), In the Lord I'll Be Ever Thankful (12), Send Forth Your Spirit, O Lord (19)

♩ begin and end with a song

LEADER   On this festive occasion let us begin our prayer.

all make the sign of the cross

LEADER   Let us all say:
We praise you, Lord God, with all our heart:

ALL   **We praise you, Lord God, with all our heart.**

It is important to mark a graduation with prayer, showing that our growth is graced and guided by God. A transition as important as the movement from grade school to high school is a notable event in our sacred journey of life.

For students in parochial school, a ritual of blessing can be added to a school assembly, or to the graduation ceremony itself. The religious education community can bless their friends during the last class gathering, to mark their transition from the elementary program to the youth group. The ritual might include parents and friends, the whole school, or just the faculty. It can be prepared and celebrated by the eighth-graders alone. It can take place in the auditorium, church, or classroom. In any case, it should be followed by music, hospitality, and something delicious to eat.

LEADER   God ever present among us,
we praise you for all you have given
and all you still have in store for us.
We thank you for bringing this class of eighth-graders
to a new time of growth and happiness.
May they always give witness
to your loving kindness.
We ask this through Christ our Lord.

ALL   **Amen.**

LEADER   As you graduate, are there memories and hopes you
can you share with us?

*the graduates may share stories or pictures from past school years
and reflections on their movement into a new phase of their lives;
when they have finished continue with the following*

LEADER   As these students move toward a new phase of life,
where new forms of maturity will be expected, let us
call upon the Spirit of God to strengthen them for
the future. What gifts do we ask of the Holy Spirit
for them?

To each petition, let us respond, "Come, Holy Spirit."

*teachers, parents, and fellow students may offer petitions that they
have prepared*

LEADER   Let us pray:
Gracious God,
hear the prayers we offer you
on behalf of our friends
who are graduating.
Protect them on their life journey.
We ask this through Christ the Lord.

ALL   **Amen.**

LEADER   Let us bow our heads and pray for these graduates.

May the Lord fill your life
with love and rejoicing.
May the Lord protect you
and keep you safe from all dangers.
May the Lord be with you
wherever you go,
now and for ever.

ALL   **Amen.**

♩ close with a song

Farewell Blessing for a Friend Who Is Leaving

Preparation: Sometimes a student or a teacher leaves before the school year is over. A blessing can be part of your goodbye.

Prepare a gift that will help your friend remember all of you. It can be as simple as a booklet of drawings, a picture of the class, or a card that everyone has signed. You may want to invite your friend's parents or another relative. If your friend is a teacher, you may want to invite their husband or wife. If you share songs or something good to eat, use this blessing just before your friend's departure.

Music option: Shalom, My Friends (20), Go Now in Peace (9)

LEADER   Let us begin our prayer.

⁙ all make the sign of the cross

LEADER   Let us say:
God is ever watchful and always near.

ALL   **God is ever watchful and always near.**

LEADER   Gracious and loving God,
you have prepared a new place
for our sister/brother N____
where she/he may continue to grow in wisdom
and in love for you.

The departure of a student or teacher before the school year is over is an important event. They should not be allowed to "just disappear" from the community. Moving away is especially hard for children, and a ceremony of farewell can settle some of their anxieties.

The Irish blessing for a traveler is also suitable for this event. See page 206.

Be with N____ on her/his journey,
Send your Son as light for her/his path,
and your Spirit as strength for new beginnings.
Bless this gift as a sign
of our friendship and best wishes.
We ask this through Christ our Lord.

ALL   **Amen.**

give the gift you have prepared

LEADER   In joy, God gathered us together. In peace, God now
leads us along separate paths. Let us bow our heads
and pray for N____.

May almighty God keep you from harm
and bless you with every good gift.

ALL   **Amen.**

LEADER   May God's word abide in your heart
bringing you comfort and wisdom.

ALL   **Amen.**

LEADER   May your path be clear and joyous
and your heart strengthened by lasting friendships.

ALL   **Amen.**

LEADER   And may God bless all of us.

all make the sign of the cross

end with a song

Prayers for the Sick

Preparation: The following prayers can be used when someone in the community is sick. The first, Theotokos, is a communal prayer. The two following can be said by a group or copied and given out to pray at home.

Music options: All Will Be Well (1), Hear Us, O God/Óyenos, Señor (10)

Theotokos

Theotokos, which means "God-bearing" is the title given to Mary, the mother of God. In the year 431 the Church Fathers from both the East and the West gathered at the Council of Ephesus and officially honored Mary with this title. Devotion to Mary as the Mother of God is reflected in art, sculpture, and stained-glass windows. We continue to ask her to intercede for us, especially in times of sickness and death.

LEADER Let us begin our prayer.

 all make the sign of the cross

LEADER Holy Mary, Mother of God,
pray for all who are sick,
especially N____.

LEADER	ALL
Mother of Mercy,	**pray for them.**
Mother of Light,	**pray for them.**
Mother of the Savior,	**pray for them.**
Mother of the Good Shepherd,	**pray for them.**
Mother of the Church,	**pray for them.**

LEADER Lord God, through the prayers of Mary, our Mother,
bring your healing presence
to all who are sick, injured, or troubled.
We ask this through Christ our Lord.

ALL **Amen.**

LEADER You see our troubles, Lord;
you know our suffering.
In your mercy strengthen all the sick
especially N____.
Ease their pain,
heal their bodies,
relieve their loneliness,
and calm their fears.

Let them know you are always near,

their healer and redeemer.

We ask this through Christ our Lord.

ALL   **Amen.**

⠿ all make the sign of the cross

Strength to the Weary

LEADER   Let us say:

The Lord gives strength to those who are weary.

ALL   **The Lord gives strength to those who are weary.**

LEADER   Even young people get tired,

then stumble and fall.

But those who trust the Lord

will find new strength.

They will be strong like eagles

soaring upward on wings;

they will walk and run without getting tired.

The Lord gives strength to those who are weary.

ALL   **The Lord gives strength to those who are weary.**

Amen.

This prayer is taken from the book of the prophet Isaiah (40:29–31). He wrote during a time of disaster and suffering for the people of Israel. He wrote words of comfort and hope. He encouraged the people to trust God and to endure.

Prayer of Saint Augustine (adapted)

LEADER   Watch, O Lord, with those who wake,

or watch or weep tonight.

Tend your sick ones.

Rest your weary ones.

Bless your dying ones.

Soothe your suffering ones.

Pity your afflicted ones,

for your love's sake, O Lord Christ.

ALL   **Amen.**

This prayer can be put on a card and taken for use as a regular part of evening prayer. Remind the students that the nighttime is usually the most difficult time for the very ill and for people with great anxieties.

Prayer When a Person in the School Community Dies

Preparation: If the whole school participates and is in a large gathering space, the sharing of memories can be organized. If the ceremony is in a classroom or small chapel, however, the sharing can be spontaneous.

Select a leader and a reader.

Music options: Come, All You Blessed Ones (5), Jesus, Remember Me/Cristo, Recuérdame (13), All Will Be Well (1)

♩ begin and end with a song

LEADER   **Let us begin our prayer**

 all make the sign of the cross

LEADER   Today we gather to pray for our sister/brother, N____, who has been called in death. Our loving God, rich in mercy, has opened wide the gates of paradise, offering her/him rest and lasting joy. Let us all say, Blessed be God for ever.

ALL   **Blessed be God for ever.**

READER   Listen to the words of the holy Gospel according to John   11:20, 21–26

When Martha heard that Jesus had arrived, she went out to meet him. Martha said to Jesus, "Lord, if you had been here, my brother would not have died. Yet even now I know that God will do anything you ask."

Jesus told her, "Your brother will live again!"

Martha answered, "I know that he will be raised to life on the last day, when all the dead are raised."

Jesus then said, "I am the one who raises the dead to life! Everyone who has faith in me will live, even if they die. And everyone who lives because of faith in me will never really die. Do you believe this?"

A shrine of remembrance is a way to honor a person who has died.

When a member of the school community dies, whether a teacher or a student or a member of the staff, the class can help prepare a simple shrine of remembrance. A picture of the person who has died might be surrounded with a few things that were identified with them, such as the teacher's pencil or mug, or the crossing guard's whistle. Flowers, cards, or decorations that are added can be given to the family of the deceased friend after the ceremony.

Assembling the shrine provides an opportunity for conversation about the deceased friend and a way of sharing sorrow or sadness. It also allows students to learn more about Christian beliefs regarding death and resurrection, and local customs for burying and honoring the dead.

It is good to allow children an opportunity to join in prayer when a member of the school community dies.

"Yes, Lord!" she replied. "I believe that you are Christ, the Son of God. You are the one we hoped would come into the world."

The Gospel of the Lord.

ALL   **Praise to you, Lord Jesus Christ.**

LEADER   It is good to remember those who have been part of our lives, and to pray for people whose work and interest have helped to make this school a good place for us. Let us share some of our memories of N____.

allow those present time to speak

LEADER   God of mercy,
receive our friend, N____,
forgive her/his sins,
and welcome her/him
into the company of your angels and saints
who share in your glorious kingdom.
We ask this through Christ our Lord.

ALL   **Amen.**

LEADER   Eternal rest grant unto her/him, O Lord.

ALL   **And let perpetual light shine upon her/him.**

LEADER   May she/he rest in peace.

ALL   **Amen.**

LEADER   May her/his soul
and the souls of all the faithful departed,
through the mercy of God,
rest in peace.

ALL   **Amen.**

The loss, the grieving, and the mystery of death do not belong to adults alone.

This prayer includes a sharing of memories. These words can be spoken by adults and children. Relatives of the deceased may appreciate an oportunity to speak about how much the school community meant to their family member.

Prayer before Studying or Making a Presentation

LEADER	O God, come to my assistance.
ALL	**O Lord, make haste to help me.**

LEADER	Let us all take a moment to be silent.

allow a few moments for everyone to quiet

LEADER	Let us pray.
ALL	**Let my words and my thoughts be pleasing to you, Lord, because you are a mighty rock and my protector. Amen.**

Psalm 19:14

Prayer before an Examination

LEADER	O God, come to my assistance.
ALL	**O Lord, make haste to help me.**

LEADER	Let us all take a moment to be silent.

allow a few moments for everyone to quiet

LEADER	Come, Holy Spirit, be light to my mind and peace to my soul, that I may work with confidence and be successful in this time of testing. To you be thanks and praise now and for ever.
ALL	**Amen.**

Prayer before a Sport Competition

LEADER Lord our God,
grant that we play with courage,
enthusiasm,
respect for opponents,
and obedience to the rules,
so that, win or lose,
we may bring honor to your name
now and forever.

ALL **Amen.**

Blessing before and during a Class Trip

LEADER Let us begin our prayer.

⁘ all make the sign of the cross

These prayers are useful before, during, and after field trips and outings of all kinds. They can also be used when a student or teacher is moving to another place.

TRAVELERS Loving God, source of all life and joy,
be with us as we travel,
make us respectful of those we meet,
grateful for those who offer hospitality,
patient and kind to one another,
alert to the wonders of your world,
and confident in new situations.
Remind us of your loving presence,
and bring us safely home.
We ask this through Christ our Lord.

ALL **Amen.**

LEADER Let us bow our heads and pray.

May the Lord bless us and keep us,
May the Lord's face shine upon us
and guide our feet into the way of peace.

ALL **Amen.**

Thanksgiving after a Journey

TRAVELERS   Blessed are you, Lord our God,
Creator of the earth and its wonders.
We thank you for our safe journey
and a place to call home.
Lead all of us along your paths in this life,
and gather us into your heavenly dwelling.
We ask this through Christ our Lord.
Amen.

Irish Blessing for Travelers

LEADER   May the road rise to meet you.
May the wind be always at your back.
May the sun shine warm upon your face;
the rains fall soft upon your fields
and, until we meet again,
may God hold you in the palm of his hand.

ALL   Amen.

Blessing of Food for Sharing

The Blessing of Food for Sharing can be used at any time of the year by a class preparing to eat food brought for a festive occasion.

Preparation: Place the basket or platter of food (fruit, cookies, or anything simple) where it can be seen. After the ritual, the food will be shared by everyone as a simple meal of friendship. Adapt the prayer for birthday treats or other treats brought by parents.

Music option: For Your Gracious Blessing (8), We Bring God's Holy Love (25)

 begin and end with a song

LEADER   Let us begin our prayer.

 all make the sign of the cross

LEADER	Blessed be the name of the Lord,
	now and for ever.
ALL	**Amen.**

LEADER	Bless, O Lord, this fruit of your good earth
	and the work of human hands.
	It comes to us through your grace
	and the loving care of many people (or N____).
	As we share this food,
	make us joyful today.
	For this food is a sign of your greatest gift:
	your Son Jesus who redeems us in faith
	and your Holy Spirit who unites us in hope.
	Let this gathering be a taste of your kingdom,
	where all things are transformed by love.
	We ask this through Christ our Lord.
ALL	**Amen.**

all make the sign of the cross

Blessing of Gifts for Giving

THANKSGIVING AND THROUGHOUT THE YEAR

Preparation: Gather around the food, clothing, or other gifts you have collected. If that is not possible, place a portion of the gifts where they can be seen. Fill in the blank lines in the blessing with a description of the gifts. Adapt the prayer according to the gifts you have prepared and the people who will receive them.

Select a leader and a reader.

Music options: For Your Gracious Blessing (8), We Bring God's Holy Love (25), or a familiar hymn such as Now Thank We All Our God

♩ begin and end with a song

LEADER   Let us begin our prayer.

all make the sign of the cross

> There are several times during the year when it is traditional to gather money, food, clothing, or other gifts for those in need. Collections are often part of our observance of Thanksgiving, Christmas, and Lent. Students preparing for the sacrament of Confirmation often are involved in a service project and collect items to give to others.

207

LEADER   Blessed be the name of the Lord,
          now and for ever.
ALL   **Amen.**

READER   Listen to the words of the prophet Joel   2:20–22, 26

The Lord works wonders
and does great things.
So tell the soil to celebrate
and wild animals to stop being afraid.
Grasslands are green again;
fruit trees and fig trees
are loaded with fruit.
My people, you will eat until you are satisfied.
Then you will praise me
for the wonderful things I have done.

The word of the Lord.
ALL   **Thanks be to God.**

LEADER   Loving God,
          in your goodness you have given us
          the food, clothing, and shelter
          that we need for life.
          You have given us family and friends
          to care for us.
          Now, because it is our turn to care for others,
          we have gathered (name the gifts)____.

          Let us lift up our hands in offering and pray.

          Merciful God, bless these gifts
          and bless the people who will receive them.
          Do not let these gifts
          be a cause of embarrassment
          but a source of joy and a sign of our respect.
          We ask this through Christ our Lord.
ALL   **Amen.**

all make the sign of the cross

Prayer at a Time of Great Joy

Preparation: Select a leader and five readers.

Music option: Come, Let Us Sing with Joy (6), Jubilate Servite (14), Sing Out, Earth and Skies (22), Sing to God with the Tambourine (23)

LEADER   Let us all say:
            The Lord has been good to us, and holy is his name.

ALL   **The Lord has been good to us, and holy is his name.**

LEADER   We bless and thank God
            for the gift that has been given to us.

        mention the reason for rejoicing

LEADER   Let us pray.

        allow a minute or two of silence

> This psalm of praise and thanksgiving is good for moments of great rejoicing, as at the birth of a sibling, recovery from serious illness, or the making of peace. The playing of instruments and bells, as the psalm mentions, would be appropriate, as is singing a joyful song.

READER ONE   Shout praises to the Lord!
            Praise God in his temple.
            Praise him in heaven, his mighty fortress.
        Psalm 150

READER TWO   Praise our God!
            His deeds are wonderful,
            too marvelous to describe.

READER THREE   Praise God with trumpets
            and all kinds of harps.

READER FOUR   Praise him with tambourines and dancing,
            with stringed instruments and woodwinds.

READER FIVE   Praise God with cymbals, with clashing cymbals.
            Let every living creature praise the Lord.

LEADER   Shout praises to the Lord!
            The Lord has been good to us, and holy is his name.

ALL   **The Lord has been good to us, and holy is his name.**
            Amen. Alleluia!

Prayers for Sad Days

Preparation: These are prayers for sad days and other times of trouble. To pray as a group, begin with the sign of the cross, then read one of the three short readings from scripture (A through C), and end with the prayer and the sign of the cross.

Select a leader and a reader.

Music options: All Will Be Well (1), Come, All You Blessed Ones (5), Jesus, Remember Me/Cristo, Recuérdame (13), Shalom, My Friends (20)

♩ begin and end with a song

LEADER   Let us begin our prayer.

⁘ all make the sign of the cross

READER   choose A, B, or C

(A) Loving God,   *Psalm 27:13–14*
I know that I will live to see how kind you are.
Trust the Lord!
Be brave and strong,
and trust the Lord!

(B) The Lord says: *Psalm 91:15–16*
When you are in trouble, call out to me.
I will answer and be there
to protect and honor you.
You will live a long life
and see my saving power.

(C) The Lord says: *Isaiah 41:10*
Do not fear, for I am with you.
Do not be afraid, for I am your God;
I will strengthen you, I will help you,
I will hold you in my hand.

LEADER   Most holy and most merciful God,
strength of the weak,
rest for the weary,
comfort of the sorrowful,

Sad events often come upon us without warning. It is good to know some prayers by heart that we can silently pray whenever we need them. The three short readings from scripture used in this prayer are easy to memorize. Then they can be used at any time.

our refuge in every time of need:
grant us strength and protect us.
Support us in all dangers,
and carry us through all trials.
We ask this through Christ our Lord.

ALL   **Amen.**

⁘ all make the sign of the cross

Prayer after an Argument

Preparation: The teacher or other adult should be the leader; select a reader.

TEACHER   Let us gather together to pray.

READER   Listen to the words of the prophet Isaiah   2:15–16, 17

The Lord says this:
No matter how much you pray, I won't listen.
You are too violent.
Wash yourselves clean!
Stop doing wrong and learn to live right.
See that justice is done.
I, the Lord, invite you to come and talk it over.

The word of the Lord.

ALL   **Thanks be to God.**

keep a few minutes of silence

TEACHER   We may now speak of the wrong we have done and
the good we have not done, that regret may come
from the heart and forgiveness be freely given.

talk over what has happened

after a brief conversation,
reconciliation is signified by a hug or handshake

> Sometimes students forget themselves and get into an argument in the classroom or on the playground. It is sometimes left to an adult to help the angry students sort out their disagreement and their feelings. When the argument is over and things have been talked out, this prayer might be used to restore peace.

TEACHER	Gracious Lord,
	you are slow to anger, full of love,
	good in every way, merciful to every creature.
	Forgive our sins and heal our weakness,
	that we may praise you
	through Christ our Lord.
ALL	**Amen.**
TEACHER	Let us pray with the words that Jesus taught us.
ALL	**Our Father . . .**

all make the sign of the cross

Prayer for Peace

ATTRIBUTED TO SAINT FRANCIS OF ASSISI

Lord, make me an instrument of your peace:
where there is hatred, let me sow love;
where there is injury, pardon;
where there is doubt, faith;
where there is despair, hope;
where there is darkness, light;
where there is sadness, joy.

O divine Master,
grant that I may not so much seek
to be consoled as to console,
to be understood as to understand,
to be loved as to love.
For it is in giving that we receive,
it is pardoning that we are pardoned,
it is in dying that we are born to eternal life.

Prayer for Universal Peace

Preparation: Select a leader. Divide remaining students into Side A and side B.

Music option: Shalom, My Friends (20)

♩ begin and end with a song

LEADER   Let us begin our prayer.

⁘ all make the sign of the cross

LEADER   Loving God,
                teach us to be people of peace:

SIDE A   Teach us to love one another,
                that there may be peace in our families.

SIDE B   Teach us to strengthen one another,
                that there may be peace in our school.

SIDE A   Teach us to live and work justly,
                that there may be peace in our city.

SIDE B   Teach us to give equal respect and opportunity,
                that there may be peace in our nation.

SIDE A   Teach us to see that people in all countries
                have food, freedom, and safety
                that there may be peace in our world.

SIDE B   Teach us to be peacemakers
                in all that we do.

LEADER   Lord, teach us
                through the power of your Spirit,
                now and for ever.

ALL   **Amen.**

Our world is always in need of greater peace. We long for peace in our families, our school, our neighborhood, and our world, and yet we find it difficult to do those loving, forgiving, and generous things that can encourage peace to grow.

This is a prayer for those times when we have peace—and the lack of peace—on our minds.

Prayer in Time of War, National Crisis, or Natural Disaster

Preparation: Adapt the prayer to the occasion through the writing of an introduction, and the choice of alternate readings and intercessions. The prayer might be shortened for a group of younger children, or for children in a single classroom. If the children bring gifts for the victims, such as clothing for people who lost homes in a hurricane, these things can be brought in procession and blessed. If you wish to include the planting of flower bulbs as a sign of hope and resurrection, use parts of the prayer on page 12 (feasts of the angels).

Prepare gifts, drawings, flowers, prayer cards or some other memento. If the whole school gathers, each class can bring some item of remembrance to the central space.

Select three leaders (adults or older students) and a reader. Leader One should be an adult.

Music options: All Will Be Well (1), Hear Us, O God/Óyenos, Señor (10), Come, All You Blessed Ones (5)

♩ begin and end with a song

LEADER ONE   Let us begin our prayer.

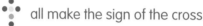 all make the sign of the cross

LEADER ONE   We have gathered today to remember in prayer . . .

name the event and say enough about it to direct the children's thoughts toward the needs of the people most affected by it, then continue

LEADER ONE   As we bring to the prayer table signs of remembrance and support for those who are suffering, let us sing of our faith in the power of God to comfort, to heal, and to renew.

♩ let all those gathered sing; let those with mementos or gifts come in procession to place them on the prayer table

LEADER ONE   May the almighty and all-loving God,
Father, Son and Holy Spirit,
bless and protect all those who suffer [who have died]
because of (name the event).
May God bless these signs of our solidarity with them.
We ask this through Christ our Lord.

ALL   **Amen.**

When a tragedy of great significance occurs, children need an opportunity to join trusted adults in praying about the event, and coming to understand its meaning. Therefore, either as part of the gathering for prayer, or before it, a "pastoral conversation" should be led by a teacher, priest, parent, or professional counselor. Once children have had a chance to have their questions answered candidly, and they have been able to express their feelings of sorrow, anger, or anxiety, they will be more able to reaffirm their faith in the healing power of God.

LEADER TWO	O God, come to our assistance.
ALL	**O Lord, make haste to help us.**

LEADER TWO	Let us all say, "The Lord is our protector, now and for ever."
ALL	**The Lord is our protector, now and for ever.**

LEADER TWO	I look to the hills! Where will I find help? It will come from the Lord, who created the heavens and the earth.
ALL	**The Lord is our protector, now and for ever.**

LEADER TWO	The Lord is your protector, and he won't go to sleep or let you stumble. The Lord is your protector, there at your right side.
ALL	**The Lord is our protector, now and for ever.**

LEADER TWO	The Lord will protect you and keep you safe from all dangers. The Lord will protect you now and always wherever you go.
ALL	**The Lord is our protector, now and for ever. Glory to the Father and to the Son and to the Holy Spirit as it was in the beginning, is now, and will be for ever. Amen.**

READER	Listen to the words of the apostle Paul to the Romans 8:38-39
	I am sure that nothing can separate us from God's love—not life or death, nor angels or spirits, not the present or the future, and not powers above or powers below. Nothing in all creation can separate us from God's love for us in Christ Jesus our Lord!
	The word of the Lord.
ALL	**Thanks be to God.**

LEADER THREE The Lord is good and listens to our prayers. Let us pray for those who need God's help.

select appropriate petitions from the following; add others as needed

LEADER THREE That those who have died
may rise with Christ on the last day, we pray:

ALL **Lord, hear our prayer.**

LEADER THREE That the families and friends of those who have died
may be comforted, we pray:

ALL **Lord, hear our prayer.**

LEADER THREE That the lost may be found
and the suffering healed, we pray:

ALL **Lord, hear our prayer.**

LEADER THREE That those who protect or rescue others
may be filled with courage and compassion, we pray:

ALL **Lord, hear our prayer.**

LEADER THREE That members of the armed services
may be kept under your protection, we pray:

ALL **Lord, hear our prayer.**

LEADER THREE That the victims of prejudice and war
may find justice, we pray:

ALL **Lord, hear our prayer.**

LEADER THREE That our troubled world
may come to know the peace that only you can give,
we pray:

ALL **Lord, hear our prayer.**

LEADER THREE May the peace of God,
which is beyond all understanding,
keep our hearts and minds
in the knowledge and love of God
and of his Son, our Lord Jesus Christ.

ALL **Amen.**

LEADER ONE   Let us pray with the words that Jesus taught us.
ALL   **Our Father . . .**

⚬ all make the sign of the cross

Prayer for Times of Crisis

LEADER   God our Father, source of our life,
              heal the suffering
              and comfort the brokenhearted.

       keep a brief silence

LEADER   Lord, in your mercy,
ALL   **Hear our prayer.**

LEADER   Lord Jesus Christ, source of our light,
              brighten our darkness
              and show us the path to safety and peace.

       keep a brief silence

LEADER   Lord, in your mercy,
ALL   **Hear our prayer.**

LEADER   Holy Spirit of God, source of our unity,
              bless our leaders with wisdom
              and our protectors with strength.

       keep a brief silence

LEADER   Lord, in your mercy,
ALL   **Hear our prayer.**

LEADER   Holy Trinity, One God,
be with us in this time of distress,
look with kindness on those in need of your mercy,
and bring us all into the joy of your kingdom.

keep a brief silence

LEADER   Lord, in your mercy,
ALL   **Hear our prayer.**
Amen.

Prayer to the Blessed Virgin Mary in Times of Need

LEADER   In our time of need, let us ask the prayers of Mary,
mother of all the living:
We turn to you for protection,
holy Mother of God.
Listen to our prayers
and help us in our needs.
Save us from every danger,
glorious and blessed Virgin.
ALL   **Amen.**

ALL   **Remember, most loving Virgin Mary,**
never was it heard
that anyone who turned to you for help
was left unaided.
Inspired by this confidence,
though burdened by my sins,
I run to your protection
for you are my mother.
Mother of the Word of God,
do not despise my words of pleading
but be merciful and hear my prayer.
Amen.

Prayers for the Jewish People

Prayer at Rosh Hashanah

Preparation: Cut apples so that each person in the group will have a slice. Prepare a bowl of honey for dipping and some napkins.

Music option: Shalom, My Friends (20)

 begin with a song

LEADER Bless, O Lord, your Jewish children
who this day celebrate Rosh Hashanah,
the beginning of a new year.
With them we praise and thank you
for the days and years
that you have given us.
Grant life, peace, and joy
to those who keep this day of beginnings.

take a slice of apple, dip it in honey, and say

LEADER Thank you, God, for the fruit of the trees.
We pray that the new year
will be a sweet and happy one for all.

ALL   **Amen.**

pass the plate of apples and the bowl of honey to all present, and enjoy the sweetness

 when all have eaten, end with a song

Rosh Hashanah is the beginning of the new year on the Jewish calendar. It occurs in the autumn. In each Jewish meeting place, a shofar, which is a ram's horn, is blown like a trumpet to call Jews to remember the past year and to practice their faith even better during the coming year. It is customary to welcome the new year by dipping slices of apple into a bowl of honey and wishing everyone a sweet new year.

The Jewish year 5761 began in the autumn of the Christian millennium year 2000. Can you figure out what next year will be on the Jewish calendar?

Prayer at Yom Kippur

Yom Kippur, the Day of Atonement, ends the ten-day period of repentance and reflection that begins with Rosh Hashanah. Yom Kippur, the holiest day of the Jewish liturgical year, is given entirely to penance and reconciliation. This is so important to the Jewish community that they do not work or travel on this day. Everything is quiet so that each person can spend the day in prayer and fasting, and in making peace with God.

LEADER   Bless, O Lord, your Jewish children
who this day
keep the Day of Atonement.
We join them in asking
for your mercy and forgiveness.
Open our eyes to see our mistakes.
Open our hearts to those who ask our forgiveness,
and teach us to walk by the light of your truth,
now and for ever.

ALL   **Amen.**

♩ end with a song

Prayer during Hanukkah

Hanukkah celebrates a miracle that occurred in Jerusalem many years before Jesus was born. After the Jewish people defeated an invading army, they had to rebuild the Temple and rededicate it to the worship of God. (The Hebrew word for dedication is "hanukkah.") There was only enough oil to light the great menorah for one day, but the light kept burning for eight days, when more oil could be obtained.

On each of the eight days of Hanukkah, the family lights one more of the candles on their menorah. Hanukkah is a happy celebration, with gifts, special foods and songs, and visits from relatives.

Preparation: Help the students to understand the significance of this day by showing them a menorah. Like the candles on an Advent wreath, the menorah candles remind the faithful of God's saving acts.

The Hanukkah prayer might be added to morning prayer around the Advent wreath.

LEADER   Bless, O Lord, your Jewish children
who keep the festival of Hanukkah.
As the menorah candles
recall your acts of saving love,
so may you always be a steady light
for the children of Israel,
giving hope in times of darkness,
now and for ever.

ALL   **Amen.**

Prayer at the Time of Passover

Preparation: Help the students to understand the significance of this day by reminding them that many times in history the Jewish people have had to leave their homes and the countries where they were raised. They hold their freedom as a treasured gift from God.

Music option: Shalom, My Friends (20)

LEADER   Bless, O Lord, your Jewish children
who this year keep the holy season of Passover.
With unleavened bread and bitter herbs
they remember times of suffering and slavery.
As once you led them safely through the sea,
and sealed your love for them at Sinai,
so now gladden their hearts,
and strengthen them in freedom.
Protect them in their homes
around the world,
now and for ever.

ALL   **Amen.**

♩ end with a song

The feast of Passover, called "Pesach" (PAY-sock) in Hebrew, is a remembrance of the Exodus, when Moses led the enslaved Israelites out of Egypt to freedom. Passover lasts eight days. It begins with a ceremonial meal called a "seder" at which special foods are blessed and eaten, and prayers of thanksgiving are said.

Prayer on Holocaust Remembrance Day (Yom ha-Shoah)

Preparation: Help the students understand the significance of this day by explaining the nature of the Holocaust. The presentation should be appropriate to their age. The point is to help them see the importance of ending the cycle of racial and religious hatred, not to frighten or horrify them.

LEADER   God of mercy and compassion,
on this day of remembrance
open our eyes to the strengths of your chosen people,
and our hearts to their suffering.
Be close to them throughout the world;
shelter them from hatred,
protect them from danger,

Twelve days after Passover, many Jewish communities keep a day of remembrance of the Jews who died during World War II. It is important for all of us to remember that many Jews suffered horribly when supposedly Christian people destroyed their homes, took their property, and sent millions to starvation and death in concentration camps. It took centuries for such hatred to build up, and it will take many years to root it out entirely. Let us ask God to cleanse us and all people of religious and racial hatred so that the world may be a place of understanding, respect, and peace.

bring them comfort in sorrow,
and peace in their homeland.

Let us pray for the millions of Jews
who suffered and died for their faith:
Eternal rest grant unto them, O Lord,

ALL **And let perpetual light shine upon them.**

LEADER May they rest in peace.
ALL **Amen.**

LEADER May their souls
and the souls of all the faithful departed,
through the mercy of God,
rest in peace.
ALL **Amen.**

Other Jewish Holidays

On any of the Jewish holy days, we can join our Jewish brothers and sisters in spirit by saying the following prayer, which is based on the beginning of the "Shema," (sheh-MAH) which Jews pray at the beginning and end of each day.

Students may recognize the prayer because Jesus spoke about it. The prayer is taken from the words of Deuteronomy 6:4–5.

LEADER Hear, O Israel,
the Lord is our God,
the Lord is one!
Blessed be God's glorious kingdom for ever.
You shall love the Lord, your God,
with all your heart,
with all your soul,
and with all your strength.
Bless, O Lord,
our Jewish brothers and sisters
who keep the feast of (name the feast).
In your unfailing mercy
strengthen and shelter them
now and for ever.
ALL **Amen.**

Prayers for the Muslim People

Prayer at the Time of the Muslim New Year
(Awwal Muharram)

Preparation: Help the students count what year it is on the Muslim calendar. Help them do research on Muhammad, or tell them something about his life.

LEADER   God, most gracious and merciful,
bless your Muslim children
who welcome on this day
the beginning of a new year.
Comfort them as they mourn,
strengthen them as they renew their trust in you.
Grant them a year of joy and peace,
now and for ever.

ALL   **Amen.**

The new year begins with the first day of the month of *Muharram*. Because Muslims count time by the moon rather than the sun, their year is eleven or twelve days shorter than the Western year. This means that the first day of the Islamic year is constantly changing seasons.

Muhammad, the prophet Muslims revere, fled from the town of Mecca to Madinah because of threats against his life in the Western year 622. Muslims count that as "year one" on their calendar in the same way Christians begin counting with the birth of Christ.

Prayer for Ramadan

Preparation: Help the students to understand how this month of prayer and fasting is similar to the Christian Lent, and how it differs.

LEADER   God, most gracious and merciful,
bless your Muslim children
who are observing the holy time of Ramadan.
Grant them pardon and peace.
Strengthen them through fasting and prayer.
Draw their families closer together,
and open their hearts to the homeless,
so that their lives may be a blessing
now and for ever.

ALL   **Amen.**

During Ramadan Muslims set aside many activities and amusements so that they can give their attention to prayer and study. They try to be kind and friendly to everyone.

At sundown each day, Muslims celebrate a breaking of the fast *(iftar)* and a festive dinner is given for family, friends, and neighbors. In many communities Christians are invited to share *iftar* and dinner at the mosque during Ramadan.

Prayer at *Id al-Fit'r*

On the last day of Ramadan, people go outside to watch eagerly for the rising of the new moon. When the thin crescent is visible, the fasting of Ramadan is over! Then *Id al-Fit'r,* a three-day feast, begins. all Muslims try to go to the mosque for prayers, which are held outside when possible.

Id al-Fit'r is a time of festivity, joy, and peace after the hard work of Ramadan.

Preparation: Help the students learn about the role of special foods in Islam. What are Muslims forbidden to eat or drink? What are some Islamic customs for celebrating the end of Ramadan?

LEADER   God, most gracious and merciful,
                 bless your Muslim children
                 whose hearts are light
                 as they celebrate the great feast.
                 Rejoicing, they feed the hungry,
                 welcome the stranger,
                 and delight in the giving of gifts.
                 May their feasting
                 be a taste of the eternal banquet
                 you have prepared for those who love you,
                 and may their lives be nourished in peace
                 now and for ever.

ALL   **Amen.**

Prayer at the Feast of the Sacrifice *(Id al-Adha)*

All Muslims try to make a pilgrimage or *hajj* to the holy city of Mecca at least once in their lifetime. The shrine at Mecca is said to have been built by Abraham and his eldest son, Ishmael. The *hajj* is an important religious duty, one of the "five pillars" of Islam. Muslims try to be in Mecca on the day of *Id al-Adha,* a holy day honoring Abraham's willingness to sacrifice his son Ishmael to God.

Preparation: Help the students learn about the tradition of making a pilgrimage to holy sites. If they are old enough, they might do research about Mecca, the holy city for Muslims.

LEADER   God, most gracious and merciful,
                 bless your Muslim children
                 who, like us,
                 call Abraham their father.
                 Let all who put their trust in you,
                 the Holy One revealed to Abraham,
                 be united in love for the poor,
                 hospitality to the traveler,
                 and awe in your presence.
                 Blessed be God for ever.

ALL   **Amen.**

Part Three

Catholic Prayers

Sign of the Cross

The sign of the cross is traced on us when we are brought to be baptized and it is traced on us again when our bodies are prepared for burial. It is the first prayer we say when we rise each morning and the last we say before falling asleep. It is the sign that we belong, body and soul, to the God who created us, who saves us, and who loves us. It is a sign of our Christian belief in the Holy Trinity.

In the name of the Father, and of the Son,
and of the Holy Spirit. Amen.

The Our Father (The Lord's Prayer)

The Our Father, which we also call the Lord's Prayer, is Jesus' response to the apostles when they asked him how they should pray. All Christians pray the Our Father.

Our Father, who art in heaven,
hallowed be thy name;
thy kingdom come;
thy will be done on earth as it is in heaven.
Give us this day our daily bread;
and forgive us our trespasses
as we forgive those who trespass against us;
and lead us not into temptation,
but deliver us from evil. Amen.

Doxology (Glory Be)

This is a short prayer of praise. It is often used at the end of a psalm, or at the end of a decade of the rosary. It used to begin "Glory be to the Father . . ." and so it is sometimes called the "Glory Be." The word "doxology" means "words of praise," and Christian doxologies always name the three divine Persons of the Trinity. The last verse of some hymns is a doxology.

Glory to the Father, and to the Son,
and to the Holy Spirit:
as it was in the beginning, is now,
and will be for ever. Amen.

Apostles' Creed

I believe in God, the Father almighty,
creator of heaven and earth.
I believe in Jesus Christ, his only Son, our Lord.
He was conceived by the Holy Spirit
and born of the Virgin Mary.
He suffered under Pontius Pilate,
was crucified, died, and was buried.
He descended to the dead.
On the third day he rose again.
He ascended into heaven,
and is seated at the right hand of the Father.
He will come again to judge the living and the dead.
I believe in the Holy Spirit,
the holy catholic Church,
the communion of saints,
the forgiveness of sins,
the resurrection of the body,
and life everlasting. Amen.

A creed is a statement of what we believe. It is named from the Latin word "credo," which means "I believe." That is the way each creed begins. This prayer gives the basic truths of our faith. It has been used by the Christian community since at least the year 753. Creeds have been used at Baptism since the very earliest days of the Church.

Come, Holy Spirit

LEADER Come, Holy Spirit, fill the hearts of your faithful.
ALL **And kindle in them the fire of your love.**

LEADER Send forth your Spirit, and they shall be created,
ALL **And you will renew the face of the earth.**

LEADER Let us pray:
ALL **Lord, by the light of the Holy Spirit**
you have taught the hearts of your faithful.
In the same Spirit
help us to relish what is right
and always rejoice in your consolation.
We ask this through Jesus Christ our Lord. Amen.

This traditional prayer to the Holy Spirit is often said during the time between the feast of the Ascension and Pentecost. It is a good prayer to use whenever we are seeking guidance for ourselves, our community, or our world.

Act of Contrition

My God,
I am sorry for my sins with all my heart.
In choosing to do wrong
and failing to do good,
I have sinned against you
whom I should love above all things.
I firmly intend, with your help,
to do penance,
to sin no more,
and to avoid whatever leads me to sin.
Our Savior Jesus Christ
suffered and died for us.
In his name, my God, have mercy.
Amen.

The Hail Mary

No one person composed this important prayer. The Christian people came to use the greeting of the angel to Mary, "Hail, full of grace, the Lord is with you" in their daily prayer. Gradually Elizabeth's words of praise to Mary were added, "Blessed are you among women, and blessed is the fruit of your womb." The second part of the prayer was added during a great plague, when many people were dying and everyone was filled with fear and grief. It begins with a declaration of faith in Mary's motherhood of God and ends with the plea of her children that she pray for them at the time of their death.

Hail Mary, full of grace,
the Lord is with you.
Blessed are you among women,
and blessed is the fruit of your womb, Jesus.
Holy Mary, mother of God,
pray for us sinners now,
and at the hour of our death.
Amen.

The Angelus

Traditionally the Angelus, a prayer of three verses, each followed by the Hail Mary, was said when the church bells tolled at 6 a.m., 12 noon, and 6 p.m. Look for a print of Jean François Millet's famous painting The Angelus.

V.   The angel spoke God's message to Mary,
R.   **and she conceived of the Holy Spirit**

V.   Hail Mary . . .
R   **Holy Mary . . .**

V.   "I am the lowly servant of the Lord:
R.   **let it be done to me according to your word."**

V.   Hail Mary . . .
R.   **Holy Mary . . .**

V.   And the Word became flesh
R.   **and lived among us.**

V.   Hail Mary . . .
R.   **Holy Mary . . .**

V.   Pray for us, holy Mother of God,
R.   **that we may become worthy of the promises of Christ.**

Let us pray.
Lord fill our hearts with your grace:
once, through the message of an angel
you revealed to us the incarnation of your Son;
now, through his suffering and death
lead us to the glory of his resurrection.

We ask this through Christ our Lord.
R.   **Amen.**

229

The Magnificat

My soul proclaims the greatness of the Lord,
My spirit rejoices in God my Savior;
For he has looked with favor on his lowly servant.
From this day all generations will call me blessed:
the Almighty has done great things for me,
and holy is his Name.
He has mercy on those who fear him
in every generation.
He has cast down the mighty from their thrones,
and has lifted up the lowly.
He has filled the hungry with good things,
and the rich he has sent away empty.
He has come to the help of his servant Israel
for he has remembered his promise of mercy,
the promise he made to our fathers,
to Abraham and his children forever.

This prayer is called a "canticle," which means that it is a psalm or hymn. According to the Gospel of Luke, these words were said by Mary when her cousin Elizabeth blessed her and the baby she would bear. In every age Christians have repeated the words of Mary as the sun sets and evening begins.

The Memorare

Remember, most loving Virgin Mary,
never was it heard
that anyone who turned to you for help
was left unaided.
Inspired by this confidence,
though burdened by my sins,
I run to your protection
for you are my mother.
Mother of the word of God,
do not despise my words of pleading
but be merciful and hear my prayer.
Amen.

Tradition tells us that this prayer was composed by Saint Bernard in the twelfth century. The title means "remember" in the Latin language.

The Hail, Holy Queen

Hail, holy Queen, mother of mercy,
our life, our sweetness, and our hope.
To you we cry, the children of Eve;
to you we send up our sighs,
mourning and weeping in this land of exile.
Turn, then, most gracious advocate,
your eyes of mercy toward us;
lead us home at last
and show us the blessed fruit of your womb, Jesus:
O clement, O loving, O sweet Virgin Mary.

The Rosary

How to Pray the Rosary: The prayers are divided into groups of ten, called "decades." Most people use a string of beads that counts out five decades. The rosary begins with the Apostles' Creed, the Our Father and three Hail Marys. Then each decade is introduced by an Our Father, followed by ten Hail Marys, and ends with the Doxology. When five decades are finished, the Hail, Holy Queen is said.

As we pray each decade, we think about a "mystery" or moment of grace in the plan of God. There are fifteen traditional mysteries and five new ones added in 2002 by Pope John Paul II. The mysteries help us to think about the revelation of God's love that is shown to us in Jesus.

The Joyful Mysteries (the incarnation and birth of the Son of God)
1. Annunciation: Mary learns that she will become the mother of God. Luke 1:26–38
2. Visitation: Mary and Elizabeth visit and tell about God's wonders. Luke 1:39–58
3. Nativity: Jesus is born in a stable. Luke 2:5–16
4. Presentation: Mary and Joseph take the infant Jesus to the Temple, and they meet Simeon and Anna. Luke 2:27–38
5. Finding of Jesus in the Temple: Mary and Joseph lose Jesus, then find him teaching. Luke 2:47–52

The Luminous Mysteries (the public ministry of Jesus)
1. Baptism of Christ in the Jordan: God's son is prepared for his mission by the Holy Spirit. Matthew 3:13–17
2. Wedding at Cana: Jesus reveals the kingdom through his saving acts. John 2:1–10
3. Preaching of Jesus: Jesus proclaims the kingdom of God and calls everyone to conversion. Mark 1:14–15
4. Transfiguration: Jesus is the light of the world; listen to him. Matthew 17:1–5
5. Institution of the Eucharist: Jesus gives himself to his followers. 1 Corinthians 11:23–26

The rosary (from the Latin for "rose garden") is a bouquet of prayers repeated so that the person can put aside all distractions and remain attentive to God's presence. People like repeating prayers when they cannot use a book, such as when they are cooking or walking or sick, or when they are praying before they fall asleep at night. When the rosary is said, it is always understood as prayer offered to God, with devotion to the Blessed Mother. A string of beads or knots can be used to count the prayers. The prayers that are part of the rosary are: the Apostles' Creed, the Our Father, the Hail Mary and the doxology (Glory Be).

In the beginning, many Christians said the 150 psalms, but as time went on and fewer of them could read, they said 150 Our Fathers instead. During the twelfth century they added the angel's greeting to

Mary ("Hail Mary, full of grace . . ."), and then Elizabeth's greeting ("Blessed are you among women. . . ."). Finally, during a time of plague, the "Holy Mary" sentence was added, and the prayer we call the "Hail Mary" was complete.

The Sorrowful Mysteries (the suffering and death of Jesus)

1. Agony in the garden: Jesus prays about the suffering he will go through. Luke 22:39–46
2. Scourging at the pillar: Soldiers whip Jesus. John 19:1
3. Crowning with thorns: Soldiers mock Jesus. Mark 15:16–17
4. Carrying of the cross: Jesus goes through the streets of Jerusalem to Calvary. John 19:17
5. Crucifixion: Jesus is crucified and dies on the cross. Luke 23:33–46

The Glorious Mysteries (the triumph of Jesus the Christ, and those joined to him)

1. Resurrection: God raises Jesus from death to life. Mark 16:5–7
2. Ascension: Jesus enters into divine glory. Acts 1:6–11
3. Coming of the Holy Spirit: The church is filled with God's courage and guidance. Acts 2:1–4
4. Assumption of Mary: She is the first to share in the resurrection of Jesus. Acts 15:20–21
5. Coronation of Mary: The Mother of God becomes queen of heaven. Revelation 12:1

Songs

A Note about Copying the Music

Purchasing this resource does not grant permission to reprint all of the material it contains. It is illegal to reproduce copyrighted text and music without the permission of the copyright owner or licensing agent. In justice to the authors, composers, and employees of publishing companies, permission must be secured in order to photocopy any of the songs included in this resource.

The copyright holder or licensing agent is named at the bottom of each song. Mailing addresses are provided here. When you write for permission, tell them which song, how many copies you want to make, and what you will be using them for. Each of the copyright holders and licensing agents has allowed their song to be included here trusting that parish and school staff members will act justly and lawfully.

Concordia Publishing
3558 South Jefferson Avenue
St. Louis MO 63118-3968

Estate of Roland Ford Palmer
c/o Reverend Peter D. Wilkinson
25 Government
Unit 209
Victoria BC V8V 2K4

GIA Publications
7404 S. Mason Avenue
Chicago IL 60638

Hope Publishing Company
380 S. Main Place
Carol Stream IL 60188

ICEL
1522 K Street NW
Washington DC 20005

Oregon Catholic Press
5536 NE Hassalo
Portland OR 97213

Selah Publishing Company
4143 Brownsville Road
Suite 2
Pittsburgh PA 15227

Walton Music
c/o Hal Leonard
7777 W. Bluemound Road
Milwaukee WI 53212

World Library Publications (WLP)
3825 N. Willow Road
Schiller Park IL 60176

Song number	Title	Vocal CD Track number	Accompaniment CD Track number
1	All Will Be Well	1	1
2	Awake, Awake and Greet the New Morn	2	2
3	Bless Us, O Lord	3	3
4	Celtic Alleluia	4	4
5	Come, All You Blessed Ones	5	5
6	Come, Let Us Sing with Joy	6	6
7	From Ashes to the Living Font	7	7
8	For Your Gracious Blessing	8	8
9	Go Now in Peace	9	9
10	Hear Us, O God / Óyenos, Señor	10	10
11	If Today You Hear the Voice of God	11	11
12	In the Lord I'll Be Ever Thankful	12	12
13	Jesus, Remember Me/ Cristo, Recuérdame (English)	13	13
13	Jesus, Remember Me/ Cristo, Recuérdame (Spanish)	14	13
14	Jubilate Servite	15	14
15	Joy to the World	16	15
16	Lenten Gospel Acclamation	17	16
17	Lift High the Cross	18	17
18	Oh, How Good Is Jesus Christ!/ ¡Oh, Que Bueno Es Jesús! (English)	19	18
18	Oh, How Good Is Jesus Christ!/ ¡Oh, Que Bueno Es Jesús! (Spanish)	20	18
19	Send Forth Your Spirit, O Lord	21	19
20	Shalom, My Friends	22	20
21	Sing of Mary	23	21
22	Sing Out, Earth and Skies	24	22
23	Sing to God with the Tambourine	25	23
24	This Day God Gives Me	26	24
25	We Bring God's Holy Love	27	25
26	We Are Marching in the Light of God/ Siyahamba	28	26
27	We Sing of the Saints	29	27

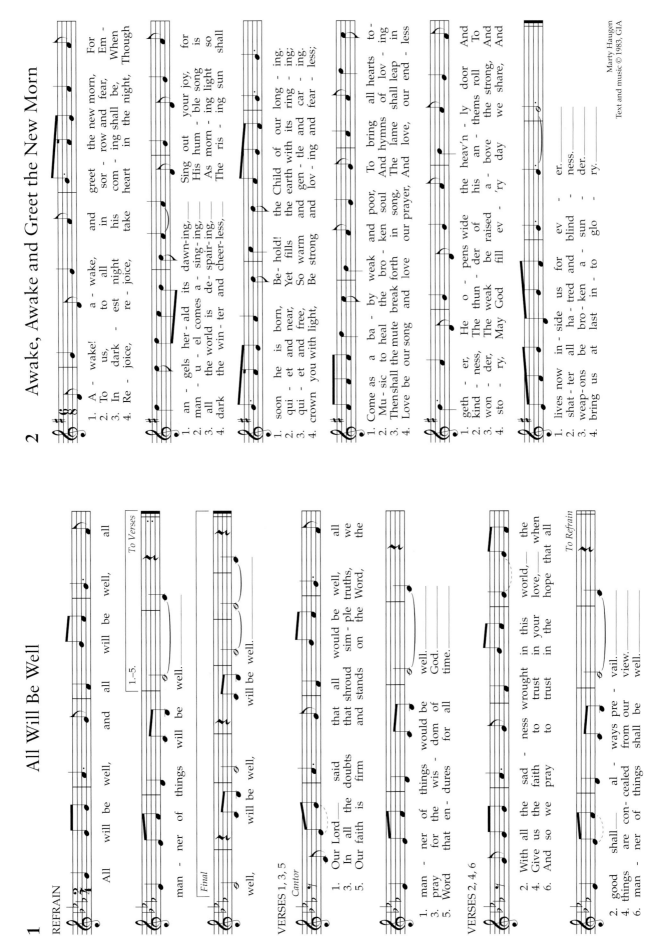

2 Awake, Awake and Greet the New Morn

Marty Haugen
Text and music © 1983, GIA

REFRAIN

1 All Will Be Well

The Revelations of Divine Love, Chapter 32
Julian of Norwich, c. 1342–c. 1416
Adapt. by Steven C. Warner

Steven C. Warner
Text and music © 1993, WLP

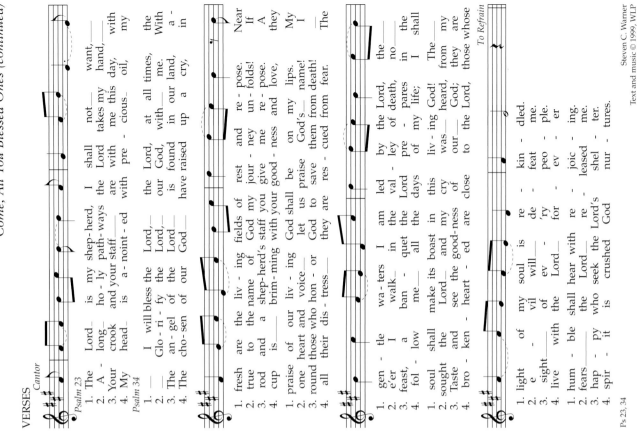

Come, All You Blessed Ones (continued)

VERSES
Cantor

Psalm 23
1. The Lord is my shep-herd, I shall not want, the
2. A - long ho-ly path-ways the Lord takes me this day, with
3. Your crook and your staff are with me. With
4. My head is a-noint - ed with pre - cious oil, my

Psalm 34
1. — I will bless the Lord, the Lord, our God, at all times,
2. The Glo-ri-fy the Lord, the Lord With
3. The an - gel of the Lord is found in our land, a -
4. The cho-sen of our God have raised up a cry, in

1. fresh are the liv-ing fields of rest and re - pose. Near
2. true to the name of God my jour - ney un - folds! If
3. rod and a shep-herd's staff you give me re - pose. A
4. cup is — brim-ming with your good - ness and love, they

1. praise of our liv - ing God shall be on my lips. My
2. one heart and voice — let us praise God's — name! I
3. round those who hon - or God to save them from death! —
4. all their dis - tress — they are res - cued from fear. The

1. gen - tle wa - ters I am led by the Lord, the
2. e'er I walk in the val - ley of death, no
3. feast, a quet me all the Lord pre - pares in the
4. fol - low days of my life; I shall

1. soul shall make its boast in the liv - ing God! The
2. sought the Lord and my cry was heard, from my
3. Taste and see the good-ness of our God; they are
4. bro - ken heart - ed are close to the Lord, those whose

To Refrain

1. light of my soul is re - kin - dled.
2. e - vil will ev - er de - feat me.
3. sight with the Lord for ev - er peo - ple.
4. live with the Lord for ev - er

1. hum - ble shall hear with re - joic - ing.
2. fears shall the Lord re - leased me.
3. hap - py who seek the Lord's shel - ter.
4. spir - it is crushed God nur - tures.

Ps 23, 34

Steven C. Warner
Text and music © 1999, WLP

3

Bless Us, O Lord

Bless us, O Lord, and bless our ta - ble, Keep us u - nit-ed in your love.

Ron Lewinski
Text © 2003, WLP
Genevan Psalter, 1551
Attr. to Louis Bourgeois, c. 1510–1561

4

Celtic Alleluia

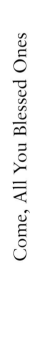

Al - le - lu - ia, al - le - lu - ia.

Al - le - lu - ia, al - le - lu - ia.

Fintan O'Carroll and Christopher Walker
Music © 1985, Fintan O'Carroll and Christopher Walker, pub. by OCP

5

Come, All You Blessed Ones

REFRAIN
Cantor/All

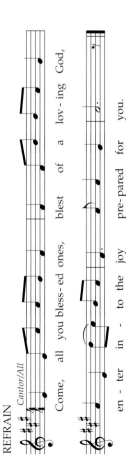

Come, all you bless-ed ones, blest of a lov - ing God,

en - ter in - to the joy pre-pared for you.

6

Come, Let Us Sing with Joy

REFRAIN

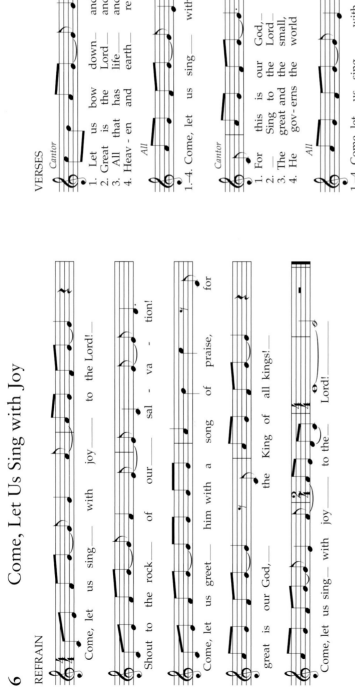

Come, let us sing with joy to the Lord! Shout to the rock of our sal - va - tion! Come, let us greet him with a song of praise, for great is our God, the King of all kings! Come, let us sing with joy to the Lord!

Come, Let Us Sing with Joy (continued)

VERSES

Cantor
1. Let us bow down and wor - ship the Lord:
2. Great is the Lord and wor - thy of praise:
3. All that has life and breath shall re - joice:
4. Heav - en and earth re - joice in his name:

All
1.–4. Come, let us sing with joy to the Lord!

Cantor
1. For this is our God, whose peo - ple we are:
2. Sing to the Lord and bless his name:
3. The great and the small, all crea - tures of God:
4. He gov - erns the world with jus - tice and truth:

All
1.–4. Come, let us sing with joy to the Lord!

To Refrain
1.–4. Come, let us sing with joy to the Lord!

Paul A. Tate
Music © 2001, WLP

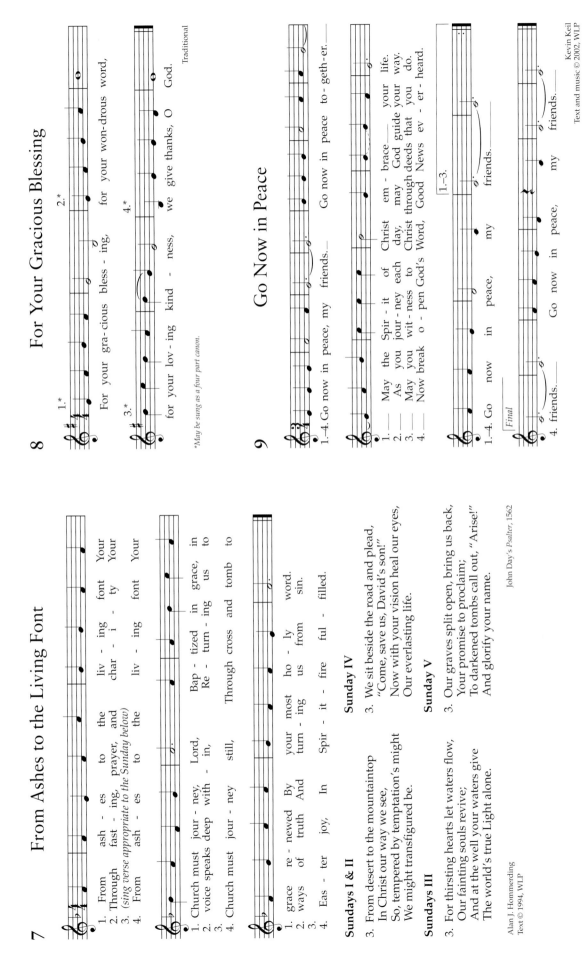

8 For Your Gracious Blessing

Traditional

*May be sung as a four part canon.

7 From Ashes to the Living Font

Sundays I & II
3. From desert to the mountaintop
In Christ our way we see,
So, tempered by temptation's might
We might transfigured be.

Sundays III
3. For thirsting hearts let waters flow,
Our fainting souls revive;
And at the well your waters give
The world's true Light alone.

Sunday IV
3. We sit beside the road and plead,
"Come, save us, David's son!"
Now with your vision heal our eyes,
Our everlasting life.

Sunday V
3. Our graves split open, bring us back,
Your promise to proclaim;
To darkened tombs call out, "Arise!"
And glorify your name.

Alan J. Hommerding
Text © 1994, WLP

9 Go Now in Peace

John Day's *Psalter*, 1562

Kevin Keil
Text and music © 2002, WLP

11   If Today You Hear the Voice of God

REFRAIN

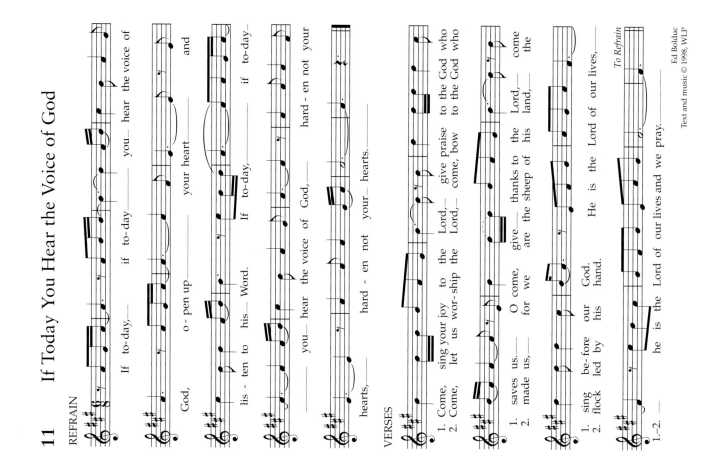

If to-day, if to-day you hear the voice of God, o-pen up your heart and lis-ten to his Word. If to-day, if to-day you hear the voice of God, hard-en not your hearts. you hear the voice of God, hard-en not your hearts.

VERSES

1. Come, sing your joy to the Lord, give praise to the God who
2. Come, let us wor-ship the Lord, come, bow to the God who

1. saves us. O come, give thanks to the Lord, come the
2. made us, for we are the sheep of his land, the

1. sing be-fore our God. He is the Lord of our lives,
2. flock led by his hand.

To Refrain

1.–2. he is the Lord of our lives and we pray.

Ed Bolduc
Text and music © 1998, WLP

10   Hear Us, O God/Óyenos, Señor

Cantor/Todos/All

Hear us, O God, hear our prayer,
Ó - ye - nos, Se - ñor, ó - ye - nos;

es - cu - cha nues - tra o - ra - ción.

Pedro Rubalcava
Text and music © 1994, WLP

12   In the Lord I'll Be Ever Thankful

In the Lord I'll be ev-er thank-ful, in the Lord   I will re-

joice!   Look to   God,   do   not   be   a - fraid;   lift   up your

voic - es, the Lord is   near;   lift   up your voic - es, the Lord is   near.

Taizé Community

Text and music © 1986, 1991, Les Presses de Taizé, GIA, agent

13   Jesus, Remember Me/Cristo, Recuérdame

OSTINATO

Je - sus,   re - mem-ber me   when you come in - to your King - dom.
Cris - to,   re - cuér - da - me   cuan - do   ven - gas en   tu   rei - no.

Je - sus,   re - mem-ber me   when you come in - to your King - dom.
Cris - to,   re - cuér - da - me   cuan - do   ven - gas en   tu   rei - no.

Jacques Berthier, 1923–1994

Text and music © 1984, Les Presses de Taizé, GIA, agent

14   Jubilate Servite

1.*
2.*

Ju - bi - la - te   De - o   om - nis ter - - ra.

Ser - vi - te   Do - mi - no   in   lae - ti - ti - a.

Al - le - lu - ia,   al - le - lu - ia,   in   lae - ti - ti - a.

Al - le - lu - ia,   al - le - lu - ia,   in   lae - ti - ti - a!

Jacques Berthier, 1923–1994

Music © 1979, Les Presses de Taizé, GIA, agent

*May be sung as a two-part canon.

Rejoice in God, all the earth. Serve the Lord with gladness.

17 Lift High the Cross

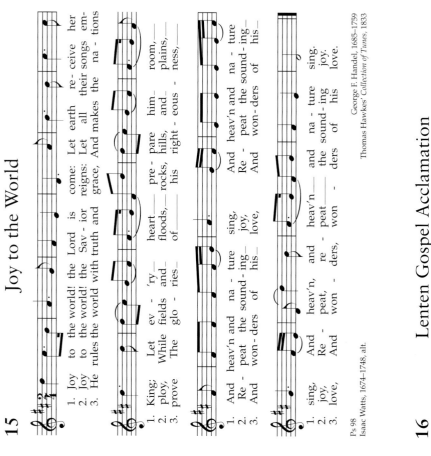

Lift high the cross, the love of Christ pro - claim, Till

all the world a - dore his sa - cred name.

1. Come, Chris - tians, fol - low where our Sav - ior trod, Our
2. Led on their way by this tri - um - phant sign, The
3. O Lord, once lift - ed on the glo - rious tree, As
4. So shall our song of tri - umph ev - er be: Praise
5.

D.C.

1. King vic - to - rious, Christ, the Son of God.
2. hosts of God in con - quering ranks com - bine.
3. on the brows the seal of him who died.
4. you have prom - ised, save us for vic - to - ry!
5. to the Cru - ci - fied!

George W. Kitchin, 1827–1912, alt.
Michael R. Newbolt, 1874–1956, alt.

Sydney H. Nicholson, 1875–1947
Text and music © 1974, Hope Publishing Co.

15 Joy to the World

1. Joy to the world! the Lord is come: Let earth re - ceive her
2. Joy to the world! the Sav - ior reigns: Let all their songs em -
3. He rules the world with truth and grace, And makes the na - tions

1. King; Let ev - 'ry heart pre - pare him room,
2. ploy; While fields and floods, rocks, hills, and plains,
3. prove The glo - ries of his right - eous - ness,

1. And heav'n and na - ture sing,
2. Re - peat the sound - ing joy,
3. And won - ders of his love,

1. And heav'n, and heav'n and na - ture sing.
2. Re - peat, re - peat the sound - ing joy.
3. And won - ders, won - ders of his love.

Ps 98
Isaac Watts, 1674–1748, alt.

George F. Handel, 1685–1759
Thomas Hawkes' *Collection of Tunes*, 1833

16 Lenten Gospel Acclamation

Praise to you, Word of God, Lord Je - sus Christ!

Text © 1969, ICEL

Charles Gardner
Music © 1992, 1993, WLP

18   Oh, How Good Is Jesus Christ!/
      ¡Oh, Que Bueno Es Jesús!

1. Oh, how good is Jesus Christ! On the cross for me he died.
1. ¡Oh, que bue - no es Je - sús! Que por mí mu - rió en la cruz.

1. On the third day he did rise. Glo-ry be to Je - sus!
1. Y en tres días re - su - ci - tó. ¡Y a su nom - bre glo - ria!

1. Glo-ry be to Je - sus! ¡Y a su nom - bre glo - ria!

1. On the third day he did rise. Glo-ry be to Je - sus!
1. Y en tres días re - su - ci - tó. ¡Y a su nom - bre glo - ria!

2. From my sin he set me free,
   Promised life eternally.
   Saved my soul and rescued me.
   Glory be to Jesus!
   Glory be to Jesus!
   Glory be to Jesus!
   Saved my soul and rescued me.
   Glory be to Jesus!

3. To the Lord my prayer I bring,
   To the Lord my song I sing.
   And my heart I'm offering.
   Glory be to Jesus!
   Glory be to Jesus!
   Glory be to Jesus!
   And my heart I'm offering.
   Glory be to Jesus!

2. Del pecado me libró.
   La vida me prometió.
   El mi alma rescató.
   ¡Y a su nombre gloria!
   ¡Y a su nombre gloria!
   ¡Y a su nombre gloria!
   El mi alma rescató.
   ¡Y a su nombre gloria!

3. Al que escucha mi oración
   yo le canto mi canción.
   Yo le dí mi corazón.
   ¡Y a su nombre gloria!
   ¡Y a su nombre gloria!
   ¡Y a su nombre gloria!
   Yo le dí mi corazón.
   ¡Y a su nombre gloria!

Traditional Puerto Rican
English translation © 2003, WLP

Traditional Puerto Rican melody

19   Send Forth Your Spirit, O Lord

REFRAIN

Send forth your Spir - it, O Lord, and re - new the
face of the earth.   Send forth your Spir - it, O
Lord, and re - new the face of the earth.

VERSES
Cantor

1. Bless the Lord, O my soul,   Lord
2. Lord, my God, great are your works!   In
3. All of your crea - tures look to you,   to

1. God, how great you are,
2. wis - dom made them all.   You
3. give them their food in time.

1. wrapped in a gar - ment of glo - ry and might,
2. Rich is the earth and filled with your life.
3. give with a - bun-dance, they gath - er it up,

                                    To Refrain

1. clothed in light as in a robe.
2. Bless the Lord, O my soul!
3. by your hands they have their fill.

Steven C. Warner
Text and music © 1996, WLP

Ps 104

21 Sing of Mary

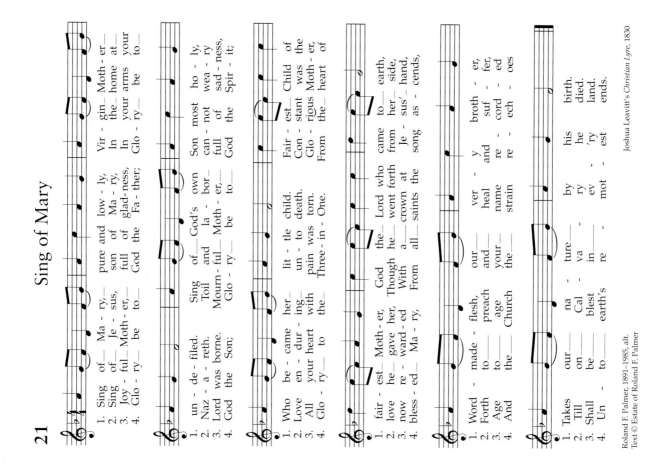

1. Sing of Ma - ry, pure and low - ly, Vir - gin Moth - er
2. Sing of Je - sus, son of Ma - ry, In the home at
3. Joy - ful Moth - er, full of glad - ness, In your arms your
4. Glo - ry be to God the Fa - ther; Glo - ry be to

1. un - de - filed. Sing of God's own Son most ho - ly,
2. Naz - a - reth. Toil and la - bor can - not wea - ry
3. Lord was borne. Mourn - ful Moth - er, full of sad - ness,
4. God the Son; Glo - ry be to God the Spir - it;

1. Who be - came her lit - tle child. Fair - est Child of
2. Love en - dur - ing un - to death. Con - stant was the
3. All your heart with pain was torn. Glo - rious Moth - er, of
4. Glo - ry to the Three - in - One. From the heart of

1. fair - est Moth - er, God the Lord who came to earth,
2. love he gave her, Though he went forth from her side,
3. now re - ward - ed With a crown at Je - sus' hand,
4. bless - ed Ma - ry, From all saints the song as - cends,

1. Word - made - flesh, our ver - y broth - er,
2. Forth to preach, and heal, and suf - fer,
3. Age to age, your name re - cord - ed
4. And the Church the strain re - ech - oes

1. Takes our na - ture by his birth.
2. Till on Cal - va - ry he died.
3. Shall be blest in ev - er - mot - land.
4. Un - to earth's re - mot - est ends.

Roland F. Palmer, 1891–1985, alt.
Text © Estate of Roland F. Palmer

Joshua Leavitt's *Christian Lyre*, 1830

20 Shalom, My Friends

Sha - lom, my friends! Sha - lom, my friends! Sha - lom! Sha - lom!
Sha - lom cha - ve - rim, sha - lom cha - ve - rim. Sha - lom, sha - lom.

God's peace be with you! God's peace be with you! Sha - lom!
Sha - lom cha - ve - rim, sha - lom cha - ve - rim. Sha - lom,
sha - lom.

Traditional Hebrew text
Tr. by Theodore Wuerffel
Tr. © 1973, Concordia Publishing House

This tune may be sung as a round at the distance of one measure.
The original text of the second phrase is "Lehitraot, lehitraot, shalom, shalom."

Traditional Hebrew melody

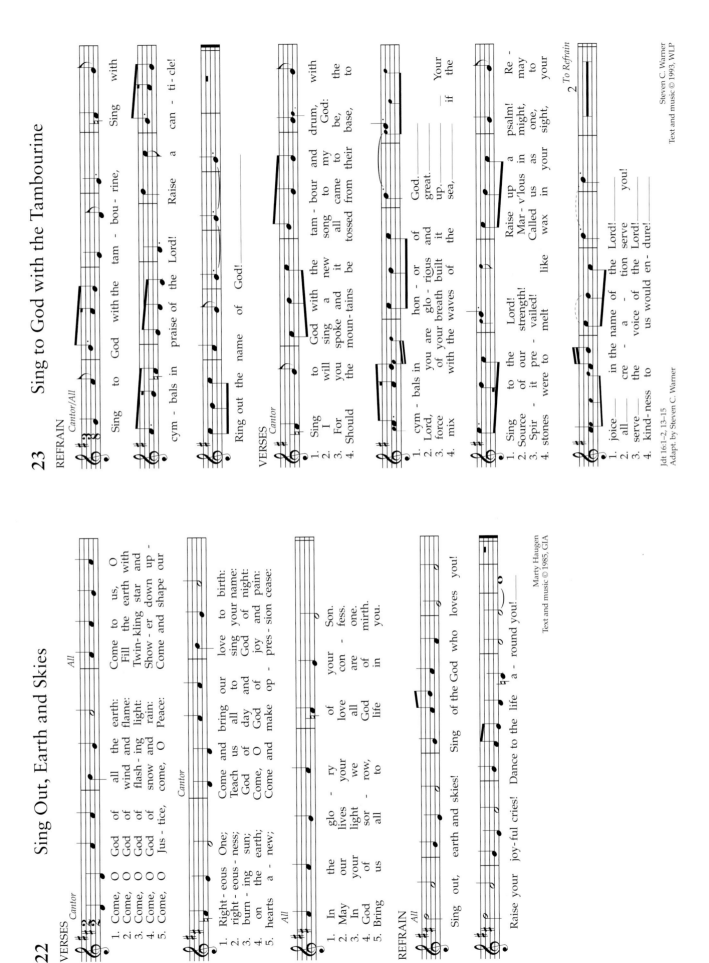

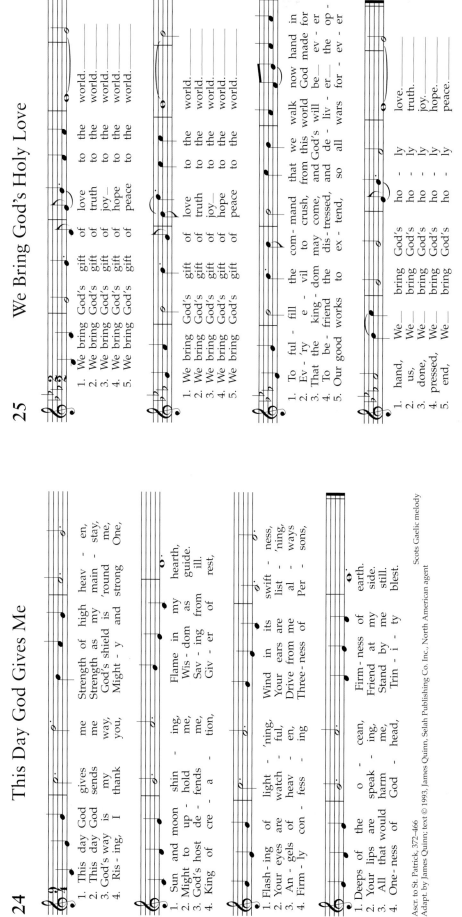

25 We Bring God's Holy Love

1. We bring God's gift of love to the world.
2. We bring God's gift of truth to the world.
3. We bring God's gift of joy to the world.
4. We bring God's gift of hope to the world.
5. We bring God's gift of peace to the world.

1. We bring God's gift of love to the world.
2. We bring God's gift of truth to the world.
3. We bring God's gift of joy to the world.
4. We bring God's gift of hope to the world.
5. We bring God's gift of peace to the world.

1. To ful-fill the com-mand that we walk now hand in
2. Ev-'ry e-vil to crush, from this world God made for
3. That the king-dom may come, and God's will be ev-er
4. To be-friend the dis-tressed, and de-liv-er the op-
5. Our good works to ex-tend, so all wars for-ev-er

1. hand, We bring God's ho-ly love.
2. us, We bring God's ho-ly truth.
3. done, We bring God's ho-ly joy.
4. pressed, We bring God's ho-ly hope.
5. end, We bring God's ho-ly peace.

African–American

Rose Weber
Text © 1971, WLP

24 This Day God Gives Me

1. This day God gives me Strength of high heav-en,
2. This day God sends me Strength as my main-stay,
3. God's way is my God's shield is 'round me,
4. Ris-ing, I thank you, Might-y and strong One,

1. Sun and moon shin-ing, Flame in my hearth,
2. Might to up-hold me, Wis-dom as my guide.
3. God's host de-fends me, Sav-ing from ill.
4. King of cre-a-tion, Giv-er of rest,

1. Flash-ing of light-'ning, Wind in its swift-ness,
2. Your eyes are watch-ful, Your ears are list-'ning,
3. An-gels of heav-en, Drive from me al-ways
4. Firm-ly con-fess-ing Three-ness of Per-sons,

1. Deeps of the o-cean, Firm-ness of earth.
2. Your lips are speak-ing, Friend at my side.
3. All that would harm me, Stand by me still.
4. One-ness of God-head, Trin-i-ty blest.

Ascr. to St. Patrick, 372–466
Adapt. by James Quinn; text © 1993, James Quinn, Selah Publishing Co. Inc., North American agent

Scots Gaelic melody

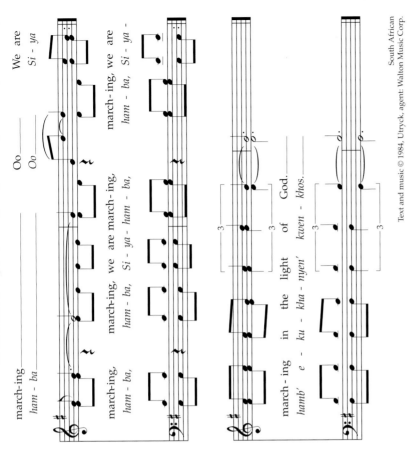

South African

Text and music © 1984, Utryck, agent: Walton Music Corp.

26   We Are Marching in the Light of God/
Siyahamba

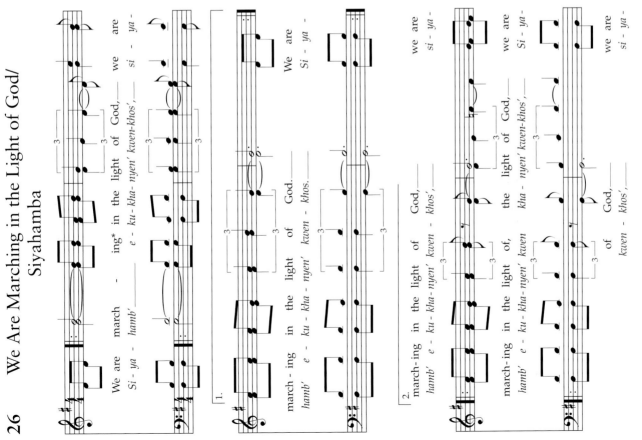

Additional verses: dancing, singing, praying, etc.

We Sing of the Saints

1. We sing of the saints filled with Spir - it and grace,
2. *(Optional verse for saint's day)*
3. We, too, have been cho - sen to fol - low the way

1. Blest wom - en and men, through all time, from each place.
2.
3. Of good - ness and truth in our stud - y and play,

1. God chose them, the ho - ly, the hum - ble, the wise,
2.
3. We raise up our song, liv - ing saints here be - low,

1. To spread the Good News of sal - va - tion in Christ.
2.
3. With heav - en - ly saints, as our praise ev - er flows.

Optional second verse for saint's days:

Feasts of Mary
A lowly, young woman
God's mother would be,
The first true believing
disciple was she.
From cradle to cross,
she would follow her Son
And share in the life
everlasting he won.

Feasts of Joseph
A carpenter, upright and
faithful, was called
To care for young Jesus,
a child weak and small.
To teach and to guide,
to embrace him in love,
Reminding him here
of the Father above.

Feasts of John the Baptist
A prophet and herald
who made straight the way
For Jesus to come,
bringing mercy's new day.
He preached to the people
to change and repent,
Preparing them as
the Messiah was sent.

March 17: St. Patrick
From Britain to Ireland
strong Patrick returned,
He baptized and preached
in the name of our Lord.
He used simple clover
to show God was One,
To teach of the Father
and Spirit and Son.

We Sing of the Saints (continued)

November 1: All Saints
There are many saints
whom we don't know by name,
For God works through people
who never find fame.
But, gathered together,
they now sing God's might,
With martyrs and prophets,
in heavenly light.

November 2: All Souls
We honor the mem'ry
of those now at rest,
Who followed the Gospel,
whose lives were so blest;
From fam'lies and friendships,
they make heaven seem
More home-like for us,
in our prayers and our dreams.

December 6: St. Nicholas
A bishop, a friend of the
poor and the weak,
Of orphans and children,
the hungry, the meek;
Saint Nicholas used all his
power and wealth
To help those in need,
to return them to health.

December 9: Blessed Juan Diego
This poor Aztec native
lived in Mexico;
Was given a sign:
roses blooming in snow.
The Mother of God
to Diego appeared,
So Jesus her Son
always would be revered.

December 13: St. Lucy
Her feast is in Advent,
her name means "the light,"
She died for upholding
what she thought was right;
St. Lucy took care of the poor
and the frail;
Her witness was brave
and her faith never failed.

July 14: Blessed Kateri Tekakwitha
The "Lily of Mohawks"
Kateri was called
For sharing God's love
with the great and the small,
She bore the name "Christian"
with honor and pride,
And now her name, "Blessèd"
is known far and wide.

August 28: St. Augustine
A great, holy man,
born on Africa's shores,
Augustine, at first, loved
the worldly life more;
He found, later on, Jesus Christ,
the true Way,
And chose the true Gospel
to live and proclaim.

September 29: Archangels
Of Gabriel, Raphael,
Michael we sing,
God's messengers: joyful,
glad tidings they bring;
Protecting the Church,
and announcing the time
When Christ shall return
in his glory sublime.

October 4: St. Francis of Assisi
Saint Francis was born
a rich, noble young man,
But God had in mind
a much different plan;
So Francis left status
and money behind,
To help many people
God's true will to find.

October 15: St. Teresa of Jesus
A woman of wisdom,
of faith and of prayer,
Teresa would speak up
when others didn't dare.
She challenged the Church
to renew and revive;
Her great love of Jesus
was always her guide.

Alan J. Hommerding
Text © 1994, WLP

Traditional Dutch melody